Through the Money Labyrinth

A CANADIAN BROKER *Guides You to* STOCK MARKET SUCCESS

Shirley E. Woods

John Wiley & Sons
Toronto • New York • Chichester • Brisbane • Singapore

John Wiley & Sons Canada Limited
22 Worcester Road
Rexdale, Ontario
M9W 1L1

Canadian Cataloguing in Publication Data

Woods, Shirley E.
    Through the money labyrinth: a Canadian broker guides you to stock market success.

Includes index.
ISBN 0–471–64113–8 (bound) ISBN 0–471–64112–X (pbk.)

1. Investments – Canada.   2. Stocks – Canada.
I.   Title.

HG5152.W66 1994   332.63'22'0971   C94–932197–4

Production Credits
Cover Illustration: Stephen Quinlan
Cover and Text Design: JAQ
Electronic Assembly: Christine Rae
Printer: Tri-graphic Printing Limited

Printed and bound in Canada
10 9 8 7 6 5 4 3 2 1

CONTENTS

Acknowledgements

I have many people to thank for this book, particularly my clients, most of whom were also friends. Working with them taught me a great deal.

Sue Buntain of Green Line Investor Services, Alison Draper of Midland Walwyn, Paul Lannan of ScotiaMcLeod, and Jamie Oyler of Nesbitt Burns all made important contributions. As did four other members of the investment community: Lloyd Garrett, Alex Gluskin, John Oyler, and Phillip Massad.

Gordon Harris of Almonte responded nobly to panic calls when my computer defeated me. Both Anice Demond of the Bank of Montreal in Mahone Bay, and George (Butch) Cook have my appreciation for sharing their specialized knowledge.

Evan Gill of the Canadian Bank Note company went out of his way to arrange for the stock certificate shown in this book, and Microstar Software graciously agreed to its reproduction.

I would especially like to thank Karen Milner, Editor, Professional, Reference and Trade Division, John Wiley & Sons Canada Ltd, for her enthusiastic support and excellent suggestions throughout this project. And I am indebted to both Elizabeth Fowler and Erika Krolman for their editorial contributions.

Finally, I must thank my daughter Julia for her sage advice, and Sandrea, my wife, for putting up with me during yet another book.

Preface

The investment scene has changed dramatically since I wrote the predecessor to this book ten years ago. The Crash of 1987 not only stunned investors (and a good many people in the business) but erased a quarter of the market's value in a single day. The Crash was followed by a reassuring recovery, but two years later the market went into another slide when the economy topped out. This recession turned out to be the worst since the Great Depression, and many blue chips were among the casualties.

Even the trust companies, traditional bastions of prudence and probity, went through the wringer. The steel companies, Canada's champions of heavy industry, also took frightful losses. Real estate became a dirty word, and both the real estate companies and the chartered banks who lent them money, paid dearly for their greed. To add to our woes, low commodity prices slashed the earnings of Canada's foremost resource companies.

On a more positive note, our weak economy brought in its wake lower interest rates. Although junk bonds—a phenomenon of the '80s—have been consigned to the junk pile, bonds enjoyed a tremendous rally in the early '90s. Unfortunately, rising bond prices also attracted a host of novice buyers, many of whom got caught when interest rates reversed their trend in 1994.

Roller coaster volatility has become part of the investment scene in the past decade. When IBM, the mother of all computer companies, lays off thousands of employees, and its stock falls to less than half its former value, there's no room for complacency. No longer can you buy blue chips and simply forget them. If you do, you may be in for a nasty surprise.

Some years ago I had a client named Steve who always blamed me for his losses, but took full credit for his wins. I accepted Steve's behaviour without comment because he was paying the commissions—and every broker has one or two clients like this. Since leaving the business and moving to the other side of the desk, I've tried to avoid blaming someone else for my financial shortcomings. I do this not from politeness, but to remind myself that I'm responsible for my financial destiny. You are too. Accountability is obvious when one buys a stock, or a bond, but it's also there when you buy a mutual fund. Yes, I agree that you pay professionals a management fee, but whose decision is it to buy the fund? Yours, of course.

Today's topsy-turvy financial world is confusing—and computers have done little to unlock the secrets of the markets. That's the bad news. The good news is that the old-fashioned fundamentals still apply. This book is designed to strip away the smoke and mirrors, and to look at those fundamentals. If you bear with me you will better understand the investment game, and you will avoid many of its pitfalls. And it may also help you to invest more successfully. I certainly hope so.

S.E.W.
Mahone Bay, Nova Scotia

1   WHY PUT YOUR MONEY IN THE MARKET?

One of my daughters, when she was very young, asked me, "Does investing mean making your money grow?" I thought at the time that it was a pretty good definition—and I still do. The growth may be a simple increase in value, or it may be added income. Sometimes it's a combination of the two.

A savings account or a Guaranteed Investment Certificate (GIC) is a typical income investment. Art or antiques, on the other hand, provide no income but may well increase in value—thus providing capital gain. A dividend-paying common stock is an excellent example of an investment that can offer a return combining both income and capital appreciation.

But, before zeroing in on stocks, bonds, and mutual funds, let's consider some of the other alternatives for getting a return on your money.

THE SAVINGS ACCOUNT

The savings account is the most popular income investment in Canada. It is theoretically risk-free, liquid (i.e., readily converted into cash), and provides a minimum return. Savings accounts are offered by all the financial institutions (including some brokers), and there's a lot of competition out there for your dollar. The banks try to outdo each other by offering accounts with catchy phrases like "plus" and "bonus," but there are really only two types of savings account: one that allows you to write cheques, and one that does not. Most institutions offer both types of account.

Savings account interest is credited on the basis of your daily, monthly, or yearly *minimum* balance, depending on the terms. The minimum feature has to be watched closely because a large withdrawal, even if it is topped up the next day, can dramatically reduce your return. The minimum is there for a purpose: to discourage you from withdrawing your money. For the same reason, chequing accounts pay a lower rate of interest than nonchequing accounts.

Here we stumble upon one of the basic principles of usury (or banking if you prefer): *the longer money is lent, the more valuable it is to the borrower.* When you make a deposit in your savings account, you are *lending* the bank your money. The bank in turn recycles your money by lending some of it, in the form of loans, to customers. The bank is able to pay you interest, because it earns a much higher rate of interest from the borrower. The "spread" between what the bank pays you and what it charges the borrower is the bank's profit. Since balances are more stable in nonchequing accounts—that is, the bank can count on having your money for a longer period—it pays a higher rate of interest for this longer-term money.

Let's take an actual example of an interest spread. As I write this, the prime lending rate (the rate banks charge their best customers) at the local branch of the Bank of Montreal is 5½ percent. The interest rate the bank pays to depositors with savings account balances of less than $5000 is ½ percent. The spread is 5 percent, or, to put it another way, the bank is charging borrowers eleven times what it is paying to depositors.

So, don't be intimidated when you ask for a loan. Remember, if you are a reasonable credit risk you are doing the bank a favour by giving it your business. Banks don't earn any money paying interest on deposits; they make it by charging interest on loans.

Years ago, when I was applying for a loan, I jocularly reminded the manager of the main branch of the Bank of Nova Scotia in Ottawa of this fact. He was not amused.

In relation to other investments, the rate paid on savings accounts is always at the lower end of the spectrum. The main advantages of the savings account are safety and liquidity. The main disadvantage is its low rate of return. When inflation is factored in, it can even be *negative*. Full taxes on interest make the picture even bleaker.

Again, let's take an example of inflation on a savings account using current actual figures. For purposes of simplicity, I will ignore the tax bite on the annual interest.

Deposited in a savings account for 1 year	$1000
Plus interest at 1/2 percent per year	5
Subtotal	$1005
Less inflation at 1 percent per year	– 10
Net	$ 995

I can't leave the subject of savings accounts without mentioning the melancholy story of my wife's great-aunt, who was known in the family as "Fat Aunt." This plump lady lived on the income from her father's estate, which was remitted to her monthly by the Royal Trust. Mindful of the need to set something aside for a rainy day, she systematically deposited her excess income in a savings account with the Bank of Montreal. After Fat Aunt went to her Great Reward, her executors discovered that she had accumulated more than a million dollars in this account. That was the good news. The bad news was that for all those years it had been earning less than 1 percent. The moral of this tale is that a savings account is a safe place to temporarily park your money, but a very poor place to invest it.

TIME DEPOSITS

Had she known better, Fat Aunt would have invested her hoard on a short-term basis, which she could easily have done with either her bank or her trust company. Most financial institutions offer plans whereby you can invest sums from one day to a year—or longer if you wish. They go under a variety of names such as term notes, deposit receipts, or time deposits. These are similar to, but not identical with Guaranteed Investment Certificates (which we'll get to later).

Time deposits bear a higher rate of interest than savings accounts because your money is invested for a given term, specified in days, for example, thirty days, with an agreed maturity date. The old rule applies: the longer the term, the higher the rate of interest. For example, a ninety-day deposit normally pays a higher rate than a thirty-day deposit. Because bigger is better in the money lending game, amounts over $100,000 receive a higher rate than lesser amounts for the same term. In this connection the *minimum* amount for a time deposit is usually from $1000 to $5000. If you want to withdraw your money before the maturity date, you'll be penalized with a lower rate of interest (this is a best-case scenario; depending upon the issuer, you may forfeit all the interest). As with savings accounts and most other debt instruments (GICs, Treasury Bills, bonds, etc.), interest is calculated on an *annual* basis. This means that if you have $1000 on deposit for one year at a rate of 4 percent, you will receive $40 in interest (4 percent of $1000). But, if you have the same amount invested at the same rate for three months, you will earn approximately $10 or one-quarter of that amount.

When you invest in a time deposit, you will probably be encouraged to buy one with a longer-term maturity. (Remember the longer the term, the more valuable it is to the borrower.) My advice is to withstand the sales pitch for a higher rate and stick with thirty- to ninety-day maturities. *This is particularly important when interest rates are low.* You will pass up a quarter or possibly a half of one percent, but you will maintain liquidity, which is the purpose of a short-term note. What you want to avoid is locking yourself in, especially at a low rate of interest. For convenience, you can instruct the bank or trust company to simply "roll over" your time deposit at maturity, which saves you the bother of going into the institution, and ensures that your money will be continuously invested at current rates. If rates go down, you'll get less; but if they spike up (as they have a number of times in the past decade), you'll get the benefit. Either way, your investment will be liquid.

Interest earned on interest—as it does when you roll over a deposit—compounds with surprising speed. For example, a sum compounded at 8 percent doubles in nine years. This might suggest that simply rolling over your money in a time deposit would be a risk-free way to invest. Unfortunately, there are two flaws to this idea: taxes and inflation. After you pay taxes on the interest and allow for inflation, you'll be lucky to break even.

GICs

Guaranteed Investment Certificates (GICs) with terms of up to five years are also very popular investments. The banks and trust companies flog GICs with great gusto, because they are a great way to lock in money for mortgage loans. I use the term "lock" with good reason. Most GICs commit you to hold the note for the full term. The only way you can get your money out early is to die—an option with limited appeal. If you are really in a bind for funds, some institutions will *lend* your money back to you, at a higher rate than you lent it to them. But the contract still stands.

GICs do have their place on the investment scene, but because of the lock-in feature one should consider the term with caution. Before buying, it pays to shop around. Recently a number of institutions have come out with some weird GIC hybrids, at least one of which is tied (with a bizarre formula) to the Toronto Stock Exchange 35 Index. As far as I can determine, the benefits of these variants are illusory or at best, minimal. If you're going to buy a GIC, you're better off choosing plain vanilla. Rates vary slightly among the major institutions and by shopping you can get the best rate for whatever term you have in mind. *The Globe and Mail* publishes a list of the current rates each week (as do a number of other major papers), which will save you endless phone calls. But don't go by the rates alone; restrict your search to the *largest and strongest* institutions. Don't be lured by a quarter point into depositing your money with one of the fringe companies. They pay more because their credit rating is not as high as the big institutions. This brings up another investment maxim: *the lower the credit rating, the higher the borrowing cost.* If you're putting money on deposit or buying a GIC, the first requirement is safety; it's senseless to risk your entire investment for a fractionally higher return.

Actually most banks, trust companies, and mortgage loan companies are members of the Canada Deposit Insurance Corporation. This crown corporation insures deposits (including notes up to five years) against loss because of the insolvency of a member institution. But there is a limit of $60,000 of coverage per institution. This means that if you have a deposit or notes totalling less than $60,000, you are covered should the issuer go belly up. If you have say, $100,000 in total, $40,000 of it won't be covered. And, in the event of a claim, you can expect to wait some weeks for settlement. Because the $60,000 limit applies to the institution, you can't increase your coverage by having accounts with several branches—the only way you can increase your protection is by having accounts with *different* institutions. So, before investing, check that the institution is a CDIC member. Remember too, that the insurance applies only to deposits and notes.

The advantages of a GIC are safety and a competitive rate that is usually (but not necessarily) fixed for the term. The disadvantages are the lack of liquidity, the fact that in some cases no interest is paid until the maturity date, and the fully taxable interest. On balance, except for special circumstances, a GIC is not a particularly good investment. Most often its best application is within a tax-sheltered RRSP.

PERSONAL MORTGAGES

Personal mortgages are another form of term investment. Personal mortgages are loans secured by real estate such as a house, a farm, or land. The term is usually five to ten years, and the rate varies with the risk. The safest type of mortgage is a first mortgage, which has first call on the proceeds from the sale of the real estate in the event of default by the borrower. A second mortgage is more risky, because it gets nothing until the first mortgage has been paid in full. A third mortgage ranks behind a second mortgage and should be bought with fingers crossed. Personal mortgages are sold to investors by mortgage brokers and some members of the legal profession. (Lawyers often take a fee on both sides of the transaction—from the lender and the borrower—and can wield their ballpoint pens with the efficiency of a revolver.) Even though a mortgage may be covered by ample assets, the rate of interest is higher than that of a GIC. This, however, is as it should be—it's a worse investment.

People often assume that because a mortgage is secured by real property, something tangible like land or buildings, it's a safe haven in bad times. The truth is that when the economy turns down, real estate prices fall with it. (If you doubt this, ask the Reichmann brothers.) Nor is a mortgage an inflation hedge; as the increments of capital are repaid, you, the borrower, get devalued dollars at the other end. Mortgage interest is fully taxable, which further reduces the true rate of return. Liquidity is another problem. Try hawking a personal mortgage.

I can think of only two reasons for owning a personal mortgage. One would be to facilitate the sale of your house by taking back a mortgage from the buyer. The other would be to facilitate the purchase of a separate dwelling for your mother-in-law.

REAL ESTATE

Real estate can be a rewarding investment if you are an *owner* rather than a *lender*. By this I mean buying real estate such as land, a house, or an apartment building with the object of selling it at a higher price. Many people have made a lot of money out of real estate. The game, however, entails an element of risk. What heightens the risk is that the secret to big profits is to use leverage—or, put more simply, other people's money. Thus when you buy, you try to borrow as much of the purchase price as possible, and put as little of your own money in as you can. This works splendidly if the value of your property rises—you get a much bigger bang for your buck—but if it falls, you're on the hook in short order.

In the '80s, when property values were rising, a great many amateurs as well as professionals made fortunes in real estate. In Toronto countless people bought houses and "flipped" them within a matter of weeks, sheltering their winnings by classifying the houses as their principal residence (a practice that can trigger embarrassing questions from Revenue Canada). At the end of the decade, the bubble burst. When real estate takes a serious hit, it goes down for the count, as did thousands of individual speculators, many of whom coughed up all their profits—and then some—in the debacle. The carnage was even more spectacular on the commercial side. Canadian chartered banks have so far been forced to write off more than $8½ *billion* in bad commercial real estate loans, Olympia and York alone accounting for nearly $2 billion of this amount. Real estate stocks have also been hammered. The most sensational of them is Camdev (a property owner and manager in the Ottawa area), whose shares plummetted from US $787½ in January 1989 to US $6 ¾ in January 1994.

The little experience I've had in real estate has been quite profitable. But I'm not an expert, and I learned this the hard way. Some years ago I had a client who was a successful real estate entrepreneur. We did business over a period of time, and I thought he was a pretty good fellow. One day he invited me into a syndicate that was going to build a large apartment building. With his track record, I figured I couldn't lose. I put in about $20,000 for a tiny slice of the pie, and made further payments in the ensuing months. Eventually, I got twitchy about my investment—the project seemed to be stalled—and started to ask questions. When I couldn't get a straight answer, I asked my friend if he would like to buy me out, which he subsequently did at my cost price. A few weeks later I was stopped on the street by an acquaintance in the real estate business who told me I had been cheated by my former partner. What had happened was that before he agreed to buy my interest he had already made a deal to sell the entire project for a fat profit. I got my share (minus hefty legal fees), but it took me three years of litigation.

What I don't like about real estate is its lack of liquidity. If you own a stock and you don't like the look of the market, you can pick up the phone and sell it in seconds. Not so with real estate; if you see storm clouds gathering, there's no guarantee that you can get rid of your property quickly. You may even be saddled with it to the bitter end. There are also other drawbacks, such as rent controls on income properties, and legislation that prohibits the purchase of farmland for speculation. I don't quibble with these laws—they are undoubtedly a good thing—but they lessen the investment appeal of real estate.

The best real estate investment for the average person is to buy your own home. I would also make it a priority to pay off the mortgage. This may sound old-fashioned and ultra-conservative, but it wasn't so long ago that mortgages were being renewed at 20 percent. And I would add that until you have substantial equity in your home—at least 50 percent—you shouldn't invest in anything else, including the stock market.

COLLECTABLES

Many people invest in collectables—works of art, stamps, coins, vintage cars, cigar bands, and much else. The list is almost endless. None of these yield any income, and all are bought for capital appreciation.

In a small way I have bought prints, paintings, and books as investments. At least that's how I rationalize their purchase. When I browse through the catalogues, I'm gratified to see that all, or at least most of my acquisitions have gone up in value. But, wait a minute. I bought *retail*; if I want to sell to a dealer I will have to accept the *wholesale* price, which is about half that of retail. Some time ago I actually did sell a number of limited edition prints, and sure enough, I netted about 50 cents on the dollar. The people who make money in collectables are the professionals, not the amateurs. For most of us, buying collectables is a hobby, not a business. Our payoff comes from owning the items, not from selling them.

LIFE INSURANCE: THE SHELL GAME

Life insurance is another popular investment. I am all for life insurance and consider it an essential form of protection. But a word of caution: the boys in the life insurance industry are highly skilled at the shell game and keep the pea moving with the speed of light.

After you cut away the frills, there are only two basic types of life insurance. One is "term" the other is "whole" life. (Variations and combinations of these two come in a bewildering array, and new hybrids appear every day.) Term insurance is like the coverage on your house or car. You pay your premiums year after year and when you stop paying that's it—there's no residual value. Whole life premiums, which are much higher for the same amount of protection, contain an increment of residual value. Both term and whole life pay off the full face value in the event of death. You can, however, cash in your whole life policy after a number of years, or when it matures, and receive a residual value. This is the reason whole life premiums are much higher than term premiums. The sales *commissions* are also much higher on whole life. This is because whole life is much more profitable for the insurance companies, and they want to encourage their salespeople to sell it.

In most cases, but particularly with heads of young families, it is a grave disservice to recommend whole life. Consider the case of a father with three young children. If he can afford only $400 a year for insurance, is it better for him to buy a $100,000 term policy, or $20,000 of whole life? If he gets run over by a truck, will his widow be happier with $100,000 or $20,000? Will she care whether it was term or whole life?

The insurance industry justifies whole life on the basis that it forces people to save, and that it is a good investment. It does force the holder to save —at the expense of coverage. But it is not a good investment compared with most other securities. If a person finds it difficult to save, he or she would be better off buying term insurance and systematically investing the surplus in a good mutual fund.

To sum up, everyone should have adequate insurance. Term insurance provides the cheapest protection, and is the best way to create an instant estate. Whole life insurance—under whatever guise—should be avoided. The only way to invest in insurance is to buy the common shares of one of the insurance companies (and be sure to choose carefully)!

AND NOW FOR THE BEST...

This brings us to the end of our tour of "alternative" investments. Each has its advantages and its disadvantages. I like to make money as much as the next person, and over the course of many years I've tried them all. But when everything is said and done, the easiest, most efficient way to make money is through the securities markets. You can buy or sell in seconds, and you can compute the precise value of your holdings at any given moment. You can also set your own pace, and pick the type of action that suits you. It has been my experience that whatever you choose, the securities markets will provide variety, liquidity, and an ongoing opportunity for profit.

2

CHOOSING A BROKER

One of your most critical investment decisions is the choice of a broker. Depending upon whom you select, doing business can range from a pleasant experience to a gut-wrenching struggle. Even more important, your broker can make the difference between your investment success and failure. To make an informed choice, you should first know something about the securities industry in Canada.

STOCK EXCHANGES

Toronto is Canada's financial centre, while Montreal and Vancouver are lesser spheres of influence. It wasn't always this way. When I entered the business in 1958, Montreal was head-quarters for many important financial institutions. Montreal still has some large securities operations, but Toronto is where the decisions are made.

In 1958 the Montreal Stock Exchange (as it was known then) was the preferred market for investment grade shares, while the Toronto Stock Exchange listed most of the speculative mining and oil stocks. Today, the TSE dominates the investment market and dwarfs the Montreal Exchange, which does about one-fifth the business. The gap would be even greater were it not for the Caisse de dépôt et placement du Québec (a government agency that invests for the Quebec Pension Plan), which directs most of its trades to the ME. Even so, if a stock is interlisted on both the ME and the TSE, the odds are that the TSE will be the better market (something to remember).

The Vancouver Stock Exchange is the reason *Forbes* magazine recently described Vancouver as "the scam capital of the world." The VSE has also been dubbed "the world's largest casino" and "Vegas North." Most of its listings—which have an average value of about a dollar—are mining and oil stocks. Neither the exchange nor the provincial securities commission are noted for their zeal in protecting the investor. Despite yet another inquiry into the scandal-ridden VSE, indications are that the members of the exchange will continue to police themselves—which is akin to putting the rabbits in charge of the carrots. My advice to anyone interested in investing (as opposed to gambling) would be to avoid the Vancouver Stock Exchange.

For practical purposes, you can also ignore Canada's two smallest markets: the Alberta Stock Exchange in Calgary and the Winnipeg Stock Exchange. Their business ethics are fine, but they account for a negligible percentage of the total volume— not quite "trade by appointment," but close to it.

SECURITIES FIRMS

Turning to the securities industry, some firms are called "investment dealers," and others are called "stockbrokers." The historic difference is that an investment dealer acts as *principal*, while a stock broker acts as *agent*. Thus, when you make a trade with an investment dealer, he will either sell to you from his inventory (take it out of his top drawer) or buy from you for his own account. The difference between the buying and selling cost is his profit on the transaction. A stockbroker, on the other hand, doesn't *own* the security at any time, but acts as your agent. The profit he makes comes from the fee (commission) he charges to do the transaction.

Investment dealers are also "underwriters" of securities. When governments or corporations want to raise money through the sale of bonds or shares, an investment dealer (or a group of dealers) will underwrite the issue. This means the dealer will buy the entire amount of the offering at a fixed price. Having bought the issue, the underwriter will mark up the price (his profit) and sell the issue to the public. If the dealer is unable to sell all of the issue, or if he's forced to discount its price, he bears the loss—not the government or corporation. For this reason underwriting entails some risk, but it can be highly lucrative. Underwriting can also benefit the economy because it provides capital for those who need it.

There are about a hundred firms in the securities business in Canada, varying in size from one-person operations to companies with over a thousand employees. Many firms, especially the larger ones, are both investment dealers and stockbrokers. In addition, some brokers act as principals rather than agents when amassing a block of shares (a point that is really only of academic interest).

To further complicate the picture, because of legislative changes made in the '80s, the four pillars of finance—banks, brokers, trust companies, and insurance companies—no longer stand alone, but have become enmeshed with each other. Banks now engage in stockbroking; brokers offer banking services; and trust and insurance companies are aggressively into the mutual fund business. Despite the blurring of boundaries, however, there is still a pecking order in the securities business.

At the bottom are the small local firms, some of which don't own a seat on an exchange. Others may have a seat, but do very little underwriting. As you climb the ladder, the size and scope of their operations increase proportionately. At the top are the full-service national houses. These firms have many branches, are members of all the exchanges, spend millions on research, and have lucrative underwriting connections. Some of the leading names are Nesbitt Burns, RBC Dominion Securities, Levesque Beaubien, ScotiaMcLeod, and Wood Gundy. All these old-line firms are now controlled by Canadian chartered banks. Richardson Greenshields and Midland Walwyn are two other national firms; both have large retail sales forces. In the investment sense, a "retail" account is an individual or small corporation with assets of up to, say, $10 million. An institution is just that; an insurance or trust company, mutual fund, pension fund, or other large government or corporate money manager. All the big houses service both retail and institutional clients. Some small investment "boutiques" also cater to institutions, but only one major player, Gordon Capital, restricts itself exclusively to large accounts. Gordon Capital is a buccaneer among the stately fleet of old-line firms, and sometimes sails very close to the wind (a practice that has provoked some high level suspensions and impressive fines by the Ontario Securities Commission).

REGULATING THE INDUSTRY

Prime responsibility for regulating the securities industry is in the hands of provincial securities commissions. The Ontario Securities Commission, which has a staff of over two hundred, is the standard setter and model for most of the other provinces. The most influential self-regulatory body within the industry is the Investment Dealers Association of Canada.

The Investment Dealers Association was founded in 1916 at the request of the Canadian government. The IDA works in conjunction with the stock exchanges and the provincial securities commissions. Its purpose—aside from the welfare of its members—is to enforce high standards of conduct and to protect the public. To this end, a National Contingency Fund was set up with the exchanges to reimburse clients if a member firm should go bankrupt. The IDA also monitors the conduct and financial position of its members. With close links to the securities commissions, the Investment Dealers Association is responsible for most of the educational courses within the industry. Because IDA firms have to measure up to certain standards and meet strict financial criteria, I would confine my search for a broker to firms that are members of the association. This shouldn't prove to be too restrictive, as there are around seventy such firms with more than five hundred offices across the country.

The IDA incidentally, should not be confused with the Broker-Dealers' Association of Ontario. The two are as different as chalk and cheese. The Broker-Dealers' Association represents a handful of small firms in the Toronto area, none of which are members of a Canadian stock exchange, and all of whom deal in unlisted resource stocks.

The mention of speculative mining and oil stocks brings up another word of warning. If you should get a long distance call from a broker who wants you to buy a "penny dreadful," say no. The typical sales pitch goes something like this: An adventurous little company has just discovered a fantastic mine (you can substitute "oil well" for "mine" if you wish). The drilling results, which are incredible, have not been released yet. But as soon as the results are known, the share price will soar. Fortunately for you, it is not too late to get in on this bonanza. By a stroke of luck, the broker has a thousand shares that are still available at the underwriting price of 70 cents. He will let you have these shares, provided you mail a certified cheque or money order to him immediately. It's the chance of a lifetime, because the stock will soon be worth eight to ten dollars!

The first thing you should ask yourself when you get this sort of call is, "If it's such a sure thing, why is a stranger taking the trouble and expense to tell me?" (You must admit that it's unlikely the Good Fairy whispered your name in his ear.) The answer of course is that you are on a sucker list. And you're not the only one. I often got inquiries from people who'd bought such stocks —sometimes second and third helpings of them. My standard advice was to get rid of the shares, but I don't remember anyone getting their money back, let alone making a profit. If you really must take a flutter, you're better off going to the racetrack—at least you'll see the horses run.

SMALL VERSUS LARGE FIRMS

Now, getting back to the choice of a broker, I would rule out any firm that isn't a member of the Investment Dealers Association. This is the first step in the process of elimination. The next thing you must decide is whether you want to deal with a large or a small firm.

Small firms usually have a single location and few people on staff. Some small firms provide excellent service. The main advantage of dealing with a small house is that you may have personal contact with the proprietor—in fact, he may look after your account. If it is a good-sized account, you will be treated like royalty. There are, however, several disadvantages to small firms, including limited trading facilities, limited research facilities, and limited access to underwritings. These shortcomings mean that you will be restricted in your investment scope.

Large firms—those with a dozen branches or more, and who are both brokers and underwriters—also have advantages and disadvantages. Known as "integrated" houses in the industry, they're like an investor's general store with commodity, money market, and mutual fund departments, as well as bond trading and stockbroking facilities. Large firms spend heavily on research, participate in many new issues, and have seats on the major North American exchanges. What does this mean to you as a client? It means convenience, and it means access to a wide variety of investment opportunities.

Research is critical to good investment decisions. If the firm you deal with publishes sound and timely information, you are well on your way to making money. Underwritings permit you to buy new issues at the original offering price without paying a commission. Often a new issue can be resold for an immediate profit. When you buy or sell stocks, the speed of the transaction depends on whether your broker is a member of the exchange on which the shares are listed. If your firm isn't a member, it must engage another broker to execute the trade. This "jitney" process can result in slow and sloppy service. If, however, you deal with a firm that is a member of many exchanges, you can expect fast and efficient executions.

On balance, I would suggest that an investor choose a large integrated house. With the caveat that the quality of research varies within the industry, and it varies from analyst to analyst within each firm. This happens for the simple reason that some people are smarter than others.

Biased research, because of an underwriting connection, is another matter. If an investment house regularly underwrites the securities of a company, don't expect to see negative reports on that company. But this is a relatively minor sin of ommission. More serious are the isolated cases where an underwriter has "primed the pump" with a glowing report just before selling a lousy issue to the public (a practice common with the fly-by-night and fringe operators). To protect investors, securities laws require that within large firms there be a "Chinese Wall" of silence between the mergers and acquisitions department and everyone else—including the sales force. The purpose of this invisible barrier is to prevent the leakage of inside information, such as news of a takeover, so that it cannot be used by people to make a quick buck on the market. Securities laws also require all firms to divulge their underwriting connections in research material. If anything, the large firms are more closely scrutinized by the securities commissions, and most bend over backwards to comply with the laws. As a client, that's to your advantage. Another point in favour of the big firms, especially those controlled by the banks, is that they have very high credit ratings.

Underwriting Canadian common and preferred shares is a multibillion-dollar business. New issues or IPOs (initial public offerings), can be tricky to judge. They are not always a boon to own—sometimes they go *down* in price after they have been sold to investors. For this reason, the decision to purchase an IPO has to be made even more carefully than the decision to purchase an existing issue. The top investment firms invariably have a better underwriting track record than the lesser firms.

A good way to select an investment firm is to ask friends or acquaintances who are involved in the market. Eventually the names of several firms—or at least one—will emerge as favourites. Having narrowed your choice to not more than three houses, your next step is to phone the managers of the local branches of these firms. The purpose of your calls is to arrange an appointment to see one of his brokers. (But, if a specific broker in a firm has been recommended to you, phone that person directly.)

When you speak to a manager, it's not necessary to tell him you're shopping, but you should give him an idea of your objectives and the potential size of your account. This information will permit the manager to match you with a broker who can best serve your needs. At least, that's the theory—he may just pass you on to the most junior salesperson (the one who's scrambling to build a clientele).

BROKERS: A PROFILE

I have used the terms "broker" and "salesperson" interchangeably, as they are one and the same. Other common names are "registered representative," "account executive," and "account advisor." Registered representative is probably the most accurate, because everyone who deals in securities must be registered with a provincial securities commission. Before obtaining a licence to deal in securities, the prospective representative must also pass an exam and have had at least three months' experience in the business. The most popular name, and the one I shall use, is broker. The word is a unisex term, and it best describes a registered representative's main function. Although the investment business has tradionally been a male preserve, today approximately 10 percent of the brokers in Canada are women. (Women are also senior executives, economists, and research analysts.) Thus, if you have a preference, you can choose a fully qualified man or woman to be your broker.

It will also help you to know that brokers are by nature highly independent. Except for discount houses, most brokers aren't paid a salary but earn their living from commissions. These commissions are generated from the business they do with their own clientele. Brokers' earnings fluctuate with the swings in the market. When the market is active, they make bags of money; when it's in the doldrums, they starve. Because a broker's clientele represents his earning power, he guards it jealously and is usually on the lookout for new accounts (which he needs to offset the attrition that takes place for a variety of reasons, including death and disenchantment). A good broker's first loyalty is to his clients, the second is to his firm. By the same token, most investors are loyal to an individual rather than to a firm. I know this to be true from personal experience—during my career I changed firms twice, and took most of my clients with me each time. And this highlights another point to consider: for practical purposes, the firm you choose will be represented by a *single* person. This is why the selection of your broker is so important.

INTERVIEWING POTENTIAL BROKERS

Now comes the phase that require's shrewd judgement on your part: choosing a broker. To make the choice intelligently, a face-to-face meeting is essential. If you rely on a telephone interview, you are only using your sense of hearing to size up a person who can make or lose a lot of money for you. By sitting down with him, you can see not only if he has shifty eyes, but you can also get an idea of the office facilities. (Forget the decor; but try to assess whether the place is being run efficiently). It is also useful to remember that while you are interviewing the broker and dangling your bag of gold before his eyes, he will be interviewing you.

To save time, you should be frank with each other. You need not fear that the information you divulge will be repeated, for brokers treat all information as confidential. This is not surprising; as personal wealth is an exceedingly sensitive subject. I suspect most people would rather talk about their marital situation than reveal their bank balance. Indeed, I once had a married couple as clients who each made me promise not to let the other spouse know of their dealings—and two brothers who insisted on the same arrangement. (The couple has since divorced, but the brothers are still together.) So you can speak freely.

One of the most unnerving interviews I ever had was with a man who was a psychic. His name was Cyril, and he was referred to me by another client. Cyril had accomplished some extraordinary psychic feats, and he undoubtedly possessed the gift of second sight. The prospect of meeting him made me uneasy, but this was offset by the intriguing potential of having him as a client. When Cyril swept into my office, I was impressed by his energy—he almost radiated sparks. During our interview, he fixed me with a glittering stare, and I was sure he was reading my mind. This made me uncomfortable, because I was thinking that with Cyril picking winners I could make a hell of a lot of money (see "tailgating" in the Glossary). Unfortunately, it didn't work out that way. Cyril opened a margin account, and with supreme confidence proceeded to pick a succession of losers. Eventually his psychic powers waned to such a degree that he was unable to recognize margin calls, even when they were sent by telegram. Our business relationship, which had started out with such promise, ended on a sour note.

The three most important things you want to learn from your interview with your broker are: whether he is competent; whether he understands your investment objectives; and whether his approach complements your objectives. Let's look at each of these questions in more detail.

Competence

Investing is more an art than a science. Assuming equal qualifications, what separates the average broker from the outstanding broker is a "feel" for the market. A university degree won't give it to you, nor will the social graces. One of the best brokers I know is a country boy who makes grammatical errors, but who consistently spots investment opportunities. His talent is his sense of the market. Some people have it, but the majority lack this gift. Experience is another valuable asset. You can find out how much experience the broker has had by casually asking when he started in the business. You may be surprised to learn that the grey-haired gentleman opposite you has only been in the industry six months, having retired from the army after thirty-five years as a cook. Or he may have been a broker for the past quarter century. What you want is someone who has been around long enough to experience both a *bull* and a *bear market*. Novice brokers are enthusiastic but naive about their firm's research. Many, like young robins, swallow it whole. Ideally, your broker will have enough experience and expertise to screen research recommendations and new issues before passing them on to you.

Understanding Your Objectives

You can't expect the broker to understand your investment objectives, if you don't know them yourself. This may sound like a stupid statement, but it's surprising how many people are unsure of what they want from their portfolio. If you don't have a clear investment goal in mind—be it capital gain, income, or a combination of both—your results will suffer. I remember interviewing a woman who had a large sum to invest, but she had no idea what she wanted from her portfolio. Although she was intelligent, well-educated, and successful, she simply hadn't given the question any thought. The problem was solved by going over her priorities, and through a process of elimination we worked out her investment objectives. One of my suggestions to her was to consult an accountant to establish her tax position. Tax is a fundamental consideration in any investment strategy, and as far as tax goes the devil is in the details. The place to get tax advice is from an accountant or a lawyer, not from your broker.

Be quite sure when you tell the broker your investment objective that you mean what you say. At the height of the last oil market—when euphoria was in the air and junior stocks were soaring—a schoolteacher named Alex came to me and said he wanted to speculate in the high fliers. I told him straight out that it was a dangerous game. Alex agreed, but said that he had $20,000 which he was prepared to risk, and if he lost the entire amount it wouldn't affect his standard of living. I chose some stocks for him and he chose some. Initially things went very well, but a few months later the market went in the tank, and Alex lost most of his money. It then transpired that he hadn't expected to lose heavily, and he was very bitter about it. The whole thing could have been avoided if he had told me at the outset that he was really only prepared to lose a modest amount. Not surprisingly, I lost Alex as a client.

My mistake with Alex (aside from disastrous market timing) was to assume that he was a genuine gambler. There are clients, and I had several of them, who love to gamble. They know the odds, and they accept their losses philosophically. What they want is *action*, and they will play any type of game to get it. When the markets are quiet, they'll hop on a plane to Atlantic City or Las Vegas—there's always action at the casinos. When stocks get active again, they return to the market. Because these high rollers generate huge commissions, they are greeted with joy by their brokers.

The mention of gamblers and losses brings up another consideration when setting your investment objective. Is your investment goal compatible with your temperament? Or, to put it more bluntly, can you stand the heat? For example, if capital gain is your first priority, this would suggest a portfolio with a fair percentage of growth stocks. By their nature, however, growth stocks are volatile and tend to have wide swings in price. Would this make you nervous? If the answer is yes, you should reconsider your strategy. It's not worth the candle to hold common stocks (even good ones) if their fluctuations make you anxious. This reminds me of Hugh and Sarah, a couple I've known for years. They like to think of themselves as cool-eyed risk takers and market sophisticates. In reality, they are worriers. When their stocks are up, they worry that they're about to fall; and when they're down, they worry that they've lost all their money. Often they worry most of the night. Sarah and Hugh would be far better of—certainly as far as stress is concerned— buying a package of growth-type mutual funds, or paying an investment counsellor to manage their holdings.

Complementary Approach

When you outline your financial position and investment objectives to the broker he will listen attentively and probably take notes. However, of equal importance to his understanding your position is whether he is genuinely interested in being of service, that is, whether he *cares* and is prepared to make an ongoing *commitment* to your investment program. Some brokers are simply "stock jockeys," who latch on to a high flier and sell it indiscriminately to all their clients. (A surprising number of brokers, even in the best firms, take this approach.) But, if you're an investor, rather than a speculator, you'll need someone with a portfolio approach, who'll consider whether a security fits into your overall program. Your broker should also keep an up-to-date list of your securities, and notify you of any significant changes to them. In addition to suggesting switches in your holdings, he should screen new issues, and only offer those that complement your objectives. Also, when the inevitable administrative screw–ups occur, it's your broker's responsibility to sort things out. A good broker not only ensures that orders are entered correctly but phones you promptly when they're executed. It's aggravating for a client to place an order to buy or sell something, and then not be told whether it's been filled. If a broker is casual about reporting back to you, he is either slothful or indifferent—or both.

Finally, you should be able to phone your broker at any time if you need advice, without feeling compelled to place an order. (Service is why you're paying him at least twice as much in commissions as a discount broker.) But remember that he has other clients, and don't waste his time with idle chat.

The topic of phoning your broker reminds me of my brother John, when he was about seventeen. John had saved a few hundred dollars from working that summer and invested part of it in a uranium stock called Can-Met. The lucky broker who executed his order (for five hundred shares at 17 cents) was the local manager of a major investment house, and an acquaintance of my parents. The day after buying Can-Met John called the broker five times for quotes; the next day seven times; and so it went. The broker, an exceedingly pompous individual, was hard-pressed to keep his temper. One could hardly blame him, because in those days, each time a quote was requested the broker had to leave his desk and pore through yards of ticker tape until he found the symbol. Several weeks later, John learned on his third call of the day that Can-Met had soared to 23 cents. While the broker held the phone and tried to control his rage, John digested this momentous news. Finally, after weighing all his options, John made his decision, "Sell half!"

As I said earlier, during your interview the broker will also be weighing you as a potential client. The first thing he will want to establish is the size of your account. Some successful brokers don't have the time to deal with small accounts. This may seem harsh, but it's a fact of life. (If you're a small account, don't lose heart, you can still build a nice portfolio with systematic purchases of mutual fund units—and you don't need a broker to do that.) The broker will also want to know if you've had any previous experience with other investment houses. If you've been dissatisfied with several other *reputable* firms, this may suggest to him that you are a chronic malcontent. Experience taught me to avoid this type of client, no matter what the size of their holdings, as they would never be satisfied. And this leads to the question of whether you, the client, plan to deal with several brokers. The advantage of having more than one broker is that you get research material and new issues from several sources. The disadvantage is that unless you are an *active trader* with a substantial portfolio, you will be an insignificant account with all your brokers. Far better to be a good account with one.

The foundation of a solid relationship between a broker and a client is mutual trust. If either party has the slightest doubt about the other's integrity, the two shouldn't do business with each other. One reason is that there are no written contracts (except for margin and special trading agreements) before a transaction takes place. Orders to buy and sell are given *verbally*, usually over the phone. If a broker deliberately misleads a client, it is very difficult to prove. If a client backs out of an order, the broker personally bears the loss. Once you have chosen a broker, you should accept his advice in good faith. Or as Bert, one of the rougher diamonds in my clientele, said to me, "Mr. Woods, if you screw up too often, you don't get no more of my business. Until then, we run!"

THE DISCOUNT BROKER

Now let's look at the alternative for investors—the discount broker. The fundamental differences between a full-service firm and a discount broker are *commissions* and *advice*. If you make your trades through a discount broker, you will save substantial amounts of commission. These savings increase with the size of the order and the price of the security. For instance Green Line, in the spring of 1994, was charging its direct trading clients:

	Full-Service Commission*	Green Line Commission	Indicated Savings
400 shares @ $4	$ 84	$ 52	38%
200 shares @$25	$126	$ 52	59%
1000 shares @$35	$590	$110	81%

*An average rate, charged by a number of leading firms.

To some extent these figures overstate the commission savings. For one thing, Green Line charges an additional $32 to register a security in your name, whereas the full–service brokers do it free. Also, for good clients, most full–service brokers will discount their commission rates by 10 to 40 percent. (But you must ask for the discount—and you may or may not get it.) Despite these reservations, you will almost always pay less with a discount broker.

Discount brokers can afford to charge lower commissions because they provide bare bones service. And while discounters in their advertising refer to the competition as "full-commission" rather than "full-service," implying in this way that their level of service is similar, this is not the case. When you enter an order with a discount house, you deal with whoever answers the phone—you won't have a specific broker. Because of this, it is prudent to *write down the name of the person you speak to, and note the time.* If an administrative problem arises (and I once encountered three with Green Line in as many weeks), you have a reference point to correct the error. I say reference point because Green Line records all its client calls.

The discount house employee who takes your order is essentially a clerk, licensed to make securities trades. These employees don't provide advice, nor are they qualified to do so. They are paid a salary, which removes the need for them to "sell," or to differentiate between large and small orders. Theoretically, every order is treated the same. Full-service brokers are paid on commission—an incentive to sell—and earn from two to twenty times as much as the discounters. Most full-service brokers, if they make an error, are personally accountable for it. This is one reason full-service houses don't make too many errors, and when they do, they are corrected at once. The possibility of having to pay several thousands of dollars out of your own pocket tends to focus your mind on getting it right. But the lack of accountability in the discount firms, combined with low wages and minimal qualifications all contribute to erratic service.

I think Green Line, a wholly owned subsidiary of the Toronto-Dominion bank, is the best Canadian discount house. It is also the oldest and by far the largest, having recently acquired its main rival, Marathon Brokerage. The other five of the"big six" Canadian chartered banks also offer discount brokerage, but in a tentative way. The reason they have only tiptoed into the business is that each of these banks controls a major full-service firm that is extremely profitable, and they don't want to jeopardize the bottom lines of these firms. The TD Bank, on the other hand, concentrates most of its efforts on its Green Line operation. Although Green Line's commission schedule is periodically undercut by its rivals, it will likely continue to be the discount leader in the field for the forseeable future.

Green Line publishes an elaborate catalogue, which is a do-it-yourself kit for investors. This catalogue contains books, investment periodicals, computer software, and research sources, all at discount prices. Indeed, in the discount business, the do-it-yourself aspect is likely to increase. Green Line has two automated services, TeleMax and MicroMax, that permit clients to place orders, check their account status, and receive trade confirmations *without speaking to an employee.* MicroMax orders are sent via your personal computer with a modem, while TeleMax orders are sent over your telephone. Both systems work, but to send a message by TeleMax, you must dial an endless string of numbers—it's far simpler just to pick up the phone and talk to someone.

The topic of phoning brings me to my final caveat about discount houses in general, and Green Line in particular: their phone systems. I don't know whether the phone capacity of discount houses is determined by cost or by client need, but I do know that in the market crash of 1987 many Green Line clients couldn't get through to the order desk. And, again, in January 1994, after Marathon Brokerage was taken over, Green Line experienced extended periods of interrupted phone service—on one occasion it took me two *days* to get through. I have since been assured that Green Line's phone system has been sorted out, and can handle heavy traffic. Time will tell.

Should you deal with a discount house? If saving on commission is your *only* consideration, the answer is yes. The person who can benefit most is a knowledgeable trader, who buys and sells frequently, in large quantities (the sort of account full-service brokers covet). This is especially true if the person trades options, which have fierce commissions. A discount house is also a good place for both large and small investors to buy mutual funds

(Green Line handles over three hundred funds) at reduced "front-end loads." Executing trades through a discount house also makes good sense if you are paying an investment advisor to manage your portfolio. In this instance your savings will offset, to some extent, the cost of the advisor's fees.

Some active investors maintain accounts with both a full-service and discount houses. This is reasonable enough—I do it myself—but it does raise an ethical question. Specifically, the temptation to take an idea from your full–service broker and to buy the stock through your discount house. There's no law to prevent this, and it happens all the time. But, in all fairness, if you pick your broker's brains, he deserves to get the business.

The average investor, in my opinion, is better off dealing with a full–service house. This assumes, of course, that your account is in the hands of a good broker. When you weigh the advantages of research material, advice, and personal service against reduced commissions, you should ask yourself one question: Am I investing *to make money* or *to save commissions*?

All this discussion about commissions reminds me of Harold, an old friend and client of mine, who used to needle me on the commissions he paid (which were substantial). His favourite way of getting his point across was with a joke—the same one—and he told it many times. It's an old chestnut, but you may not have heard it.

The setting is the yacht basin at the foot of Wall Street, in New York. Two men are standing on the pier; one is a native New Yorker, the other is a rube from out of town. With a sweep of his arm, the New Yorker points to the flotilla of luxury craft and says, "Those are all brokers' yachts."

The yokel gazes at them in awe for several minutes. Finally, he turns to his friend and asks, "But where are the customers' yachts?"

3

RULES
OF THE GAME

If you're going to invest, it helps to know the rules. Boring, but necessary. Even if you consider yourself an old pro, you may pick something up from this chapter—because knowledge of an arcane rule could save you grief, or money.

THE NEW CLIENT APPLICATION FORM

If you're a novice investor, the first thing you should know is how to open an account with a broker. It's quite simple and can be done by phone, fax, or by mail, as well as in person. All the broker has to do is to fill out the *new client application form*. Completion of this form is a legal requirement in the industry, and must be completed by the broker—and accepted by his firm—*before* you can make a transaction.

The information you provide will be treated confidentially. The first questions are your name, address, telephone number, and social insurance number. Also, you will be asked whether you want a cash or a margin account, or both. The difference between the two is: with a *cash account* all purchases are paid in full, but with a *margin account* the broker lends you a percentage of the purchase price. Assuming it's a cash account, the broker will need to know whether you want the firm to hold your securities, or to register and mail them out to you. If it's a margin account, you will have to sign a *margin agreement,* and your securities will be held by the broker as collateral. Any special instructions, such as those to do with the mailing of confirmations (invoices) or the delivery of certificates to your bank, will be noted. In this connection, if you want to open a joint account, a supplementary form is required that must be signed by you and your spouse or partner. The broker will supply this form. In certain cases a *guarantee* may be required for an account. Again, the broker has a standard form. If the account is a personal holding company or a corporation, a signed and sealed copy of the *corporate resolution* must be given to the broker.

Often one person will enter orders on behalf of another person—such as a husband for his wife. This is perfectly legal, providing a *trading authorization* is on file. This document, signed by the owner of the account, authorizes a specific person to trade on his or her behalf. I remember a woman I met at a cocktail party telling me that her husband, without her knowledge, had instructed her broker to sell her favourite stock. The stock subsequently went up threefold, and she was not a happy camper. I asked her if she had signed a trading authorization in favour of her husband. She hadn't, thus both her husband and her broker (who should have known better) were at fault. If she'd wanted to, she could have taken legal action against her broker. So, for everyone's protection it's prudent to have a signed trading authorization.

Other questions on the new client application concern your business and occupation. Your marital status is also of interest; if you're married, your spouse's name and occupation must also be recorded. The broker, for his part, states whether he has met you, how long he has known you, and whether you were referred by another client. He must also declare if he has a direct interest in your account. The interest is direct, for example, when the client is a spouse, relative, or a business partner. If the broker has direct interest, all the orders must be marked "PRO" (for professional) and are subject to the *preferential trading rule.* This rule ensures that when a regular client places an order to buy or sell a security at the *same price* as a PRO order, the regular client's order takes precedence.

Among the more personal questions on the form are your age, annual earnings, and net worth (which is arrived at by totting up your assets and deducting your debts). Your net worth need not be precise; only an estimate is required. But your earnings should be a fairly accurate figure. You will also be asked where you bank and the name of a contact at that institution. This is the normal extent of the credit check—and many brokers don't even bother to phone the bank. I rarely did, and was never stuck with a bad cheque.

The last section of the application deals with your investment objectives and your knowledge of the market. Both are very important. Your objectives are categorized as "income," "long-term growth," "speculation," and so on, and each is assigned a percentage figure. For example, your objectives might be "50 percent income" and "50 percent growth." Your investment knowledge will be graded as "excellent," "good," "fair," or "nil." This part of the questionnaire is *designed to protect you*, and to ensure that your broker's recommendations complement your objectives. If a widow, who was interested in safety and income, lost money on a raft of speculative securities, the new client application could be used as evidence against her broker. This actually happened some years ago in Toronto. An elderly grandmother sued her broker for her losses, but the case was dismissed because the new client application showed clearly that she was a "shooter" and played only highly speculative junior mines and oils.

The new client application ties in with the cardinal rule of the investment industry, which is, *know your client*. This maxim is drummed into brokers from the first day they enter the business. Knowing your client serves two purposes: to ensure that investment recommendations are appropriate for the account, and to protect the broker. Financial risk is, of course, the main reason the broker needs protection. When the application is completed, it is signed by your broker and an officer of the firm. Once this is done, you can start trading.

PLACING AN ORDER

For those who haven't invested through a broker before, it might be useful to go through what happens when you place an order. Let's say you want to buy two hundred shares of BCE Inc. You phone your broker and ask him what the "market" is on Bell common shares. He can give the answer in the blink of an eye, because he has a video terminal on his desk. By punching certain letters on the keyboard he has access to a variety of stock exchanges and can also retrieve a host of research data. After accessing the appropriate exchange, your broker enters the symbol for BCE Inc (which is "B"), and reads you the information on his screen. What you want to know is the "bid" and the "ask" on the stock, and the last price at which it traded.

The "bid" is the price at which someone is willing to *buy* a "board lot" of shares, and the "ask" is the price at which someone is willing to *sell* a board lot of shares. A board lot is a standard trading unit—in this case, one hundred shares. Whenever possible, you should trade in board lots (as opposed to "broken lots" or "odd lots"), because with board lots there is a smaller spread between the bid and the ask, and they are more marketable. In response to your question about the market on Bell, your broker might say "It's fifty to a half, trading at a quarter." This means the bid is $50 even; it is offered at $50.50; and the last trade was at $50.25. These different prices are due to the fact that stock exchanges are *auction markets*. Although most orders of less than a thousand shares are executed by CATS (the computer-assisted trading system), floor traders on the exchanges still communicate with hand signals and transact business by open outcry. On a busy day the floor of an exchange looks and sounds like a mob storming the Bastille.

The price you pay for Bell is up to you. You can tell your broker to buy the shares "at market," which will guarantee a fast execution, and you'll probably pay the offering price. Or you can stipulate any figure you wish *below* the asking price. If you stipulate a lower price, you may pick up a relative bargain. Then again, you may not buy the stock at all. My advice is once you've made up your mind, trade at market. When I say this, I think ruefully of the times I've bid for stocks below the going price, trying to be clever, and have missed them. The last one was a bid for a thousand shares of Magna International that I missed by one-eighth of a point, or 12½ cents a share. This happened a few months ago—since then, Magna has gone up over $30 a share! The only time I wouldn't go in at market is if the stock is an infrequent trader, which usually means a wide gap between the bid and the ask. In this situation you will pay more for the shares or get less for them than you should. Either stipulate a price, or better still, stick to actively traded stocks.

Let me briefly review some of the other types of orders. For instance, you can stipulate a time limit, such as "good to the 15th of February." This might be done to receive a dividend on a stock that trades "ex-dividend" (in other words, doesn't qualify for the dividend) after that date. In this connection, there are three dates to watch with dividends: the *ex-dividend date* (which the stock exchanges use to determine who gets the dividend); the *record date* (which the transfer agent uses to determine who will receive the dividend); and the *payment date*. The earliest is the ex-dividend date; the last is the payment date.

You can also enter an "open" order, which will be valid for thirty days. A "day" order is just that, good for the day. An "all or none" order means that unless it can be filled at one swoop, it will not be executed. The latter is chosen to avoid picking up small lots over a period of days and paying a minimum commission each time—or to ensure that you get a significant chunk rather than bits and pieces. Similarly, a "fill or kill" order means that the trader has moments to execute it before it is cancelled. Unless you're an institution and don't want to disturb the market, there's no justification for this type of order. Of more relevance to the average investor are "stop loss" and "stop buy" orders. Their purpose is to limit your loss by an automatic sale or purchase when the stock trades at a certain price. As soon as the stock reaches that price, your order becomes a *market* order, and it may be filled *above or below* the stop loss price. Finally, "contingent" orders are orders in which the purchase of one stock is dependent upon the sale of another, or vice versa, at a predetermined price spread between the two stocks. Contingent orders are tricky, and many brokers no longer accept them—unless you are a very big trader.

Getting back to your purchase of BCE Inc. shares let's suppose you tell your broker to buy them at market. He will write out your order on a special blue form. (Blue forms are used for buy orders, pink for sell orders—the colour contrast is to help prevent errors, which can be hideously expensive.) The blue ticket is either telexed or handed to the order desk. From the order desk it will be routed through CATS, the automated system. If the order is large, or has special conditions are attached to it, it will be sent to one of the firm's traders on the floor of the exchange. The trader will then walk to the post where the stock is traded and execute it. These may sound like drawn out procedures, but in practice most orders are executed within seconds.

As soon as your shares of BCE have been purchased, a wire is sent to the originating office. Your broker is handed a time-stamped copy of the order, which shows the price paid for the shares. If he's a conscientious broker—and he's not enmeshed in something else—he will immediately pick up the phone and call you with the news of your purchase.

Before leaving the subject of stock orders, let me mention one more point. Whether you're buying or selling, always describe your order by the number of shares, not by its dollar value. Dollar value is fine if you're buying potatoes or filling your car with gas, but not if you're trading equities. I had a new client, a doctor, who gave me an order to buy "four thousand of Bank of Commerce." I bought him four thousand shares of CIBC, and when he received the contract he nearly fainted. What he had meant was four thousand dollars *worth* of Commerce, which at that time would have been two hundred shares. (The tale has a happy ending, though: he made a quick profit before selling out.) About the only time dollar value is used in trading equities is with mutual funds. Even then, many people trade in units rather than gross dollar value. (With mutual funds you can do it either way.) To be on the safe side, always have your broker repeat your order back to you before you hang up the phone.

The Settlement Date

Following on the heels of any security trade will be a written confirmation from your broker. *Confirmation* is the term used in the investment business for a bill or an invoice.

Midland-Walwyn Confirmation

MIDLAND WALWYN

AS AGENTS, WE CONFIRM THE FOLLOWING FOR YOUR ACCOUNT ON THE
TORONTO STOCK EXCHANGE

APR 4, 1994

400   ROYAL BANK OF CANADA   26.25   GROSS $10,500.00

SOL   COMMISION   193.31

SPECIMEN ONLY

Client accounts are protected by the Canadian Investor Protection Fund within specified limits. A brochure describing the nature and limits of coverage is available upon request.

Les comptes de clients sont protégés en vertu du Fonds canadien de protection des épargnants jusqu'à concurrence de certaines limites stipulées. Une brochure décrivant la nature et les modalités de cette protection est disponible sur demande.

Interest Payable on Overdue Accounts/Intérêt imputé sur les comptes en souffrance

Net Amount
Montant Net $10,693.31

Payment for purchase or receipt of securities sold is due on settlement date.

Le paiement pour l'achat de titres ou la livraison de titres vendus sont exigibles à la date de règlement.

FOR SETTLEMENT ON APR 11, 1994

Bought or sold & confirmed by
Payment & Settlement at

Acheté ou vendu et confirmé par paiement ou règlement au

77 WESTMORLAND STREET, SUITE 130
FREDERICTON, NEW BRUNSWICK
E3B 6Z3   TEL: (506)4588322

Please retain for tax purposes/Veuillez conserver cet avis d'exécution pour fins d'impôt

JOE INVESTOR
ANYTOWN
N.B.

	Type Genre	SEC.	# 0000
		REF.	1111
	AGIG	CUSIP	780087102

Account No.
N° de compte
T95 09-1010-0

ALISON DRAPER
Financial Advisor/Représentant

You will notice the confirmation shows the number of shares, whether they were bought or sold, a description of the security, its price, and the amount of commission charged on the transaction. In addition, there are two dates on the confirmation: the *transaction date* (the day the order was executed), and the *settlement date*. The one to watch is the settlement date. On or before this date you must "settle" the account by paying for the shares or delivering the securities you have sold. A personal cheque, which usually does not have to be certified, is the normal form of payment. It is also your responsibility if you have done several transactions, such as a number of buys and sells, to know the net amount you owe—and to pay it by the settlement date. If you're not sure of your calculations, your broker will sort out the net amount. The settlement date applies to the broker as well—on that date he must pay any balance owing to you.

If you fail to pay for a purchase by the settlement date, or fail to deliver the certificate for a sale, the broker has the legal right to "sell you out" or to "buy you in." This means he can sell the shares you haven't paid for, or buy back the shares you haven't delivered. He would do this to avoid financial loss, as he is acting as your agent and must make good on the transaction with a third party. In the event of being sold out or bought in, the client bears the expense. Most brokers will go to great lengths to avoid selling out or buying in a client (because that's usually the end of the relationship), but they have the right to do so.

Settlement dates vary, depending upon the type of security. Listed stocks settle *five business days* after the transaction date, as do most unlisted stocks, bonds, and mutual funds. (This is easy to remember, except when statutory holidays intervene, it's exactly one week from the day of the transaction.) Options usually settle *one day* after the transaction; some bonds settle *two days* after the transaction; and Treasury Bills settle the *same or the following day*. Again, if you're in doubt, check with your broker *before* you make the trade.

New issues are an entirely different kettle of fish. A new issue, be it debt or equity, can settle up to six weeks from the date of the transaction. Another peculiarity about new issues, which puzzles many people, is the phrase "if as and when issued," printed on many confirmations. This is a boilerplate phrase, which for all intents and purposes can be ignored. It's there to protect the underwriters in the unlikely event that there is a glitch—such as a legal problem—which forces them to delay or cancel the issue. But this is most unusual. By the time you receive your confirmation, even though it says "if as and when issued," it is usually a done deal. And you are on the hook for it.

The Prospectus and the Right of Rescission

You do, however, have one legitimate avenue of escape: your *right of rescission*. When you receive your confirmation, you will also receive a *prospectus*, which is a legal document that provides comprehensive information on the issue. If the prospectus contains a false or misleading statement, you can, if you wish, exercise your right of rescission and rescind (cancel) the contract. You will rarely get this opportunity, because lawyers pore over the prospectus—and are challenged on the smallest technicality by the securities commissions—until it is virtually letter perfect. A prospectus is a most revealing document and should be read *before* you commit yourself to buying a new issue. (One of the old saws in the business is "investigate before you invest," which may sound trite but it still make sense.)

If you can't get a "definitive" prospectus, you can often get hold of a "preliminary" prospectus from your broker. Known in the trade as a "red herring," a preliminary prospectus contains most of the vital information, except for the price of the issue.

The Certificate

When you buy a security and tell the broker you want it registered in your name, this will be done only *after* you've paid for it. Physical delivery of the certificate may take five or six weeks. The reason for the time lag is that the certificate is issued by the company's transfer agent, usually a trust company, and trust companies are not noted for their speed. Nevertheless, from the moment you buy the security you are, for practical purposes, the beneficial owner. If you wish, you can sell it fifteen minutes later, even though you don't yet possess the certificate. This is feasible only if you buy and sell through the *same* broker (because the security is on his books), but if you sell through another broker you may have a late delivery problem. Remember, settlement is five business days and the broker can, at his discretion, levy a late delivery interest penalty.

A few months ago I bought two thousand shares of a new issue: one thousand shares from a full-service broker and a thousand from Green Line. The stock stumbled out of the starting gate, and continued to falter for the next few weeks. I had intended to hold the shares as an investment, but they acted so badly that I changed my mind. When I sold them through Green Line, I knew that the certificate from the full-service broker might be a few days late, but it seemed a minor consideration. Not so. I was nine days late in delivering the certificate, and Green Line charged me interest at an annual rate of 21 percent. Ironically, the full-service broker would have charged an interest penalty of only 7 percent. Twenty-one percent interest really smarts, and it was a painful reminder to have the certificate in hand before you place a sell order.

Another common problem is "good delivery" of the certificate. Good delivery means that the certificate must not only be on time, but in transferable form (i.e., in a legal form that permits it to be transferred to the buyer). If the security is registered in your name, you must sign it on the back, before it can be considered good delivery. This can also be accomplished by signing a power of attorney form, which is then attached to the certificate. Never sign a power of attorney unless it specifies the security and the certificate number. And be sure to get a receipt whenever you deliver a certificate.

A stock certificate is an interesting piece of paper. The more expensive ones are engraved with special inks and have the feel of a banknote. (This is not surprising; in Canada most certificates are made by the two principal banknote companies.) Certificates often contain a vignette of one or more human forms—typically, a muscular man or a voluptuous woman in clinging robes. This is not cheesecake but a device to foil counterfeiters, as it is almost impossible to reproduce subtle flesh tones and the texture of cloth in a steel engraving.

Some securities, such as Treasury Bills, come in "bearer" form, which means they are not registered in anyone's name.

This type of certificate, or one that has been previously signed off, is as negotiable as a banknote and should be treated with the same care. Whatever type of certificate you present to your broker, it must be in good physical condition. If your baby has vomited on it, or the dog has chewed it, it may not be considered good delivery.

This reminds me of a call I got one day from the agitated wife of a grumpy client. That morning, when the postman put the mail through the slot, their dog had snatched an envelope and shredded it. Unfortunately, the envelope contained a certificate for seven hundred shares of Imperial Oil that belonged to her husband—and her husband was not fond of the dog. I sent the tattered remains of the certificate off to the transfer agent with a flowery request for rush service. We were lucky; just two weeks later the new certificate arrived in the mail. The dog didn't get his teeth into it, and my grumpy client was none the wiser.

Always keep your certificates in a safe place. If a certificate is lost or stolen, it's sometimes possible to replace it, but this is a long and expensive process, and involves the purchase of an idemnity bond. Yet, many people treat them casually and leave them lying around the house. The best thing to do is place your certificates in a safety deposit box, or leave them with your broker. Normally brokers don't charge for safekeeping, but they usually insist that the securities be held in the firm's name. The main advantage of leaving certificates with your broker is the convenience. When you sell, you don't have to worry about delivery and the broker collects all your interest and dividends. At the end of the year the firm sends you a T5 form for tax purposes. There are some disadvantages, though. When a broker holds your securities, you may not receive annual and quarterly reports, unless you specifically request they be sent. There is also an element of risk. If one of the firm's employees takes off to Rio de Janeiro with your securities, the firm's insurance would probably cover the loss. But if the firm went belly up, it would be another matter. In this instance, however, the contingency fund might fill the breach. I would add that if thieves tunnelled into your bank and removed the contents of your safety deposit box you'd have an equally serious problem. These hazards notwithstanding, a bank or brokerage firm is a much safer place for your securities than your bureau drawer.

Microstar Software Stock Certificate

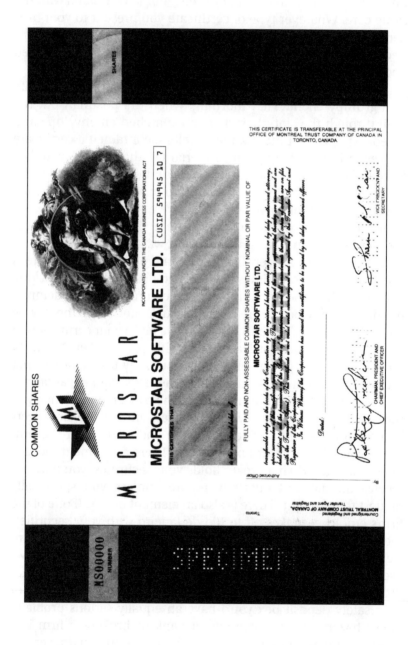

INVESTING ON MARGIN

If you invest *on margin* (that is, through a margin account, which was described at the start of this chapter) you will have no choice as to who holds your securities—your broker will, as collateral. There are other things you should also know about margin. First, buying on margin means you're playing with borrowed money. This gives you leverage on your investments. The good thing about leverage is that it can magnify your winnings. But leverage is a two-edged sword—it can also magnify your losses. With margin the broker lends you a stated percentage of the value of the security at the outset of the transaction. You put up the balance and pay the broker interest on the loan. If the stock falls, the value of the broker's loan declines with the shares, and you must make up the difference. But if the stock rises, you build up a cash credit, which you can make withdrawals on, or use to finance another purchase.

Before you can invest on margin you must, as mentioned near the start of this chapter, sign a margin agreement. Regardless of the firm you choose, the wording is standard—and odious—in all margin agreements. Of the dozen or so clauses, the one that most people choke at permits the broker *at his discretion*, to sell them out or buy them in *without notice*. Brokers very rarely invoke this clause, and when they do, it is to protect themselves (and often the client). Indeed, brokers encourage margin accounts for two very good reasons. First, a client on margin is playing with more money and hence generating more in commission. Secondly, the broker makes a profit on the loan to the client. The rate of interest is usually 1 percent above prime, because the broker normally charges 1 percent more than it costs the firm to borrow from the bank. Close scrutiny of a margin agreement makes unpleasant reading and I once had a couple of lawyers who refused to sign. Eventually, however, they realized there was no way around it, and we got on with their business.

Your margin requirement is always stated as a percentage, which you must put up in cash or securities. The percentage varies with the perceived risk of the security and its price. Thus, short Canada bonds may be purchased for as little as 3 percent margin, while some low-priced stocks require 80 percent. Other stocks are not marginable at all. A typical rate for a stock listed on the Toronto exchange is 50 percent margin. Here is an example, using this rate, of how margin works:

Client buys 500 shares @$12		cost $6000
Broker's loan to client 50%	$3000	
Client puts up 50%	$3000	
	$6000	$6000

If the shares decline to $10, the client will receive a *margin call*, and have to put up an additional $500, as the following calculation shows:

Value of shares now	$5000		cost $6000
Broker's loan now (50% of $5000)		$2500	
Client's deposit (50% of $6000)		$3000	
		$5500	$6000
Margin requirement (shortfall)		$500	

Had the shares risen in price to $14, the client would have had surplus margin, and could have withdrawn up to $500.

Value of shares now	$7000		cost $6000
Broker's loan now (50% of $7000)		$3500	
Client's deposit (50% of $6000)		$3000	
		$6500	$6000
Excess margin (surplus)		$500	

Not all brokers offer margin to their clients. The exchanges and regulatory bodies set the *minimum* margin requirements, but a firm can set higher requirements if it wishes, and can also decide what securities it is prepared to finance on margin. Some firms get criticized for taking too strict a stance on margin, especially for stocks on the Vancouver Exchange, but those are also the firms whose clients usually stay out of trouble.

Margin accounts are monitored by the exchanges and the Investment Dealers Association. If a broker permits clients to trade with insufficient margin, the firm is subject to heavy fines. For this reason brokers keep a close eye on their accounts and issue a margin call whenever a client is under margin. A margin call is a demand for more money—usually made by telephone or telegram—and the recipient must respond immediately. Both brokers and clients hate margin calls. Jesse Livermore, the legendary Wall Street plunger who had direct lines to thirty brokers, had this to say on the subject: "I know but one sure tip from a broker. It is your margin call. When it reaches you, close your account. You are on the wrong side of the market."

Unlisted Stocks

Most unlisted stocks are not marginable. The unlisted market is really a floating crap game in that it has no premises, and transactions are done between dealers over the phone. Trades on the exchanges are executed by *auction* (or by computer), whereas on the unlisted market they are done by *negotiation*. So, not only is it difficult to regulate the unlisted market, but it's also difficult to keep track of what's happening there. These last two factors create so much risk that unlisted stocks are considered too dangerous for margin purposes. My advice is to avoid unlisted stocks, except for newly issued shares of senior corporations that are about to be listed on an exchange.

Short Sales

All short sales are made on margin. You make money with a short sale when the price of the stock goes *down*. Margin is needed because you are selling shares you don't own, and the broker must lend them to you. The strategy of a short sale is to sell borrowed shares at a relatively high price and to buy them back ("cover the short sale") at a lower price. Your profit is the difference between what you sold them for (remember you didn't *own* them) and what it cost to buy them back.

A short sale is a perfectly ethical way to make money. But it's not a particularly easy way, because of the hazards and restrictions.

Before making a short sale you must check with your broker to see if he can borrow the stock for you. Assuming that he can, your order must be marked "short sale." This means that your trade cannot be executed at a lower price than the previous trade. (The purpose of this rule is to prevent a stock from being hammered into the ground by short sellers—which is known as a "bear raid.") Having sold short, you may be forced to buy the shares back without warning if the lender demands delivery of his stock. At best, your maximum profit is the amount you sold the shares for. On the other hand, if the stock goes up, your potential loss is *limitless*. If you think a stock is headed lower and you want to profit from the decline, your best course is to buy "puts." Puts will be discussed in the chapter on options.

Margin works best when interest rates are at the *low* end of the cycle. The interest rate factor is often overlooked, but it can have a powerful influence when rates are in the double-digit range. For example, if you're paying 12 percent margin, over the course of a year your investments have to appreciate by at least half that percentage *just to break even.*

The great appeal of buying on margin is that you can play with more chips. Equally compelling are the negative consequences, which can be disastrous if you lose playing with borrowed money. On balance, margin is for the experienced trader. It is not for the average investor.

4
SOURCES OF INFORMATION AND ADVICE

As an investor, you owe it to yourself to know what is going on in the business world and in the markets. Failing to keep abreast of events can cost you money in the shape of missed opportunities—as well as outright losses. With apologies to Rudyard Kipling, if you can keep your head while all around you others are losing theirs, you probably haven't heard the news.

NEWSPAPERS

One way to keep informed is to read a good newspaper. My favourite is *The Globe and Mail*, which is printed simultaneously across the country and is available the same day in most cities. The Report on Business section in the *Globe* provides excellent financial coverage. In addition to business news, the ROB devotes many pages to the markets, including bar charts (with matching volume charts) of both the Toronto Stock Exchange and the New York Stock Exchange. And, as well as regular coverage of mutual funds, each month there is a special section devoted exclusively to funds. The *Globe* also publishes an annual reference work, the *Canada Company Handbook*, which covers all the current and former companies that comprise the TSE 300 Index.

The Financial Post is on a par with the *Globe* for coverage and content. This is not surprising because the paper is entirely dedicated to business and market matters. If anything, the *Post* covers the markets in greater depth, and focuses more on the global picture. The *Post's* huge stable of writers is as good as any in the business—I particularly enjoy Diane Francis and Patrick Bloomfield. *The Financial Post* also publishes several books annually that are standard reference works in the investment industry. Two of the most useful are the *Survey of Industrials* and the *Survey of Mines and Energy Resources*. Both are comprehensive and relatively expensive.

If you don't subscribe to the *Globe* or the *Post*, you can still keep in reasonable touch with the markets through dailies such as *The Toronto Star, the Vancouver Sun, The Gazette*, and *The Chronicle-Herald*. But if you're a serious investor, you should make sure to read the *Post* or the *Globe*—and it wouldn't hurt to read both.

For investors interested in the American market, or who want a broader view of the financial scene, one daily stands out above the rest—*The Wall Street Journal*. It needs no introduction. *The Wall Street Journal* contains masses of information and is noted for its superb editorials. Unfortunately, it arrives on the stands a day late in most Canadian cities, and is unavailable in many parts of the country.

The Financial Times of Canada is a long-established weekly paper that was taken over by the *Globe and Mail* and downsized in the process. In larger Canadian cities *The Financial Times* is a supplement to the Saturday issue of the *Globe*, but it is also sold separately (especially in rural areas). The *Times* used to be the leader in mutual fund coverage, but this is no longer the case. It does, however, have a monthly mutual fund issue, and it also publishes a series of personal finance books. What I find most useful are the stock trend tables. These tables provide concise information on the stocks listed on the SE and give a trend rating for each one. Over the years I've found these ratings to be suprisingly accurate.

The Northern Miner is another venerable weekly, which caters to investors and people in the mining industry. It's not a source of hot tips—by the time drilling news appears in *The Northern Miner*, it's already been discounted in the market. But it does provide a lot of information on what's happening in the field. If you work in the mining industry, or if your main interest is mining stocks, it would be worthwhile subscribing to *The Northern Miner.*

MAGAZINES AND PERIODICALS

Business magazines, because of the time lag in publication, are really only good as sources of background information. But, as such, they do have their place. In this country, *Canadian Business* is probably the best. South of the border the choice is much greater, with *Barron's, Business Week, Forbes*, and *Fortune* leading the pack.

After business magazines come investment periodicals. There are scores of them in the United States, and if I had to choose only one, it would be the *Value Line*. It is an information service, which is supplied in weekly instalments. The *Value Line* covers approximately sixteen hundred leading North American companies, most of which are listed on U.S. exchanges. Each company is summarized on a single page, which includes a stock chart, statistics, a description, *Value Lines's* opinion of the company, and a rating on its timeliness as a buy and its safety. For those interested only in Canadian securities, *Value Line* publishes a separate Canadian Edition. The *Value Line* have had a good batting average and a solid reputation for many years.

Turning to Canadian "market letters" or investment periodicals, *The Investment Reporter* is the dean of them all, having been around in one form or another for more than half a century. Published weekly, it dispenses conservative no-nonsense advice. Each month it also sends out an Investment Planning Guide, which usually involves an analysis and restructuring of a hypothetical portfolio. Because *The Investment Reporter* stresses a portfolio approach, it is not for the trader—you won't get rich quick by following its recommendations. But if you're interested in building a quality portfolio, it's well worth the subscription price.

The *Money Letter* is another seasoned periodical, and it enjoys the largest circulation in Canada. The format of the *Money Letter*, is that of a panel of experts offering specific recommendations on a variety of stocks, bonds, currencies, and mutual funds. The senior editor is Gordon Pape, best known as Canada's leading mutual fund guru. Among the other regular contributors is a chartered accountant, David Louis, who's been with the *Money Letter* for years, and who comments on tax shelters and related topics. A fair percentage of The *Money Letter's* recommendations turn out to be winners. But not all of them, so some judgement is required on your part. Aside from this *caveat* , I would say the *Money Letter* is an excellent choice for the aggressive investor.

Investor's Digest is also a well-established periodical. It's published every two weeks and provides, through brokers' research reports, an insight into opinions on the Street. As well as its regular contributors—headed by Patrick McKeough—each issue features an interview with a top analyst or investment manager. One of the most interesting sections of this letter are the three or four pages devoted to earnings estimates by various brokers. *Investor's Digest*, which is one of the MPL Communications stable (along with *The Money Reporter* and *The Investment Reporter*), is a nicely packaged reference product for sophisticated investors.

Money Digest is the journal of the Investors Association of Canada (a private enterprise). It is published monthly, and there are three special issues each year: an Annual Investment Guide, a Guide to Mutual Funds, and an Investors Resource Directory. This letter covers a broad range of personal finance topics including insurance, estate planning, and home ownership. *Money Digest* has a competent editorial board, and also draws on some big names for its special issues. However, the level of information in the *Digest* is fairly basic, which suggests it may be aimed at the novice investor. On the other hand, it's an excellent value: a subscription to *Money Digest* costs about one-third of what comparable market letters charge, and includes membership in the Investors Association of Canada.

MARKET LETTERS

The main methods used to forecast prices are *fundamental* analysis and *technical* analysis. These are explained in a later chapter, but I mention them now as a means of introducing Ian McAvity, who is one of the most successful technical analysts around and a Canadian. He publishes a bimonthly market letter, *Deliberations*. This letter covers a broad spectrum, which includes interest rates, currencies, precious metals, and stocks. *Deliberations* is designed for the sophisticated investor, and attracts subscribers from all over the world.

As a general observation with regard to market letters, it's fair to say that all are right part of the time, but none are right all the time. And I would add that flat statements, such as "this stock will hit $70 by May" or "the market will fall in the next thirty days," should be taken with a grain of salt. No one has been able to foretell market prices *consistently*, although some have had brief and sensational spells of being right. Joe Granville comes to mind. Joe, the flamboyant author of *The Granville Market Letter*, attained astounding prominence in the late '70s. By 1980, his market pronouncements were having such an effect that New York stocks he recommended would be delayed in trading because of the influx of orders. With uncanny precision Granville predicted the top of the market, and told his subscribers to sell out. The market fell, and continued to do so for many months. Everyone held their breath, and waited for Joe to tell them when to buy in again. Joe boasted that when he gave the buy signal, there would be such a stampede that the exchanges would have to close. He may have been right. But we'll never know because Joe never gave the buy signal—even after the market bottomed in August 1982 and proceeded to make a slow rebound. Joe told his disciples that it was a false rally and instructed them to short the market. This proved most unfortunate, because during the next sixteen months the Dow Jones industrial average rose more than five hundred points. Those who followed Granville's advice lost their shirts and Joe lost his reputation for infallibility (as well as many of his subscribers).

The market is made up of those who think stocks will go up (bulls) and those who think they will fall (bears), so also do writers of market letters break down into bulls and bears. Most market pundits are bulls, although they will change their tune from time to time. But the bears take more persuading to change their song, and some never do—these are the "professional bears." The hallmarks of professional bears is that they are not only down on the market, but they also have a jaundiced view of both the economy and the currency. Almost invariably, the only investment they recommend is gold. Because of the cyclical nature of securities markets, professional bears are right several times each decade. Rather like a stopped clock (but a stopped clock is right twice every twenty-four hours.)

MARKET LETTERS THAT SELL SECURITIES

So far we have been looking at periodicals or market letters that only provide information and advice—they don't sell securities—and in every instance, you must pay for the publication. Now we come to market letters published by brokers and mutual fund dealers. These are free, and their objective is not only to inform, but also to create demand for their products or services. Market letters from the better investment houses are well worth reading, and frequently contain good research and useful recommendations.

Legitimate market letters shouldn't be confused with "tout sheets" or brochures sent out by stock promoters. These fly-by-night operators try to imitate the format of an ethical market letter, and usually begin by referring to senior resource stocks. This is to lull you into a false sense of security. Then mention is made of a major discovery by a company like Noranda. (Noranda is a favourite because it has mines all over the place.) Now, watch for it, here comes the dart. A mere nine hundred kilometres north of the Noranda discovery, an *identical* ore body has been found by Moose Pasture Mines. The rest of the letter goes on to extol the virtues of Moose Pasture Mines, and urges you to buy its shares. File this type of "market letter" in the wastebasket.

INVESTMENT COUNSELLORS AND FINANACIAL PLANNERS

Turning away from publications and towards people, we come to investment counsellors and financial planners. In the case of financial planners, some are well qualified to provide advice, while others are merely mutual fund or insurance vendors. An easy way to determine which is which is to ask whether the financial planner charges a fee. If no fee is involved, you can be certain that mutual funds or insurance (possibly both) will enter the picture. Financial planners, who are primarily concerned with money management for individuals, normally charge by the hour or ask a flat fee for the entire program. Investment counsellors, on the other hand, focus on the securities markets and portfolio management. They are licensed to dispense advice, and don't sell anything other than their expertise. For a fee, investment counsellors will advise you on your holdings, or they will manage your entire portfolio (and place the orders for you). Most of the country's investment counselling firms are in Toronto, but there are also some in Montreal, Vancouver, and other Canadian cities.

Investment counsellors are not for small investors as the *minimum* account most will accept is usually between five hundred thousand and a million dollars. Their fees are on a sliding scale, and range between ½ and 3 percent of the value of your portfolio. The larger the portfolio, the lower the fee percentage. Some counsellors have an arrangement whereby they charge a relatively low fee, but also get a bonus depending upon the performance of the portfolio. (This type of remuneration is only suitable for aggressive accounts—not for widows and orphans.) With a managed portfolio, custody of your securities is normally with a chartered bank, and you will have to sign a limited or full power of attorney and a discretionary authority. A discretionary agreement allows the firm to trade, at their discretion, on your behalf. A limited power of attorney means that the counselling firm can only circulate your funds within your portfolio, whereas a full power of attorney permits the firm to withdraw funds, even from your bank account. Because there's a major element of trust involved, it is prudent to ask around—some are better than others—and to check carefully into the background of a counselling firm before signing on the dotted line.

Green Line Investor Services has published *Green Pages*, a booklet that lists most of the investment counsellors in Canada. It contains a concise review of each firm, including fees, the amount of assets under management, and each firm's investment philosophy. The amount of assets under management is relevant because, though it doesn't necessarily indicate competence, it does show how well the firm is established. *Green Pages* also discusses the questions you should ask when shopping for an investment counsellor or financial advisor. All in all, it's an extremely useful book.

Portfolio management is also available from the major investment houses. For a comparable fee, you can get the same services that are provided by the investment counselling firms. Some houses will even put trades through other brokers (to get you new issues), and will discount your commissions. If you decide to have your portfolio managed professionally by a broker, you should be aware of two potential problems. The first is that being a broker, the firm may "churn" your holdings to generate commissions. The second is that being underwriters, the firm might dump new issues into your account that it can't sell elsewhere. Both have happened in the past, but there is little risk of these abuses occurring today.

TRUST COMPANIES

Depending on the size of your account and your threshold of pain, you can also pay a trust company to manage your portfolio. This would make sense if you decided to place all your assets in the hands of a single custodian. A trust company—for a hefty fee—will look after your financial needs while you live, and administer your estate after you die. This would not, however, be a good idea if you are looking for above average performance from your portfolio. Trust companies are by nature (except when mortgaging real estate) very conservative investors.

FREE ADVICE

Now we come to free advice, and there's lots of it around. Among the sources of investment tips are bartenders, hairdressers, people at cocktail parties, Aunt Becky, your brother-in-law, and sundry acquaintances. If properly approached, you may also get free investment advice from your lawyer, your doctor, and your bank manager. Ignore them all, especially your bank manager (who will either try to sign you up for a long-term GIC, or refer you to the person in the branch licensed to sell mutual funds).

BROKERS

I've deliberately not mentioned another source of advice—your broker. The downside of asking your broker for advice is that he may sell you something. Having got that out of the way, you'll have to admit that he's the logical person to speak to because the market is his livelihood. If your broker doesn't know the answer, he can ask someone in the firm's research department. Unless you have a computer with special software, your broker is the only person who can give you up-to-the-minute market reports. In addition to his video terminal connected to the exchange, he also has access to an astonishing amount of research information—much of it generated in-house. It need hardly be added that your broker has a powerful incentive to give you good advice. If he gives you bad advice, he may lose your account. But if he can make money for you, you'll do more business with him—and you may recommend him to your friends. In essence, this is a stick-and-carrot situation.

Many people think it's impossible to make big money in the market unless you have inside information. The accepted belief is that unless you've got a friend who's a corporate bigwig, or you're sitting beside your broker when he gets a phone call from an insider, you're out of luck. And by some form of osmosis, the closer you are situated to Bay Street or Wall Street, the better your chances of making money. This is not true. Let me tell you about Victor.

Victor was a client of mine for years. A retired civil servant, he lived on the outskirts of Ottawa. One day a man came to his door who was selling cemetery plots. This was a longer-term investment than Victor cared to make, but he was intrigued and asked the man in for a cup of coffee. They chatted about the cemetery business and Victor learned it was booming. After the salesman left, Victor hustled down to the public library and looked up the financial information on the cemetery company. The name of the company was Arbor Capital, and it had cemeteries across Canada. Its shares, which traded infrequently, were listed on the Toronto Stock Exchange.

Victor started off by buying 2000 shares of Arbor Capital at $1.07. Over the course of the next year he bought more and eventually accumulated a total of 12,000 shares at an average price of $2.31 per share. He placed most of the stock in his Registered Retirement Savings Plan. This was a wise move because the shares took off, and three years later—after a two-for-one split—were worth the equivalent of more than $25 per share. Because the stock was in his RRSP, Victor had a tax-sheltered profit of $275,000. A few years later he converted his Arbor Capital winnings into a handsome Registered Retirement Income Fund. Victor had no inside information—but he was smart enough to recognize an investment opportunity when it knocked on his door.

SOFTWARE

In addition to all the investment information available in hard copy, there are many programs on disk for personal computers. These programs allow you to access markets for up-to-the-second quotes; they'll draw charts for you; using them, you can enter orders and check your brokerage account; and they'll keep a running tabulation of your portfolio. And that's only a sample—there are many more programs. I'm not going to list brand names, because software is constantly changing. But if you're interested in investment software you should read the ads in the financial press and check with your full-service broker, or Green Line, to learn what's currently available.

TELEVISION

Investors can also get market reports and other investment information from the radio and television. *Wall Street Week* is probably the most popular TV program on investments in North America. Shown on the PBS network on Friday nights, it has a good many million viewers. I used to watch *Wall Street Week* faithfully, thinking I would learn what was really happening in the American market, and pick up some gems of wisdom. Alas, what I discovered was that some of the high-powered guests knew what they were talking about, but some did not. My problem was to know who I should believe, and this stumped me. What I did conclude was that the regular panelists, who appear on every show, were usually wrong in their assessment of the market. Eventually, I quit watching the show.

Instead, I have been tuning in to *Business World* on the CBC Newsworld network (on cable). This half-hour program is broadcast nightly during the week, and there's a slightly different show on the weekend. Co-hosts Christina Pochmursky and Ron Adams are well informed and conduct knowledgeable interviews. The format of the show is to begin with a review of the day's business events (often with an interview). This is followed by a report on the Canadian and other major markets. Then, after a commercial break, a broker, or someone in the investment business, is interviewed by Adams or Pochmursky. The final quarter of the program is usually devoted to a fairly general topic.

Business World also has a strong roster of regular guests. Dunnery Best, a former editor of *The Financial Times* and now a broker, is one of my favourites. As well as being articulate, Best has an excellent grasp of the market. But what endears him to me is his enthusiasm and unquenchable optimism. I spoke of professional bears earlier in this chapter; Dunnery Best is the nearest you'll get to a professional bull. At the other end of the spectrum, there's the economist Arthur Donner who comments sagely, but with a certain amount of reservation, on weighty matters like unemployment, budgets, and other financial data.

I've watched *Business World* now for several years and find it a painless way to keep informed. In my opinion it's as good a show as there is on the tube. I recommend it to any investor interested in the Canadian market.

5

BONDS

Bonds are the foundation of any balanced investment portfolio. And because the bond market is tied to interest rates, bond prices profoundly affect the stock market. Trading value in the bond market is more than ten times the combined value of all trades on Canada's stock exchanges. So, even if you're only interested in stocks or mutual funds and have no intention of owning bonds—you should know something about them.

A bond is a promissory note with a specified face value and a term of from one to thirty years. When you buy a bond, you're *lending* the issuer your money for a stated period. In return, the borrower pays you an agreed rate of interest during that period, and when the time is up you get your money back. The amount you get back when the loan matures is the face value on the certificate. Interest is paid, usually twice a year, by cheque or by coupons attached to the certificate.

Interest rates differ among credit risks, but one rule holds true: *the higher the risk, the higher the rate of interest.* Government of Canada bonds pay the lowest interest, while, at the other end of the spectrum, weak corporations pay the highest rates—these high-risk, high-yield bonds are known as "junk bonds."

Bond prices rise and fall with interest rates. The relationship between interest rates and bond prices is the same as a seesaw. *When interest rates decline, bond prices go up.* Conversely, *when interest rates rise, bond prices go down.* There is a logical reason for this relationship.

Let's assume that the prevailing rate of interest for a bond maturing in ten years is 8 percent. This means that people with money to invest can buy ten-year bonds to *yield* them 8 percent. ("Yield" is the return, expressed as a percentage, from a security.) Now suppose you have to sell a ten-year bond that has a rate of interest (*coupon*) of 7 percent. If you ask the full face value (one thousand dollars) for it, no one will buy it because the yield will only be 7 percent—which is less than the going rate of 8 percent. However, if you *reduce the price* of the bond sufficiently, the *yield will equal 8 percent*—and you'll be able to sell it. Figuring out the discount is done using a mathematical formula, and the investment dealer will calculate it for you. Here's the bottom line:

> A bond pays $70 per year, which at $1000 yields 7 percent.
> If the bond price is discounted to $930, a ten-year bond paying $70 per year yields 8 percent.

Therefore, to sell your 7 percent bond at a competitive price, you would have to *discount* it to $930. Although bonds normally have a face value of $1000, dealers always express the price in $100 units, thus 930 would be referred to as 93.

Now, if the prevailing rate of interest on ten-year bonds were to *drop* to 6 percent, your bond would go *up* in value. In this scenario, people with money to invest would have to be satisfied with 6 percent—the going rate. You would be in the fortunate position of owning a bond that was trading at a *premium*, that is, at a price greater than its face value. In this case, 107. Here are the figures:

> A bond pays $70 per year, which at $1000 yields 7 percent.
> If the bond price is increased to $1070, a ten-year bond paying $70 per year yields 6 percent.

As previously mentioned, the return on a bond—which consists of its coupon plus or minus the *amortized* discount or premium—is known as its yield to maturity. Most often it's simply referred to as yield. Because the bond market marches to the tune of interest rates, yields are constantly changing. As we have seen, when the yield changes on a bond, *so does the price of the bond.*

You can make money on bonds by buying them when interest rates are falling, or by selling (shorting) them when interest rates are on the rise. Because the trading is done "over the counter" rather than on the stock exchanges, the average person hears little about the bond market. Strictly speaking, it is part of the unlisted market, as trades are done by negotiation over a network of telephones. But it is infinitely more liquid, and the participants differ from those who trade unlisted stocks. In Canada, about a hundred investment dealers, banks, trust companies, and insurance companies trade bonds. The Bank of Canada is the dominant player, and its actions influence the direction of the market.

TYPES OF BONDS

Bonds are categorized as long-term, mid-term, or short-term. Long-term bonds mature in more than ten years, mid-terms between three and ten years, and short-terms in less than three years. Normally, the longer the term, the higher the yield. The reason for higher long-term rates is not only the "money rental" factor, but to compensate the lender for the increased risk of insolvency, the inevitable erosion of capital, and possible lost opportunity from a further rise in rates. When you compare bonds of similar quality, but differing maturities, you can plot out a "yield curve" on a piece of paper. A *normal yield curve* (see page 63) resembles the flight of a helicopter making its departure. Yields start low, and then go almost straight up from the short end, before gradually levelling off at the long end.

When the economy overheats and short-term rates rise above long-term rates, you get an *inverted yield curve* (also illustrated on page 63), which spells trouble. This condition is unsustainable and unnatural because the lender receives a higher return for less risk. An inverted yield curve is bad news for everyone. When it is in force, funds are sucked out of the long bond market and the stock market by the lure of high-yield, low-risk returns in the short-term market. As a result, both the bond market and the stock market decline.

In plotting a yield curve be sure to compare bonds of similar quality (e.g., Government of Canada bonds). And remember, the yields by themselves tell you little, it's their *relationship to each other* that's indicative. In other words, you can have a normal yield curve when interest rates are high; by the same token, you can have an inverted curve when rates are low. If you wish, you can make a simple yield curve diagram yourself. Just look at the box with bond prices in your local paper, or check the Globe and Mail or Financial Post. Then pick a selection of Government of Canada bonds—short-, medium-, and long-term—and note their yields and maturities. For a quick scan all you need is four or five maturities. For the short end, you might also use the latest issue of 91-day Treasury Bills.

TREASURY BILLS

Treasury Bills are short-term notes of a year or less; the most popular maturities are 91 and 182 days. Every Tuesday, the Bank of Canada auctions Treasury Bills to investment dealers, banks, and other financial institutions. The average yield of the 91-day Bills is used to set the bank rate, which is always twenty-five basis points above the average yield of the T-Bills. (A basis point is one-hundredth of 1 percent, therefore twenty-five basis points is equal to one-quarter of 1 percent). The *bank rate* is the rate of interest that the Bank of Canada will charge on money it lends to the chartered banks. This is useful to know because most of the chartered banks add 1 percent to the bank rate to arrive at their *prime rate*—the rate at which *they* will lend money to their best customers.

By putting in its own bid for all or part of the Treasury Bill issue at the weekly auction, the Bank of Canada can manipulate interest rates. In fact, it can play rates like a piano. In addition to controlling interest-rate levels, the Bank of Canada can also control the money supply by buying and selling securities in the

Normal and Inverted Yield Curves

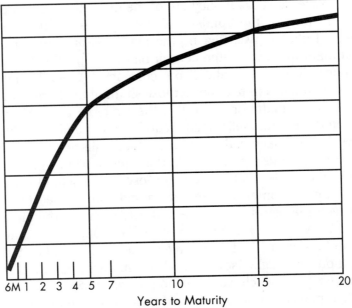

NORMAL YIELD CURVE

Years to Maturity

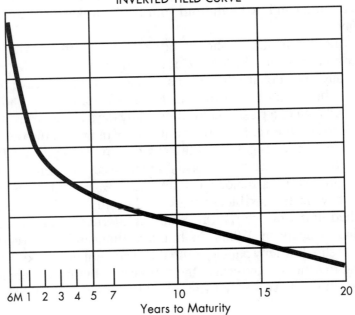

INVERTED YIELD CURVE

Years to Maturity

open market. When it buys bonds, it pumps money into the system. Bond prices rise and interest rates ease. When the Bank is a heavy seller, it sucks money out of the market (because dealers have to pay for the bonds) and bond prices decline. Interest rates, of course, rise. Rigging the market is an important and legitimate function of the central bank. Another of the Bank's responsibilities is to stabilize our currency. If Canadian interest rates get too low in relation to those south of the border, money will leave Canada for deposit in the United States. When this happens, investors sell Canadian dollars and buy U.S. dollars. As a result of the selling, the Canadian dollar falls in price.

Treasury Bills are peculiar in that they don't pay interest but are sold at a discount. For tax purposes the discount is treated the same as interest—not as capital gain. The difference between the discount and the maturity price (or the price you sell at) is your return. For example, if you bought T-Bills maturing in 87 days to yield 3.48 percent, the price would be $991.77 per thousand. Eighty-seven days later (maturity date) you would receive $1000, which would be an increase of $8.23, or a return of 3.48 percent on an annualized basis. Because of their safety and liquidity, Treasury Bills are a good place to park short-term funds. You can buy them from your bank, broker, or trust company.

Another feature I should bring to your attention is that Treasury Bills come in "bearer" form and are as negotiable (theoretically) as a dollar bill. For this reason you should leave them with the financial institution for safekeeping. This advice reminds me of a close call from my early days in the investment business in Ottawa. There were only two of us in the office and we used to take turns going to the Bank of Canada to pick up Treasury Bills. We were pretty casual about security (in those days mugging wasn't a major pastime). We always went alone, and would walk the six blocks back to the office with the T-Bills stuffed under our shirts. One summer afternoon I had about a million dollars in T-Bills (in hundred-thousand-dollar certificates) slip down my pant leg onto the pavement on Sparks Street. I had to scramble to recover the certificates, but none were lost. Since then, I have treated Treasury Bills with considerably more care.

GOVERNMENT OF CANADA BONDS

The Bank of Canada also dominates the new issue market for bonds. Government of Canada bonds are underwritten by investment dealers and subsequently sold to other institutions and to the public. The timing of these issues is basically whenever the government needs money. Some Canada issues are retractable or extendible. A *retractable bond* may be cashed in at a specific time *before* the maturity date. This is an attractive feature when rates are on the rise. Conversely, an *extendible bond* allows you to *extend* the maturity date within a fixed period. Thus the holder has the opportunity to lock in a relatively high yield when rates are declining. These two features underline the fact that while Government of Canada bonds offer the greatest safety and liquidity, they can still fluctuate *widely* in price. The Canada Conversion Loan of 1958 is a prime example of what interest rates can do to even the best quality bonds. This rollover of existing Canada bonds resulted in three giant issues, the longest having a twenty-five-year term. During the *entire* twenty-five years the long bonds never traded as high as their par value, and at one stage they sank as low as 67 cents on the dollar.

The only Government of Canada bond issues that don't fluctuate are Canada Savings Bonds. These are offered to the public each fall. The great advantage of CSBs is that they can be redeemed *at any time, at full face value*, without charge. They are only available to individuals or estates; the amount you may buy is limited; and the rate of interest is lower than "regular" bonds of a similar maturity. Also they are nontransferable, (you can't sell them to someone else), so you can't make a profit on them. Nevertheless, CSBs, because of their safety and liquidity, are an excellent investment. Indeed, a Canada Savings Bond is one of the few investments you can buy with the certain knowledge that you won't lose money—except through inflation.

REAL RETURN BONDS

Inflation is probably the greatest drawback to owning bonds. In essence, when you buy a bond you can expect devalued dollars at maturity, and your interest payments will also be devalued over

time. The problem of devalued interest has been relieved to some
extent by the introduction of Real Return Bonds (RRBs). These are
"stripped" Government of Canada bonds designed to give you a
"real" or *after-inflation* return of a specified amount. If the consumer price index (CPI) for the year showed inflation of 2 percent,
your yield would be increased by that amount to maintain your
real rate of return. Thus an RRB has a *floating* interest rate, which
is tied to the CPI and adjusted annually. Don't be fooled by the low
apparent "real return"—to *net* 4½ percent for twenty-five years
may require a *gross* yield in the double digits down the road. RRBs,
because there are a form of stripped bond, don't pay annual interest, but the interest is taxable. For this reason they are most suitable for an RRSP or other tax-sheltered account—and it's a
comfort to know the Real Return Bonds in your RRSP won't be
diminished by inflation.

FEDERAL, PROVINCIAL, AND MUNICIPAL BONDS

If you want to speculate in bonds, stick to regular Government of
Canada issues. The reason I say this is that Canada bonds are the
most marketable, hence you (and all the other players) can buy
and sell them in quantity. You should also know the action in the
bond market is in the long end, which has the biggest swings. In
this connection, low-coupon bonds tend to fluctuate more than
high-coupon bonds. Because the price fluctuations are actually
quite small, you should trade in sizeable amounts. The bond
market is one area where it makes sense to trade on margin. The
margin requirement for Canada bonds depends on their maturity and on the dealer, but is usually 2 to 3 percent.

People sometimes get confused as to whether they hold regular Government of Canada bonds or Canada Savings Bonds.
First off, read the face of the certificate, if they're CSBs it will say
so in the upper left-hand corner. CSB certificates, as a convenience, are also smaller than regular Canada certificates. On
page 67 is a drawing of a CSB certificate (it's against the law to
reproduce a detailed facsimile).

The provinces also issue bonds from time to time, and there
are a great many provincial issues outstanding. Provincial bonds
yield a little more than federal government bonds because of the
greater credit risk. In addition, the yields differ among the

Canada Savings Bond Certificate

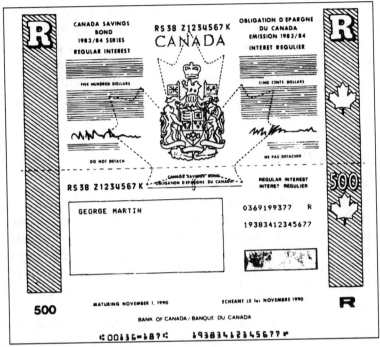

provinces for the same reason. Two private companies, Canadian Bond Rating Service of Montreal and Dominion Bond Rating Service of Toronto publish credit ratings on debt issues, including those of the provinces. In most cases, bonds guaranteed by the province (such as those for Ontario Hydro) get the same rating as the province. As a point of interest, in the spring of 1994, here is how the provinces were rated by the market:

1. Alberta, British Columbia
2. Ontario, Quebec
3. Manitoba, New Brunswick
4. Nova Scotia, Prince Edward Island
5. Saskatchewan
6. Newfoundland

The municipalities come next in the bond pecking order. They offer higher yields than the provinces, but I can't recommend them. Indeed, I suggest you avoid all municipal issues. They lack marketability, and the spread between the bid and the asked price can sometimes be frightful—which means whether you're buying or selling in the after market, you will inevitably get shafted. The only justification for buying a municipal bond is to help out your home town. But don't consider it a good investment; think of it more as a donation (although, hopefully, you will eventually get your money back).

CORPORATE BONDS

Corporations are theoretically at the bottom of the credit pile. But some companies, such as Bell, have so high a credit rating that they can borrow at lower rates than most municipalities, and even some of the provinces. Corporations issue a variety of bonds. It's the cheapest way for them to raise capital, because bond interest is paid out *before taxes*, whereas dividends are paid out *after* taxes. This is why bond interest, regardless of the issuer, is *fully taxable* in your hands.

First mortgage bonds are the senior security of a corporation. These bonds are secured by a pledge on fixed assets. *Second mortgage* or *general mortgage bonds* are also secured by fixed assets but rank behind the first mortgage bonds, which have first call against all assets.

First and second mortgage bonds should not be confused with *mortgage-backed securities*. The latter are not true bonds, but *units in a pool of mortgages* issued by a life insurance company, a trust company, or a bank. Mortgage-backed securities offer safety as well as diversification, because they are guaranteed by the Central Mortgage and Housing Corporation. MBS units come in two forms: prepayable or nonprepayable. Prepayable certificates carry a higher yield to compensate you because the mortgagors (that is, the borrowers) can prepay their loans and you could lose out on some of the term. Sometimes called "Cannie Maes" (a takeoff on "Fannie Maes," the American counterpart), mortgage-backed securities are offered in minimum amounts of $5000 with a minimum term of five years. Their main drawback is that you receive a portion of the principal with each monthly payment. At maturity you have nothing left, and along the way you have had the problem of reinvesting relatively small amounts of money. The interest portion is, of course, fully taxable. And the bonds are thinly (infrequently) traded, so liquidity is also a potential problem.

Getting back to "true" bonds, let's take a look at *collateral trust bonds*. These aren't secured by fixed assets, but by securities. A debenture isn't secured by any specific assets, it's secured by the general credit of the issuer. (All Government of Canada "bonds" are, in fact, debentures.) Corporate bonds and debentures often have a *sinking fund*, which is merely a covenant that sets a certain amount of money aside with a trustee for the eventual redemption of the issue. In practice, the sinking fund usually buys back and retires a specified amount each year. A sinking fund is a good feature because it helps to support the price of the bonds in the after market. Bonds can also be *callable* or *redeemable*, which means the company may call in or redeem them at a fixed price, in whole or in part, at its option. To compensate you for having your bonds redeemed, the price is always at a premium, which declines over time. Thus, if your bonds were redeemed three years after the issue was floated, the corporation might pay you 102; but if it happened a year before maturity, you would probably just get par. The call feature should always be checked *before* buying a bond at a significant premium—otherwise you could be in for a nasty surprise.

Occasionally a company will issue an *income bond* or *debenture*. Income bonds only pay interest if the company can earn it. Obviously this type of bond carries a substantial element of risk. But, the good thing about income bonds is that the interest is treated for tax purposes in the same way as dividends, and qualifies for the same tax credit. There are also *floating rate debentures* that pay a rate of interest tied to the prime rate or some more exotic financial index, such as the LIBOR (London Interbank Offered Rate).

Floating rate debentures are designed to give the investor some protection against an upward interest rate surge. They are one of the many innovations designed by the investment community to sell bonds to a reluctant public. This may sound odd in view of the strong bond markets of the last five years, but it makes sense when you consider that bonds were in a bear market for the previous *thirty* years. Another gimmick is to attach warrants or a similar "kicker" to a new bond issue. Warrants permit the holder to buy common shares of the company at a fixed price for a given period of time. As such, they normally have value, and dress up the merchandise. You can either exercise your warrants or sell them on the market; either way you get something for nothing. But a word of warning. You should only buy a bond with a kicker if the company is sound, and the outlook for its common shares is bright.

These same criteria apply to convertible bonds. A *convertible bond* is the most interesting and potentially the most profitable of all bonds. It doesn't have warrants, but it may be converted into common shares of the company. The number of shares is determined at the time of issue and is stated on the certificate. There are several advantages to owning a convertible bond. For one thing, if the underlying common shares go up in price, so will the bond. And if interest rates fall, the coupon will cause a convertible bond's value to rise. Should interest rates rise, and the underlying shares fall—the worst possible scenario—a convertible bond will perform better than a "straight" bond and show a smaller percentage loss than the stock.

But you must do your homework before buying a convertible bond. First, do you like the outlook for the company's stock? Unless you're bullish on the stock, *don't* buy the bond. What is the conversion rate (i.e., the number of shares that can be exchanged for the bond), and how long will it be in effect? It should be a realistic conversion rate, and you should have enough time—say four or five years. Is the bond callable, and if so, when and at what price? This is important because you could pay a big premium and then have the bond called at a lower price. (You will have time to convert before complying with the call, but this is only feasible if the converted value is higher than the call price.) What about the yield on the bond, and how does it compare with the yield on the stock? Normally the bond yield should be *significantly* higher than the stock yield. (But, because it's convertible, the yield will be less than a similar straight bond.) The *payback period*—the time it takes the bond to recoup the premium through its yield, compared with the yield on the stock—should be two years or less. To explain these points, let's take a hypothetical example.

You are considering the purchase of a convertible bond at 112. The bond yields 6 percent and is callable at 104 in 1997. It is convertible into 45 shares of common stock until 2001. The common is currently trading at $23 and yields 1 percent.

To figure out the premium, multiply the number of shares by their current price and deduct the total from the cost of the bond:

$$45 \text{ shares} \times \$23 = \$1035 - \$1120 = \text{premium of } \$85$$
$$\text{expressed as a percentage, the premium } = 8.2\%$$

To calculate the *payback period*, take the difference between the bond and the stock yields, and divide it into the premium:

$$6\% - 1\% = 5\% \text{ divided into } 8.2\% \text{ premium} = 1.6 \text{ years}$$

Theoretically, *providing the company is sound*, this convertible bond would appear to be a reasonable buy.

Convertible bonds are inherently safer than common shares because the "bond" aspect gives them a prior call on the company's assets in bankruptcy. At the same time, the conversion feature ensures that the bond appreciates at a similar rate to the common shares. For these reasons convertibles are an ideal investment for Registered Retirement Savings Plans. In an RRSP both the interest and capital gains are sheltered from tax. Aggressive investors like convertible bonds because they can be margined at a lower rate than the common stock, and the interest paid by the bonds helps to offset margin charges. Convertibles are also an excellent "hedge" against a short sale of the common; but mind you do your math! (Hedging will be discussed in detail in the chapters on options and commodities.) For the average investor, convertibles offer the best opportunity to make significant money in the bond market.

Stripped or ("zero coupon") *bonds* are a relatively new concept in the bond market, and they have been immensely successful. Stripped bonds don't pay interest but are sold at a deep discount. They are created by "stripping" or detaching the coupons from the certificates of high-grade bonds such as Government of Canada or provincial issues. As no interest is paid, *both* the certificates for the principal and the coupons are sold to investors. The main advantage of a stripped bond is that you get a huge bang for your buck. For example, a stripped bond maturing in twenty years, with a yield of 8.25 percent, will return a sum equal to five times your original investment. Another advantage of stripped bonds is that they eliminate the problem of reinvesting the interest. The only downside is that even though interest is *not* actually paid out, it must be reported each year and you must pay tax on it. Because of the tax, these bonds are really only suitable for nontaxable accounts. For this reason, the best place for stripped bonds is in your Registered Retirement Savings Plan—and in an RRSP, they are an ideal investment.

When a new bond issue or any other issue of securities is sold, an advertisement appears in the financial press. This advertisement gives the details of the issue, and the name of the underwriter. If there's more than one underwriter (as is usually the case), they are listed in order of precedence. Appropriately enough, the advertisement is known in the business as a "tombstone." By the time you see a tombstone (illustrated on page 73) in the paper it is too late to buy the issue. (Unless it's been a failure, in which case you don't want it anyway.)

After a new issue is sold, the price fluctuates with supply and demand. When you buy or sell in the after market, you will be given a "subject" or a "firm" quote. A *subject quote* means "subject to confirmation," and the dealer is *not* obligated to do the trade. A *firm quote* means that the dealer is *committed* to do the trade at that price, but only for a specified period of time.

BOND CONTRACTS

The confirmation or contract you receive from the broker when you buy or sell a bond is different from a stock confirmation. Because the broker is acting as a principal, not an agent, the confirmation will say "sold to you" or "bought from you." It will also debit or credit you with accrued interest. This requires an explanation. When you buy a bond you are *charged* accrued interest from the last day interest was paid on that bond. This is only fair, because the person who sold it would not receive their interest from that date, even though they were the beneficial

Tombstone

These securities having been sold this announcement as a matter of record only

Additional issue

CFCF INC.

$31,875,000

2,500,000 Subordinate Voting Shares

Price: $12.75 per Subordinate Voting Share

Scotia McLeod Inc.　　　　　　　　　Richardson Greenshields
　　　　　　　　　　　　　　　　　　of Canada Limited

Toronto Dominion Securitites Inc

owner of the bond. You will recoup the interest when the next interest payment rolls around. That is, you will be paid the *full* amount by the issuer—thus the charge cancels itself out. When you sell a bond, you will be *credited* with accrued interest from the last payment date. Should you sell bonds with coupons attached to them be sure to detach all the coupons, except the current one. On page 74 is an illustration of a bond contract.

You may be surprised to see that a commission is not shown on your bond contract. There is no commission on new issues, but when bonds are traded in the after market, the dealer adds or subtracts his commission from the bond price (depending upon whether you are buying or selling). As a general rule, the longer the term, the greater the commission. For example, the dealer's commission—which is whatever he chooses—might be 10 cents a hundred for short-term bonds, and 50 cents a hundred for long-term bonds. If you think the price is out of line,

Scotia McLeod bond contract

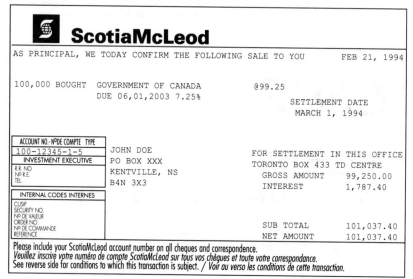

you can ask the dealer what he's charging on the trade. The best protection against being ripped off is to deal with a reputable firm, and with an individual you can trust.

Commissions are really a minor factor when trading bonds. The big challenge is to predict the direction of interest rates. If you can do that correctly—most of the time—you will be well on your way to consistent profits.

6

COMMON STOCKS

If you're looking for action, common stocks are the odds-on favourite. And with good reason; common stocks are usually, but not always, a high-risk, high-reward investment. All of us know someone who's taken a shellacking in stocks. On the other hand, when someone boasts he's made a bundle, it's almost certain he did it with common shares (stocks and shares are one and the same).

There is, however, more to common shares than meets the eye. Some stocks are a crap shooter's delight, while others are almost as staid as a bond. Canadian insurance companies (which are regulated by the federal government) hold hundreds of millions of dollars worth of common shares in their portfolios. One of the reasons insurance companies buy common stocks—and a reason why *you* should—is that stocks are an excellent hedge against inflation.

Common stock represents the *equity* or *ownership* of a company. When you buy common shares in a company, you become a part owner. As such, you are exposed to the risks and the rewards of ownership. If the company does well, your equity in the company and the value of your stock will increase. You will also participate in the earnings of the company, which may be reflected in increased dividends paid out to you on a regular basis. If the company does badly, your equity in the company will shrink and so will the value of your stock. Should the company go belly up, you could lose your entire investment. (When a company goes bankrupt, the common shareholders are last in the line of creditors to be paid, after the bank, the bondholders, and the preferred shareholders.) I have a friend who built his dream house on the profits he made in common stocks. And I know of another fellow who ended up papering his bathroom wall with worthless share certificates. So, you should know what you're doing *before* you buy common stocks, because the results can be dramatic.

Normally, each common share carries one vote in the election of the company's board of directors. Thus, common shareholders have a voice in the management of the company. At the discretion of the directors, shareholders are awarded dividends, usually four each year, which are paid quarterly. Unlike bond interest or preferred share dividends, which are at a fixed rate, there is no set rate for common share dividends.

DIVIDEND TAX CREDITS

Dividends on common shares are paid *after* taxes, and are not cumulative. Noncumulative means that if a dividend is skipped, there's no obligation for the company to make it up later. That's the bad news. The good news is that Canadian common and preferred share dividends qualify for a special tax credit.

There are two reasons for the tax credit. One is that the company has already paid tax on the dividend it's disbursing to you, and the money shouldn't be fully taxed twice. The other is to give Canadians an incentive to invest in Canadian companies.

The tax credit works as follows. First, your dividend is inflated or "grossed-up" by 25 percent. Next, your federal tax is calculated on the grossed-up amount. Then, the credit, which is 13 ⅓ percent of the grossed-up amount, is deducted from the federal tax payable on the dividend. For example, let's suppose you receive $800 in dividends. Here is the tax calculation, compared with $800 in bond interest:

	Dividends	Bond Interest
Amount received	$ 800	$ 800
25% gross-up	+$ 200	N/A
Total reported	$1000	$ 800
Federal tax 30%	$ 300	$ 240
Less dividend tax		
credit at 13⅓%	–$ 133	N/A
Net federal tax	$ 167	$ 240
provincial tax		
at 55%	+$ 92	+$ 132
Combined federal		
and provincial tax	$ 259	$ 372

This may look complicated; in addition to everything else I've included provincial tax. But, as both the actual and the grossed-up dividend figures are on your T5, the calculation is relatively straightforward. What is plain is that on an after-tax basis—the one that counts—dividend income is much more valuable to you than interest income.

But I don't want to dwell on dividends, because the main reason to buy common stocks is for *capital gain.* In any case, many common stocks pay little or no dividends, including the shares of some first-rate "growth" companies. Numerous studies have shown that over the long term common stocks have consistently outperformed bonds. So let's keep the primary purpose of the two investments separate: bonds for income, common stocks for appreciation.

EVALUATING COMMON SHARES

Common stocks range from "blue chips" to "penny dreadfuls." A *blue chip* is a seasoned performer with a strong balance sheet, while a *penny dreadful* is a speculative stock whose main asset is hope. Before going into the various types of shares, let's look at some of the basics.

The *capitalization* of a business can cause confusion. Some novice investors have the impression that all capitalizations are the same. If the shares of company "A" are trading at $10, and the shares of company "B" at $15, they think the shares of company "A" offer better value. However, even if the two companies are the same size and their business prospects are identical, the $15 shares could be the better buy. It all depends on the capitalization.

Think of two pies that are exactly the same size. One is cut into six pieces, the other into seventeen pieces. Now substitute "company" for "pie," and "shares" for "pieces." Shares represent pieces of the corporate pie, and a key factor is how big or how small the pieces of that pie are. Assuming both companies are the same size, if company "A" had one million shares, and company "B" only two hundred thousand, theoretically the shares of company "B" would be five times as valuable. Let's say their net worth is one million, here's the calculation:

1,000,000 shares divided into $1,000,000 = $1 per share
200,000 shares divided into $1,000,000 = $5 per share

It should be mentioned that there are *two* figures to note when checking the share capitalization of a company. One is the number of *authorized shares*, the other is the number of *issued shares*. The authorized amount is the total number of shares the company is allowed to issue under its charter. The issued amount is the total that have actually been issued and are in the hands of shareholders. Of the two, the issued number is the one that counts. Also common shares have a *par value* (expressed in dollars) or *no-par-value*. The par value of a common share is its stated face value as assigned by the company's charter. It bears no relationship to the *market value*, and is so irrelevant that most companies now only issue NPV (no-par value) common stock.

When I was a boy, I found a sheaf of mining certificates that had belonged to my grandfather. Many of the certificates were engraved with the words "Par Value One Dollar," and a quick count showed that at least fifty thousand bore this magic inscription. Astounded at the bonanza I'd stumbled upon, I rushed to my father with the certificates. Dad riffled through them, and to my chagrin told me they were worthless. It was then that I learned what par value means to common shares—nothing. It does, however, have considerable significance to *preferred shares*, which will be dealt with in the next chapter.

A common stock's *yield* is the annual dividend expressed as a percentage of the price of the shares. It's easy to calculate; simply divide the price of the stock into the dividend. For example, if a stock trading at $25 pays a dividend of $1.25, the yield is 5 percent.

Here is the way a stock quotation appears in most newspapers:

TransAlta Stock Quote

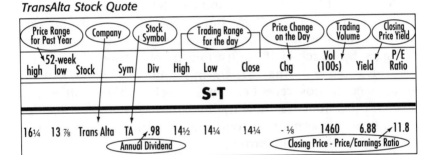

How do you value a stock? Both the number of shares outstanding, and their yield (if any) should be considered, but this is only the tip of the iceberg. Two other important measurements are the price of the stock compared to its book value, and compared to its earnings per share. Both are simple to figure out. For the *book value*, simply deduct all the company's debts from its assets, and then divide the number of shares into the residue. So, if the shareholders' equity or residue is twelve million dollars, and there are one million shares out, the book value would be $12 per share. This figure should then be compared to the market price of the shares. The price-to-earnings ratio is equally simple to calculate. First, get the *earnings per share* by dividing the company's net earnings by the number of issued shares. When you have this figure (the earnings per share), divide it into the market price of the stock. Assuming the earnings are $1.25 and the price of the stock is $12.50, the price-to-earnings or P/E ratio would be ten. A P/E ratio of ten means that the shares are trading at ten times the company's annual earnings.

The P/E ratio is probably the most popular yardstick for measuring whether a stock is overvalued or undervalued, and is also used to compare stocks within a given industry. The *Monthly Review*, published by the Toronto Stock Exchange, (available from your broker), lists the major industries and their average P/E ratios.

Don't, however, blindly follow the readings on your calculator. You must also keep an eye on the stage of the economic cycle, because it can play hob with earnings and throw the ratios out of whack. For instance, in 1993 BCE's earnings had been depressed by the recession and the shares were trading at a P/E of 23:1, which was about twice as high as normal. On the face of it, BCE should have been sold immediately. But earnings were expected to recover and investors—who always *discount the news six to nine months in advance*—were paying for *future* earnings. By March of 1994, just four months later, BCE shares had advanced a further $7. By this time the company had announced its most recent earnings, which included stiff write-offs, and the stock was now trading at an astronomical P/E of 250:1. Investors seemed unconcerned with the "old" news and kept betting that good earnings were just around the corner. This brings up another investment rule: after you do your historical calculations, you must also try to assess what's ahead for the company—don't only look at the past, look at the future.

Book values and earnings ratios differ with each industry. For instance high tech companies and resource companies normally trade at much higher P/E ratios than banks and utilities. Yields also differ, and, taking the same industries as an example, banks and utilities pay much bigger dividends than high tech and resource stocks. Price-to-book value ratios also vary from one industry to another. After doing your maths, you have to exercise judgement in comparing the results—always compare apples with apples, (don't try to compare a bank to a gold mining company). And remember that even if you're careful with your calculations and your comparisons, you can still be fooled by erroneous information.

Royal Trust is a classic example. In 1992, when the institution was in its death throes, management glossed over the seriousness of the situation. On paper, Royal Trust looked like a wonderful buy: a fine old company with a big dividend, trading at less than book value, and (according to management) the business outlook was positive. I bought shares at $8. A couple of months later the stock was trading at $6, and the technical picture looked awful. Royal Trust's theoretical value was still there but something was obviously wrong—despite protestations to the contrary by management. The market action on the stock was trying to tell me something. Eventually I got the message and sold out. At $6.50, this was not a pleasant loss, but considerably better than 36 cents, that Royal Trust common traded at a few months later. There are several lessons to be learned from this melancholy confession. The first is to be skeptical when management says one thing and the market says another—when in doubt, rely on the market. The other is to take your losses quickly, and let your profits run. If you do that, you'll always be able to play another day.

THE GRADING SYSTEM

Within the two broad categories—growth stocks and income stocks—are a number of subgroups. But before looking at them, let's discuss the grading system that applies to all stocks. At the top of the list we have "blue chips," a term which came to the investment industry via the gambling casinos. Blue chips are proven companies with strong balance sheets and consistent earnings. Among the blue companies are names like BCE, Canadian Pacific, Imperial Oil, Molson, and the chartered banks. The next level, where many good stocks are found, has smaller companies or companies with less impressive earnings records. The third tier contains stocks that are described as "businessman's risk" situations. The term "businessman's risk" is an industry euphemism which spares the need for the broker to tell his client "If this one goes in the tank, no crying towel is provided." At the bottom of the heap are the "specs" or "penny dreadfuls" (the latter, a term lifted from English nineteenth-century pulp literature).

GROWTH STOCKS

Growth stocks can be subdivided into senior (established) companies and emerging ones. The emerging ones are the most sensational performers—and the most susceptible to disaster.

When I think of growth stocks, I think of Mitel and its two founders, Michael C.J. Cowpland and Terence H. Matthews. Cowpland and Matthews grew Mitel from nothing, and later in 1979, "went public" at a price of $10 per share. During the next few years the company roared ahead and the stock was split three for one (see p. 86 for a discussion of "stock splitting"). By the early '80s, the original shares reached the equivalent of $150 per share. Then the company faltered and went into a prolonged decline. Matthews and Cowpland left Mitel and went their separate ways, starting up new companies: Newbridge Networks Corporation and Corel Corporation. Shares of Newbridge and Corel (classic businessman's risk situations) did phenomenally well in the market recovery from the spring of 1993 to the spring of 1994. During this period Newbridge went from $33 to nearly $100 per share, and Corel rose from a low of $8¾ to more than $30. Whether Newbridge or Corel will eventually become blue chips remains to be seen. But one thing is certain, had you invested in Mitel, Newbridge, or Corel when they were *emerging*, you would have been handsomely rewarded for the risk. And risk there is—for every winner there are at least a dozen losers. It should also be mentioned that junior growth stocks are the hardest hit when the market encounters a down draft, and even the most senior ones will fall dramatically during an extended downturn.

CYCLICAL COMPANIES

Companies in cyclical industries are not, strictly speaking, growth stocks, but if you buy them at the right time they can produce huge capital gains. Cyclical industries are the ones that are especially sensitive to the general economy or to changes in commodity prices. They include auto makers, parts suppliers, mining companies, cement producers, steel companies, and the forest products industry—a hefty percentage of all the stocks on the TSE. The cyclical nature of their business can be seen by a glance at the forest products industry. When the economy enters a recession, the amount of newspaper advertising drops sharply and construction activity dwindles. Pulp and paper companies sell less newsprint, and lumber companies sell less lumber. The result is a drop in their earnings. When the economy picks up, so does the pace of construction and the demand for newsprint. Eventually, both earnings and share prices recover in the forest products industry. This "boom and bust" cycle produces a roller coaster ride for investors—so timing is critical.

Debt leverage is another factor that contributes to wide swings in the earnings of many cyclical companies. If a company has a lot of debt (bonds) in relation to its equity (common shares), this means a heavy fixed charge on earnings. During bad times there is little or nothing left over for the common shareholders, but in good times the earnings of the common shares can increase dramatically. For example, let's assume that a company must earn $800,000 to service the annual interest on its debt. If it estimates earnings of $1,000,000, there will be $200,000 left over (before taxes) for the common shareholders. Now let's see what happens if the company suffers a 20 percent *decline* in estimated earnings.

Actual earnings	$ 800,000
Cost to service debt	–$ 800,000
Amount available for common shareholders	0

That's the bad side of debt leverage. Now let's look at the good side. In this case we'll assume that the company has a 20 percent *increase* in estimated earnings. Look at what this does for the common shareholders:

Actual earnings	$1,200,000
Cost to service debt	–$ 800,000
Amount available for common shareholders	$ 400,000

Note that a 20 percent increase in estimated earnings has increased the pre-tax amount available for shareholders by 100 percent.

Astute investors watch cyclical stocks closely. The trick is to buy them when the industry is in the doldrums, and to ride them up with the recovery. The problem, however, is that when they should be bought—in *advance* of a recovery—investors' morale is at its lowest point, and damned few analysts have a good word for the cyclicals. If a cyclical stock is heavily leveraged, so much the better, for you'll get an even bigger lift. Like all stocks, the cyclicals reach a crest, usually at the tail end of a boom, and then go into a long descent. So the timing of your *sale* is as important as the timing of your purchase.

Although the demand for their products, (aluminum and nickel), has been weak for some years, Alcan and Inco are two of the best cyclical stocks in Canada. The three major steel companies, Stelco, Dofasco, and Ivaco, are also first-rate cyclicals. If you want a double or even a triple play on cyclical stocks, you might consider Noranda Inc. This diversified resource company has three main divisions: mining, forest products, and oil and gas. The scope of Noranda's operations is extraordinary; in the mining division alone it produces copper, zinc, aluminum, lead, nickel, potash, gold and silver.

INCOME STOCKS

Preferred shares (see Chapter 7) are the quintessential income stocks, but some common shares also qualify as income stocks. Companies that pay out a high percentage of their earnings as dividends fit into this category. Typically, this type of company has consistant earnings, with little potential for earnings growth. Therein lies the trade-off for investors: generous dividends versus captial appreciation. Because of their staid earnings performance, income stocks are characterized by low price earnings multiple and above average yields.

Utilities

The shares of telephone, power, and gas utilities are classic income stocks. Companies in these industries also issue rights (see p. 87) on a fairly regular basis, which increases the effective yield on their shares. Some of the more familiar names are BCE, Maritime Tel & Tel, Fortis, TransAlta, Canadian Utilites, and Consumers Gas.

Because these companies operate government-regulated monopolies, they are considered to have limited growth potential. Regulation acts as a drag on earnings, which frequently lag behind the pace of inflation. On the plus side, regulated companies can predict their earnings with reasonable certainty and can safely pay out a high percentage in dividends. Another advantage of the utilities is that they rarely have a problem with accounts receivable. If you don't pay your gas or electric bill, the service will be disconnected. The fact that you can't switch to another supplier is a powerful incentive to pay your account on time.

Investors looking for growth usually ignore utility stocks. I don't and would urge you to look at them carefully. As I mentioned, they pay generous dividends, and these dividends *increase* over the years. You can't say the same thing for a bond. Most utilities and banks (as well as some other companies) have dividend reinvestment programs. This means you can elect not to receive your dividends in cash, but use the proceeds to buy more shares. The shares will be bought at a reduced commission, and you may even get them at a discount. TransAlta, for example, buys dividend reinvestment shares at a 5 percent discount from the average market price. No one—not even a discounter—can match this deal.

MATURE COMPANIES, "DEFENSIVE" STOCKS, AND BANKS

In the zone between growth stocks and income stocks, there are several groups to watch. One consists of mature companies that pay a reasonable dividend, while also offering reasonable growth. Canadian Pacific, Moore Corporation, and National Trust are typical of this category. Then we have the "defensive" stocks, which offer essential services or products that are little affected by a recession. This type of company can also pass on price increases to its customers. Food stores, brewers, and utilities fall into this group. During a recession people must eat; they will continue to drink (the cheapest alcoholic beverage); and they must have phones as well as light and heat. Some of the names that come to mind are Dominion Stores, Loblaw, Labatt, Molson, Consumers Gas, BCE, BC Tel, TransAlta, and Nova Scotia Power.

The third group consists of the banks. In the past twenty years greedy loan practices have nearly destroyed the chartered banks on three occasions. The first time it was indiscriminate lending to the oil and gas industry, which came back to haunt the banks when world oil prices fell. Then it was a raft of ill-considered loans to Third World countries, many of which had to be written off. The most recent was a reckless spate of real estate loans—a folly that is still being paid for by bank shareholders. Despite these blunders, Canada's chartered banks continue to enjoy an enviable reputation for strength and stability. I may not admire banking practices, but I consider bank shares a fine investment (far better to be an owner than a borrower). The chartered banks' role in the economy is similar to a croupier or a pimp—every time someone plays, they take a rake-off. Moreover, bank shares trade at relatively low price-to-earnings ratios and pay out relatively big dividends. If the banks could learn to control their greed—which does such appalling things to their collective judgement—they would be superior growth stocks. But even with their flaws, *I would strongly recommend that a chartered bank stock—or several—form the core of your equity portfolio.* If you are a novice, I would suggest restricting your purchase (unless you have an account with the National) to the Big Five. They are, in alphabetical order: Bank of Montreal, Bank of Nova Scotia, Canadian Imperial Bank of Commerce, Royal Bank, and Toronto-Dominion Bank.

SHARE SPLITS, RIGHTS, AND WARRANTS

Stock Splitting

From time to time the banks split their shares. The most recent was a two-for-one split by the Bank of Montreal in 1993. A stock split means that the shares you hold are subdivided into smaller units. For instance, if the split is on a three-for-one basis, each one of your "old" shares will become three "new" shares. As a result of the split, the shares will *drop* in price because the theoretical value of the new shares is one-third of the old. (Remember, the pie is still the same size, but now the pieces are smaller.) The main reason for a stock split is to bring the shares down to a popular price level—say $10 to $25—and make them more attractive to investors. A second reason is to improve the marketability of the stock by increasing the "float" or the number of shares outstanding. Investors like stock splits because the split shares usually (but not always) take a little jump in price, which results in an immediate gain in the total value of their holdings.

Rights

The chartered banks, as well as other companies, also issue rights. The purpose of this is to raise additional share capital. A "right" permits the shareholder to purchase stock at a discount price. Usually the shareholder receives one right for each share. Rights may be exercised (to buy more stock) or sold. Either way, they are a benefit to the shareholder, and increase the return on the stock. The purchase formula varies, but usually one or more rights *plus cash* buys an additional share. For instance, if the shares of a company are trading at $25, it might take five rights plus $20 to acquire one new share. This would give each right a theoretical value of $1. Here is the calculation:

    5 rights + $20 = $25 (one share)
    5 rights   = $25–$20
    5 rights   = $ 5
    1 right   = $ 1

As I mentioned, the reason a company issues rights is to raise additional equity capital. (In the case of the chartered banks, their lending capacity is tied to their capital base.) The logic behind issuing rights to existing shareholders is to allow them, if they wish, to maintain the percentage of their holding in the company. After a rights issue is announced the stock trades *cum rights* (*cum* is Latin for "with") for a short period. Anyone who buys the shares during the cum rights period is entitled to the rights. If you sell your shares before they go *ex rights* (*ex* is Latin for "out of"), you forfeit your rights. There's always an active market for rights, so it's easy to buy more (to round out your holdings) or to sell all or part of them. But you must act promptly; rights are usually only valid for a few weeks, after which they become worthless. I often had clients come in with a sheepish look and a certificate for expired rights. If you allow them to expire, it's the same as throwing away money.

Warrants

In the investment sense, a "warrant" can mean one of two things. It is either a certificate for rights, or a long-term right to buy shares. Because warrants have a long-term call on stock, they usually have a time value as well as their intrinsic value. For instance, Air Canada warrants allow you to buy Air Canada stock at $6.25 until 6 December 1995. In March of 1994, when Air Canada was trading at $7.75, this warrant had an *intrinsic* value of $1.50, but was trading at $2.90—a premium of nearly 100 percent. The premium was the time value. As the time runs out on the life of a right or a warrant, the premium declines to its intrinsic value. The way to determine the intrinsic value is to deduct the exercise price (or strike price) from the current price of the stock. In the Air Canada example:

Price of Air Canada common share	$7.75
Less strike price of warrant	−$6.25
Intrinsic value of warrant	$1.50

Sometimes a warrant has no intrinsic value—no tangible value at all—and trades purely on its time value. In March 1994, Hollinger warrants to purchase the common at $20 per share were an example of this phenomenon. At that time the common stock was $15.50, and the warrants (good until 30 September 1998) were trading at $3.50. If we do our sums on these numbers, we'll see that the stock was $4.50 *short* of its strike price, and buyers were paying an *additional* $3.50 for the warrant—which had no intrinsic value. This translates into a whopping $8 time premium. Or, put another way, by expiration of the warrant, the stock would have to rise more than 50 percent to break even. Here are the figures:

Hollinger strike price	$20.00
Cost of warrant	+$ 3.50
Price to break even	$23.50
Less current price	−$15.50
Increase needed	$ 8.00 or 52%

The Benefits of Rights and Warrants

Both warrants and rights are leveraged investments because a small price change in the underlying stock can make a huge percentage change in their value. This gives rights and warrants great speculative appeal. They are also a good way to play expensive stocks with a minimum cash outlay. But don't forget—inevitably rights and warrants expire. When that happens, it's game over.

SECONDARY OFFERINGS

A *secondary offering* is the only time a broker can sell you shares at a discount from the market price. This type of transaction occurs when a block of stock comes up for sale that is too large to be absorbed in regular trading. To facilitate the sale of the block, the shares are discounted by a small amount and usually sold at a net (i.e., commission included) price. Often there is little warning before a secondary is made, because the stock price would weaken in anticipation of the offering. When a secondary offering takes place on the floor of an exchange, it must be completed in a very short time. For this reason, when your broker phones he will press you for a quick decision.

Unless you've been waiting for an opportunity to buy the stock, you should probably pass up a secondary offering. The discount is *not* sufficient reason to buy, and there's a good chance the seller is unloading because he thinks the stock is fully valued (that is, at its maximum price). Even if there's a valid reason for the secondary, once it's completed the stock will probably decline in price. This is not surprising when you think about it—the secondary will have sopped up the buying interest for the short term. This doesn't mean you should ignore *all* secondary offerings, but I suggest you view them with suspicion, and a critical eye.

SPLIT SHARES AND STOCK RECEIPTS

Split shares and stock receipts are two other stratagems devised by the investment industry to promote sales. While the motive behind their creation may be less than noble, both types of securities can be useful to the average investor.

Split shares are fashioned from stocks that have good dividends and reasonable growth records. An underwriter or a syndicate buys a large block of stock and then "strips" the shares, which are subsequently offered to the public. The stripped or split shares have their capital gain and income split into two parts. All the capital growth above the issue price accrues to the capital portion (known in the industry as a special capital gain security or SPEC). All the dividend income accrues to the other portion (which is called a payment enhanced capital security or PEAC). On a predetermined date, both portions are cashed in. At that time, providing the underlying shares haven't sewered, the PEAC holders get their money back. The SPEC holders—who are highly leveraged—receive the difference between the income portion and the actual stock price at maturity. Let's take a hypothetical example:

underlying share price $28   div. $1.50   yield 5.35%

<u>Issue Prices</u>
income or PEAC portion $20   div. $1.50   yield 7.5%
capital or SPEC portion $ 8   nil   nil

<u>Redemption Prices at Maturity</u>
underlying share price $33   div. $1.65   yield 5%
income or PEAC portion $20
capital or SPEC portion $13

In this example the income or PEAC holders get their money back, and have received all the dividend income (including the annual increase from $1.50 to $1.65). The capital or SPEC holders also get their money back, plus the growth in the underlying stock above the issue price (which in this case amounts to $7 per share, or a gain of 87 percent on their investment).

Because of the income requirement, most split shares are derived from utility or bank stocks. Sometimes, for greater security, a basket of shares is marketed—such as Can-Banc, which is a pool of five Canadian chartered bank shares. Split shares are listed on the major exchanges and trade freely. Their main risk—as with most investments—is their future performance. To minimize this risk you should only buy top-quality PEAC or income shares, and ensure that they have an ample margin of safety. (The margin of safety is the difference between the underlying share price and the PEAC price.) If you're going to buy a SPEC or capital share, make sure the company has promising growth prospects—some utilities have little to offer in this respect. Carefully chosen, split shares can maximize after-tax income for conservative investors or provide impressive capital gains for those willing to accept more risk.

Share Receipts are even more interesting because they *combine* leverage and income. Receipts—which represent a downpayment only—are used as an incentive for buyers to purchase a new or secondary offering of common stock. Because you pay only 40 to 60 percent down to beneficially own a full share, receipts provide attractive leverage. And, as you receive the full dividend, your initial yield is very generous. The term of a receipt is usually a year to eighteen months, after which the balance is payable. In the interim, your shareholding is evidenced by a printed receipt—hence the name share receipts.

When Nova Scotia Power went public in August 1992, it offered residents of the province the opportunity to buy the shares through receipts. Nova Scotians could acquire their shares by putting up $6, and paying a further $4 in August 1993. Everyone else had to pay the full offering price of $10. As Nova Scotia Power shares carried an initial dividend of 75 cents, the yield on the receipts was a whopping 12½ percent! (And by the time the final payment was due, the underlying shares had appreciated by close to 20 percent.) Note that not all share receipts go up, so all the normal caveats apply—plus two extra ones. First, check when the receipts are due, because you could end up buying them after they've paid their last dividend. Second, you must pay the final instalment on time, or suffer the consequences.

Share receipts shouldn't be confused with *American deposit receipts*. The latter, also known as ADRs, are certificates of ownership of a foreign security held in an American bank, and traded on a U.S. stock exchange. Most of the South African gold mining shares and most of the European securities traded in North America are represented by ADRs.

AMERICAN SECURITIES

If you're a serious investor, you simply can't ignore the American stock market. In Canada, a high percentage of our stocks are resource-oriented, and even the supply of these companies is dwindling as a result of takeovers and amalgamations. The U.S. market is much broader-based, and offers a cornucopia of investment goodies. To give you an idea of its variety, here is a selection of common stocks listed on the New York Stock Exchange:

Advanced Microsystems	Fruit of the Loom	Pfizer
Allied Signal	General Dynamics	Pitney Bowes
American Express	General Electric	Polaroid
Avon	Glaxo	Procter & Gamble
Bally	Grumman	Quaker Oats
Bausch & Lomb	Harley Davidson	Raytheon
Boeing	H.J. Heinz	Reader's Digest
Broken Hill Properties	Helene Curtis	Rubbermaid
Burger King	Hershey	Sara Lee
Caterpillar	I.C.I.	Smucker's
Champion Spark Plug	Kellogg	Sothebys
Chris Craft	Lockheed	Thiokol
Chrysler	Matsushita Electric	Tiffany
Colgate-Palmolive	McDonald's	Unilever
Daimler Benz	Merrill Lynch	Vigoro
Delta Airlines	Nat'l Semiconductor	Wells Fargo
Digital Equipment	Nike	Winnebago
Eastman Kodak	Outboard Marine	Wrigley
Eli Lilly	Owens-Corning	Xerox
Ford	Pepsi Cola	Zenith

The two largest stock exchanges in the United States are the American Stock Exchange and the New York Stock Exchange. The senior of the two is the New York Stock Exchange, which has many more listings, stiffer listing requirements, and the larger trading volume. The two main *stock markets* (as opposed to exchanges) are the NASDAQ and the NYSE. NASDAQ is the acronym for National Association of Securities Dealers Automated Quotations, a highly efficient computerized over-the-counter facility. NASDAQ stocks tend to be less seasoned than companies listed on the NYSE, and are less rigorously screened before being allowed to trade. This doesn't mean that there aren't good companies on the NASDAQ, but it does suggest that extra care should be taken, because whatever way you look at it, a NASDAQ listing doesn't have to meet the same standards as a New York Stock Exchange listing.

In addition to the huge choice available, I like U.S. stocks for a number of reasons. They are more volatile than Canadian stocks, so if you pick a good one you won't have to wait long for your reward. The markets are also highly liquid, which means the bid and ask prices are close to each other, and you can get in and out in a hurry. Also, because American stocks are bought and sold in U.S. dollars, they are an excellent currency hedge. No matter how patriotic you are, it makes sense to have some of your assets in American funds. Dividends from U.S. stocks are always useful, particularly if you vacation in the United States or the Caribbean.

There are two principal drawbacks for Canadians owning U.S. stocks. First, dividends are subject to an automatic 15 percent witholding tax. This tax is deducted at source, so there's no way around it. And, unlike Canadian dividends, you don't receive any tax credit on foreign dividends. However, Revenue Canada allows you to claim the amount of witholding tax you have paid on your Canadian income tax return. Second, and more important, if you have U.S. stocks in your name when you die, your estate may be subject to succession duties from the states in which the companies are domiciled. To avoid the succession duty problem, leave your shares with your broker, a Canadian bank, or a Canadian trust company and make sure that the certificates are registered in that institution's name, not in yours.

If you plan to trade U.S. stocks on a regular basis, you would be well advised to open a U.S. funds account with your broker. If you do this, you won't have to convert from Canadian to U.S. dollars (or vice versa) every time you do a transaction. In addition to the convenience, you will avoid being "whipsawed" by currency swings.

On the subject of converting U.S. or Canadian funds, you will get a significantly better rate from your broker than from your bank. The reason is that the broker is willing to take less on the transaction to facilitate the trade—which is where he makes his money. And it should be obvious that a Canadian broker who is a member of the New York Stock Exchange will give you better service than one who is not.

A FINAL WORD

Finally, if you're going to invest in common stocks, put your business through the major stock exchanges. Forget the unlisted markets—they can't be monitored or regulated as closely as the exchanges. In Canada, stick to the Toronto Stock Exchange or the Montreal Exchange. In the United States, restrict yourself to the American or New York stock exchanges. If you're a shooter, you can add NASDAQ to the list.

7

PREFERRED SHARES

Preferred shares are a staid, grey sort of investment—not a good bet for those who want action, but an odds-on favourite for income investors. Why? Because preferred shares are a hybrid security with some of the safety of a bond, plus the after-tax return of a common share. This combination—a big dividend and the tax credit—ensures a generous yield.

Because preferred dividends are paid from after tax-earnings, the tax credit is the same as for Canadian common shares. When making your return you "gross up" the actual dividend by 25 percent, then deduct 13⅓ percent of the grossed-up total from your federal tax. If your investment income is solely dividends from Canadian corporations, an astounding amount will be tax-free. Tax legislation changes frequently, but in 1994 a single person with no dependents could receive more than $20,000 in dividends, and not pay a cent of tax!

Although preferred shares lack glamour, more than three hundred issues, with a market capitalization of nearly twenty billion dollars, are listed on the Toronto Stock Exchange. Like common shares, preferred shares are part of the equity of a company.

But they are a safer investment. They are called preferred shares because they have preference over the common on both the earnings and the assets of the company. In the event of dissolution, preferred shares rank behind the the bank and the bondholders but ahead of the common shareholders. When a dividend is declared, the preferred shares have first call on the earnings.

On the negative side, preferred shares don't participate in the growth of a company (unless they're convertible). Nor do they have a vote in the company's affairs. The dividend is set at a fixed rate like the coupon on a bond. This rate—which may be "floating"—doesn't change, even if the company's earnings and common dividends increase. (A floating rate is normally a fixed percentage of another rate, such as the prime rate. Thus, although the percentage is fixed, the dividend "floats" with the underlying rate.)

A preferred share is also similar to a bond in that it has a par value. The par value is its *stated value*, and is important for two reasons. First, the par value is a claim on the assets of the company and must be satisfied in full before anything is paid to the common shareholders. This means that the owner of a preferred share with a par value of $25 is entitled to $25 in the event of the company's winding up or dissolution. Second, the dividend is often expressed as a percentage of the par value. For example, a $25 par preferred paying $1.50 (which is 6 percent) may be described as a $1.50 preferred or a 6 percent preferred. Both terms are correct.

Under existing tax laws, issuing preferred shares is the most expensive way to raise capital (because dividends are paid out of earnings after taxes, whereas bond interest is paid before taxes). If it's so expensive, why, you may wonder, do companies issue preferred shares? There are various reasons. In the case of the chartered banks, it's usually to increase their equity base. Some companies issue preferreds because they don't want to dilute their common shares. Others resort to preferreds because their credit isn't good enough to float a bond issue. (Brokers gloss over the latter case by saying, "The market is not receptive to a debt issue at this time.")

ASSETS COVERAGE AND DIVIDEND COVERAGE

There are two important ratios that you should scrutinize before buying a preferred share: the asset coverage and the dividend coverage. Check the figures for the past *five years*, and note the *trend*. If the figures are adequate but the trend is weakening, move on to another prospect.

The source of this information is the company's balance sheet, which is in every annual report, and many research reports. The first thing to note is the section on the asset side of the sheet called "shareholders' equity"; this shows the common shares outstanding as well as any preferred share issues. Simply divide the number of preferred shares into the total shareholders' equity. The resulting number is the asset coverage per preferred share. Here is an example, when there's only one preferred issues outstanding, of the asset coverage calculation:

Shareholders' equity	$45,000,000
500,000 6% $20 par preferred	
Asset coverage per preferred share	
($45,000,000 ÷ 500,000)	= $90
Expressed as a ratio, 4.5:1	or 4.5 times

If the same company were to issue more shares, say 400,000 7 percent preferred with a par value of $25 which rank *junior* to the 6 percent preferred, you would calculate the asset coverage on the new issue this way:

Shareholders' equity	$ 45,000,000
Less 500,000 6% $20 par preferred	–$ 10,000,000
Balance available for new preferred	$ 35,000,000
Asset coverage per new preferred share	
($35,000,000 ÷ 400,000)	= $ 87.50
Expressed as a ratio, 3.5:1	or 3.5 times

The asset coverage ratio is critical because it represents the cushion of equity in the event of liquidation. As a rule of thumb, the *minimum* asset coverage ratio for utility preferreds should be 2:1 and for other companies 3:1 per share.

The dividend coverage ratio is also very important. It can be calculated by a complicated formula or by a slightly less precise, but simple one. I prefer the simple way which is to divide the total preferred dividend into the total net earnings (excluding nonrecurring items). If there is only one preferred outstanding, this is how it's done:

Company net earnings $2,400,000

500,000 6% $20 par preferred dividend requirement
(500,000 x $1.20)   = $ 600,000
Dividend divided into earnings   = 4
Dividend coverage ratio 4:1   or 4 times

If there are two or more preferreds that rank *pari passu* (a Latin phrase meaning "equally"), subtract the total dividend requirement and apply the resulting ratio to *all* the issues. On the other hand, if one issue ranks senior to another, this is the way you calculate dividend coverage for the junior preferred (we'll use the previous example of a 7 percent second preferred):

Company net earnings $2,400,000
Less 6% preferred dividend   –$ 600,000
Balance available for 7% preferred $1,800,000

400,000 7% $25 par preferred dividend requirement
(400,000 x $1.75)   =$ 700,000
Dividend divided into earnings balance   = 2.57
Dividend coverage ratio 2.57:1   or 2.57 times

The minimum acceptable coverage for utility shares is two times the dividend requirement; for other companies, it is three times. So, in the foregoing example if the issuer was a utility, both preferreds would have sufficient coverage, but if it was another type of company, the second preferred wouldn't measure up.

EARNINGS TRENDS AND RATING SERVICES

As mentioned earlier, the earnings trend must be taken into consideration, especially when calculating dividend coverage. An erratic or a downwards trend are both bad signs. To get a valid trend you must check the common share earnings for the past five years or more. Here is an example of a solid earnings trend:

1994	1993	1992	1991	1990	1989
$3.28	$2.92	$2.40	$2.17	$2.03	$1.79

For those who don't want to punch a calculator, the rating services publish credit ratings on most of the actively traded preferred issues. Both agencies use the same scale, in which P1 is the highest and P5 the lowest. But not infrequently assessments among the rating services vary. To be on the safe side, you should restrict yourself, (unless you're taking a calculated risk) to issues that have at least a P2 low rating.

TERMS AND CONDITIONS OF THE ISSUE

Having worked out your ratios, or checked the agency ratings, your work isn't over. Now you have to look at the terms and conditions of the issue. For instance, is the dividend cumulative or noncumulative? A *cumulative dividend* means that if a quarterly dividend is passed (i.e., payment to investors is skipped), it remains an obligation on the books of the company. Sometimes a company will get into financial difficulty and pass its preferred dividends for several years, and then, after it recovers, pay them back. Stelco Preferred C shares are a recent example. If the shares, however, are noncumulative and the company passes its preferred dividend, you're out of luck. So it's prudent to buy only cumulative preferreds. The only exception would be preferreds issued by the chartered banks, which are often noncumulative. The banks scrap the cumulative clause because they don't want anything to jeopardize their long histories of paying common share dividends.

Another thing to watch out for is the "call" or "redemption" feature. Many preferred shares can be redeemed by the company on or after a set date, at a fixed price. Usually the company will pay a premium in the early years, but this premium declines with the passage of time. The reason for the premium is to compensate the holder for the loss of his investment. The rationale behind the declining premium is that the longer the shares are held, the less painful the loss. Some shares are noncallable, particularly "straight" preferreds (described below), but they are the exception rather than the rule.

If your shares are called and you've paid a big premium for them, you stand to lose money. (This is not necessarily the case with convertible preferreds, because you may be able to convert them into the underlying common.) The hazard is particularly great if you've bought high-coupon preferreds in the after market. The closer the redemption date, and the higher the coupon, the greater the potential for loss. A high coupon is like a red flag to the issuer, who knows it can be refinanced at a lower rate. But the further away the call date, the more time you have to write off your premium. As the call date approaches, the time element overrides the relative yield. This is particularly noticeable when the stock is trading ex-dividend just before the call date.

I should also mention that a company may have the right to redeem its shares, but it is *not* obligated to do so. Nevertheless, when assessing a preferred share, you should *always assume that it will be called on the redemption date.* This way you won't be in for an unpleasant surprise. The best solution is to buy redeemable preferreds when they are first offered, or at not more than the issue price. Or, you can avoid the hazard completely by only buying nonredeemable shares.

STRAIGHT PREFERREDS

Until relatively recently, there was only one kind of preferred share—the "straight" preferred. It is akin to a perpetual bond in that it has no maturity date. Aside from those cases where there is a redemption feature, the only way these shares are removed from the market is if the company buys them back. This is sometimes done by a company, if it has a "sinking fund" for making periodic purchases in the market. Because preferreds are essentially a fixed-income security, they respond to interest rates exactly like a bond: when interest rates rise, the price of preferred shares fall. Conversely, when rates decline, the price of preferreds rise. Since rates peaked in the '80s, preferred shares as a class have done very well. But, having said that, I must also tell you that preferred shares were in a bear market for a quarter of a century before rates peaked. Indeed, in the early '80s, not more than half a dozen straight preferred issues were readily marketable.

A bear market for straight preferreds could happen again. All that's required is a prolonged rise in interest rates. Straight preferreds are a pure interest play, and a poor one at that. Based on many years of experience, I would suggest you *avoid all straight preferreds, regardless of the yield.* When rates rise, as they inevitably will, if you hold straight preferred shares, you're trapped. The only way out is to take a loss. And the longer you procrastinate, the worse it will be.

Investors sometimes confuse class "A" and class "B" *common* shares with straight preferred shares. Whether they are class A or B (or class X or Y, for that matter), common shares *participate* in the earnings of the company. Often class A shares don't have a vote, but have first dibs on the earnings. After the class A shares have been paid a given amount, the class B shares are paid a like amount. Then, both classes share equally in any further dividend payments. Molson class A and B shares are a good example. Molson class A shares don't have a vote but are entitled to a dividend of 20 cents before anything is paid to the class B shares, which have a vote. After both classes receive 20 cents, they share equally in any additional distribution.

When there are two classes of common shares to choose from, you should theoretically buy the one with the vote. The logic behind this choice is that in the event of a takeover, voting shares will be more valuable. Nowadays, however, securities legislation usually ensures equal takeover treatment for both voting and nonvoting shares. But each company is different and should be assessed on its own merits. Quite often *marketability* is more important than the vote—as in the case of Molson A and B shares. Molson A shares have no vote, but trade at a premium to the B shares because they're more marketable. This paradox is true of several major Canadian companies.

CONVERTIBLE PREFERREDS

Convertible preferred shares are the only preferreds with a tie to the common. Convertibles are more volatile than straight preferreds and offer much greater profit potential. Convertible preferred shares—which are both an income and a growth investment—can be exchanged for common shares of the company. Conversion terms vary with each issue, but the effect is to lock in a set price for the common, for a given period of time. For instance, each preferred share might be exchangeable for one share of common for seven years. Thus, if the underlying common shares rise (or, if interest rates fall), a convertible preferred will increase in value. Should the common shares decline, a convertible has some downside protection because the dividend provides a measure of support.

Although convertible preferreds offer the best of both worlds, they must be chosen with care. The first thing to ask yourself is whether you'd like to own the common stock. If you don't like the common, forget the convertible preferred. You should also know that when convertible preferreds are issued, their yield is usually *less* than other preferreds, and the conversion price is always *above* the current market price of the common. The difference between the conversion price and the market price is known as the "time premium" or simply as the "premium." A convertible preferred might be issued at $20 (its par value) and be convertible into one common share that is currently trading at $16. The $4 difference between the cost of the preferred and the market price is the premium, which is normally described as a percentage—in this case, 25 percent.

To determine whether the premium is reasonable, you will have to consider several factors. One is the *payback period*, or the amount of time required for the additional yield on the preferred to recoup the premium. Taking our previous example of a 25 percent premium, if the preferred yield is 5 percent and there's no dividend on the common, the payback period will be five years. Here's the calculation:

Convertible preferred yield	5%
Less common yield	0

Additional yield on preferred   5%

Divide yield difference of 5% into premium of 25%
Payback period   = 5 years

In assessing the payback period, there are a few maxims you might want to consider. First, if you're a conservative investor, don't buy a convertible preferred unless there's enough time to pay back your premium. Second, if the underlying common has a large and secure dividend, don't bother with the convertible preferred, buy the common. For years BCE had a convertible preferred that eventually had its dividend *surpassed* by the dividend on the common—into which it was convertible on a one-for-one basis! Third, and this is one of my pet beliefs, if you think a stock has explosive growth potential and the conversion period is long, don't be too concerned with the payback period (providing it's not outrageous).

The call feature should also be scrutinized. If you pay a big premium for a convertible with less than three years to redemption, you could be vulnerable. Should the shares be redeemed, you'll be given a month or so to convert, which is no problem, providing the common shares have risen enough to cover your premium. If they haven't, you are certain to take a loss. To minimize this loss, choose whichever is higher: the redemption price or the conversion value. For example, if you paid $30 for a preferred that is being redeemed at $25 and the value of the underlying common stock is $27, it would obviously be wiser to convert and sell the common. If, however, the two values are almost the same, you'd probably be better off to let your shares be redeemed because of commission costs. When a stock is called, the price, by the way, is always "net"; there's no commission charge.

You should also pay close attention to what happens on the expiry date of the conversion privilege, if there is one. Some convertible preferreds on that date revert to being straight preferreds. Others continue to be convertible at a higher price, or at several higher prices on an escalating scale. Before you buy any convertible, whether it is a new or outstanding issue, you should study the terms carefully. If you have any doubts, get a copy of the original prospectus, which your broker can provide. But I should warn you that the terms can sometimes be tough to understand. For example, here is an excerpt describing the conversion feature of the Toronto Dominion Bank, noncumulative U.S. pay class A first preference shares, series 6:

> On or before January 31, 2004 each preferred share shall be convertible at the option of the holder on the last business day of January, April, July, and October in each year on not more than 90 and not less than 65 days' notice into that number of fully paid freely tradable common shares of the bank determined by dividing U.S. $25.00 together with declared and unpaid dividends to date fixed for conversion by the greater of U.S.$1.00 and 95% of the U.S. dollar equivalent of the weighted average trading price of such common shares on the TSE for the 20 trading days ending on or before the fourth day prior to the date fixed for conversion.

Did you have to read that sentence twice to grasp its content? So did I. For those of you who didn't bother to hack through the legal verbiage, it says that four times a year, until January 2004, you can convert the shares into TD common at a 5 percent discount. My glib interpretation, however, leaves out some important details, such as the requirement of at least 65 days' notice before conversion. Let me repeat: if you're not sure about the precise terms of a convertible issue, read the fine print.

VARIABLE RATE OR FLOATING PREFERREDS AND RETRACTABLE PREFERREDS

In the late '70s, aside from a few convertibles, the preferred market consisted solely of straight preferreds. As rates had been rising for twenty years, everyone was losing money. New issues were tough to sell and the preferred market appeared doomed. To save this facet of the business—which, in former days had been extremely lucrative—the securities industry came up with two new types of straight preferred shares. One was the *variable rate* or *floating preferred*, the other the *retractable preferred*. Both were designed to protect the buyer's capital, and both proved highly successful. Since the late '70s, Canadian investors have bought literally billions of dollars worth of floating and retractable preferred shares.

A variable rate or floating preferred is the same as a straight preferred with one important exception—the amount of the dividend is not fixed, but is tied to prevailing interest rates. The dividend is stated as a percentage of the Canadian prime rate, or (if the the issue is denominated in American funds) the U.S. prime rate. There's no set formula, but normally the payout is between 60 and 80 percent. Sometimes the "floating" dividend doesn't commence for a number of years, but for the first years is fixed. These are known as *delayed floaters*. It's well to remember that in this type of issue your interest rate hedge doesn't kick in until the dividend starts floating (and you must also watch the redemption feature). Some floaters have a minimum dividend that ensures that even if rates decline dramatically, you'll still receive a reasonable income. This is a useful feature. On the other hand, some floaters have a ceiling on the maximum yield. This is a limitation to avoid, because it exposes you to risk should interest rates soar (as they have so many times in the past).

The main purpose of a floating rate preferred is to provide a hedge against rising interest rates. Ideally, a floater should have a hefty minimum dividend, and a waiting period of not more than a year before the variable rate commences. It should also measure up to all the other standards of a good preferred. Remember, a floating rate preferred is a defensive investment—so stick with quality.

Now, let's take a look at *retractable preferreds*, the other '70s innovation. A rectractable preferred doesn't have a floating dividend, but it does have an escape clause: the holder can sell the shares back to the company, at issue price, on a future date. This makes a retractable preferred similar to a bond in that for both the return of your capital is assured, and there's a fixed rate of income. In the creditors' line, retractable preferred holders rank behind the bondholders. On the other hand, preferred dividends (unlike bond interest) qualify for the tax credit.

Retractables proved to be an instant hit with investors. In the spring of 1994 more than fifty issues were outstanding, and many were trading at premiums. Because retractables often trade at a premium, you can't simply buy them on a yield basis. You must check the terms of each issue.

One of the things you must watch for when considering retractables is the redemption or call feature, which we spoke of earlier in this chapter. Virtually all retractable preferreds are redeemable as well as retractable. The difference between the two is that a redemption is at the company's pleasure, while a retraction is your choice. Sometimes the redemption and retraction dates are different, but more often they're the same date. Because of the redemption and retraction features, you have three yields to consider: current yield, yield to retraction, and yield to redemption. The ones that count are yield to retraction and yield to redemption. Here is an example that shows their importance. The issue is TransCanada Pipelines, retractable preferred, "Series N" which has a par value of $50 and pays a $4.50 dividend. It is redeemable and retractable on 1 February 1996, at par. This was the market at the beginning of 1994:

Security	Price	Div	Current Yield	Retrac Yield	Redem Yield
TransCanada Pipelines	$56	$4.50	8.04%	3.73%	3.73%

As the example shows, if you look only at the current yield you can be fooled. In this case, TransCanada is paying a 9% dividend on the "Series N" preferred, which is expensive to service. With only two years to go, unless interest rates move substantially higher, it is likely the company will redeem the shares at $50 and refinance at a lower rate. Should this happen, and you paid $56 for the preferred, you would incur a $6 capital loss per share when your shares were called. In the meantime, your actual yield would have only been 3.73 percent.

Now let's look at the effect of redemption and retraction yields on two PEACs. As you may remember, PEAC is the abbreviation for payment enhanced capital securities, or in plainer English, the income element of stripped common shares. Both PEACs are based on BCE shares, and are similar to standard retractable preferreds. The first one, BNT Dividend Equity, receives the full BCE dividend and has a par value of $27.50, which is also its redemption and retraction price on 20 April 1995. As a "kicker," if the underlying BCE common is trading at over $65 on that date, the BNT redemption price is increased by 20 percent of the amount over $65 (BCE at the time was trading

at $48). The second PEAC, First B Inc., has a par value of $26.50
and receives $2.50 of the BCE dividend until the BCE dividend
(currently $2.68) reaches $4, at which point it receives the excess
above that amount. First B Inc. is redeemable and retractable at
$26.50 on April 23 1996.

Security	Price	Div	Current Yield	Retrac Yield	Redemp Yield
BNT Div Eqty	$29.75	$2.68	9.01%	2.92%	2.92%
First B Inc	$25.00	$2.50	10.08%	12.51%	12.51%

While it's true these two PEACs mature twelve months apart,
and their terms are not identical, they're comparable on a fundamental basis. Viewed from any angle, it's difficult to see why
anyone interested in income—the prime reason for a PEAC—
would choose BNT Dividend Equity shares at that price. Whereas First B Inc. shares are the opposite—their price is below par;
their current yield is great; and the redemption/retraction yields
are truly sensational.

If you're thinking of paying a premium for a retractable preferred, always assume the worst—that your shares will be
redeemed at the earliest possible date. As a rule of thumb, you
shouldn't pay more than a 20 percent premium for a retractable.
Some retractables have several retraction dates, while others have
only one. Occasionally you'll encounter a "soft retraction," which
means that, instead of cash, you'll receive the equivalent value in
securities on the retraction date. Westcoast Preferred D, which is
retractable into $25 of Westcoast common at a 5 percent discount
in July 1997, and July 1998, is a good example of a soft retraction.
Regardless of how many retraction dates there are though, after
the last (or only one) has passed, the security becomes a *straight*
preferred. So, if you hold any retractables, make a note of the
retraction dates. You don't, under any circumstances, want to end
up owning a straight preferred.

In the past decade some convertible preferreds have come
out with a retraction feature. Alternatively, some retractable preferreds have enhanced their sales appeal with equity ties, such
as warrants to buy common shares of the issuer. A few preferreds
have a variable dividend that is adjusted to ensure that the

shares trade around par (a concept introduced by the Bank of Commerce). Quite a few retractables have been issued in U.S. dollars, with the option to receive dividends in Canadian or American funds, which provides a currency hedge. Income investors have done very nicely with these innovations. But it hasn't only been widows and orphans who have profited from these income securities. Marvin, one of my largest and most sophisticated clients, also did well.

Marvin is a high roller in industrial stocks who never trades less than five thousand shares at a crack. Although he was in sea-soned companies, his portfolio got badly battered in the 1981-82 recession. At the peak of the market his holdings were worth about ten million dollars. Then came the long slide. As the prices fell day after day Marvin's health began to suffer. Finally, he sold out and took a loss of about three million dollars. The only thing he kept was a hundred thousand shares of BCE. Marvin then departed for a long holiday in Florida to recover from a bleeding ulcer. While he was recuperating down south, he gave the matter a lot of thought and decided to change his investment strategy. From now on he would be an ultra-conservative investor. At that time interest rates were at their peak, and he shrewdly bought large chunks of the best retractable preferred and convertible preferred issues. When interest rates began to decline and the market perked up, Marvin was in excellent shape. By the end of 1983 he had regained his health, he had an assured income, and a paper profit of more than one million dollars. All by investing in preferreds at the right time.

ONE MORE OBSERVATION

In closing this chapter on preferreds, let me leave you with one more observation. When I was in the business I was sometimes asked to recommend a security that combined absolute safety, high income, and excellent growth. Of course, is there no such thing. It's a myth. But I do think that a convertible preferred is about as close as you'll get to this will-o'-the-wisp. A good con-vertible preferred is relatively safe; it has a generous yield; and it offers potential for capital gain. It's my favourite investment.

8

MUTUAL FUNDS

Τhere are over six hundred mutual funds in Canada with more than 130 billion dollars in assets. If you wish—and many people do—you can restrict yourself to mutual funds and never look at another investment. Next to bank accounts, mutual funds are the most popular place for people to invest their money. During the bull market of 1993, Canadian funds increased their assets by 70 percent, and by 1994 there were more than ten million mutual fund accounts.

A mutual fund is a company or a trust whose assets consist of securities. These securities are managed for the benefit of the shareholders. Thus a shareholder owns a small piece of a large investment portfolio. For as little as a few hundred dollars you get diversification and professional management. And, after you plunk down your money, you can forget about it because your investment is looked after by someone else.

Recent surveys show, however, that many people buy mutual funds without knowing what they're getting into, or they buy them for the wrong reason. For instance, a surprising number of people who switch from GICs to money market, bond, or mortgage funds, assume these investments are insured (like their GICs). They're not. And many novice investors, as well as GIC "refugees," don't understand market dynamics nor the risks associated with equity funds. With the huge variety of funds available, and the hype surrounding them, it might be useful to review what's out there. If nothing else, this may help to cut through the blarney, and allow you to assess the situation more objectively.

OPEN-END AND CLOSED-END FUNDS

Basically, there are two types of mutual funds: "open-end" and "closed-end". The open-end fund is by far the most common, and the one we will concentrate on in this chapter.

An open-end fund doesn't have a fixed capitalization, but continually offers and redeems its own shares (thus the number of shares and total assets in the fund are constantly changing). Normally the shares are redeemed at their "net asset value", which is their actual value. Some funds deduct a redemption fee from the net asset value. Many funds are sold to the public at a premium, with the fee being stated as a percentage of the net asset value. An increasing number of open-end funds, however, are being offered and redeemed without charge—these are known as "no load" funds. Because open-end funds make their own market, their shares are not listed on the stock exchanges.

Closed-end funds, also known as *investment trusts*, have a fixed number of shares and are listed on the exchanges (or traded over the counter). Like regular companies, they may also have bonds and preferred shares outstanding. Unlike open-end funds, the shares of closed-end funds can trade at a substantial premium or discount to their net asset value. Usually they trade at a discount. The reason for the discount is that investors know the fund is unlikely to liquidate all its assets and distribute the proceeds. On the other hand, the premium is often due to euphoria, and unless there are special circumstances (such as the fund converting to open-end), *a closed-end fund trading above its net asset value is a candidate for sale.*

As a matter of interest, there are two kinds of closed-end funds: investment companies and holding companies. Investment companies, such as Canadian General Investments and

United Corporations, simply supervise a portfolio of securities. Holding companies, like Power Corporation and the Traders Group, own controlling blocks of shares in companies, and play an active role in their management.

In total there are less than twenty closed-end funds in Canada, and they're not of much consequence to the average investor. So, let's get back to open-end funds. As mentioned earlier, there are more than six hundred open-end funds, and they offer something for everyone. Despite the number of funds, it's easy to keep track of them. *The Financial Post* and *The Globe and Mail*, as well as other Canadian daily papers, publish extensive mutual fund listings. *The Financial Times* has a weekly report, and both the *Post* and the *Globe* publish a monthly survey of mutual funds. These surveys are well worth studying; they will give you both a good idea of what's available and how the funds stack up against each other. To simplify your quest, the *Globe* separates the funds into categories. These categories are:

Balanced Funds—Canadian Equity Funds—Bond Funds—
International Bond Funds—International Equity Funds—
Dividend Funds—U.S. Equity Funds—Real Estate Funds—
Money Market Funds—International Money Market Funds- -
Sector Equity Funds—Mortgage Funds

Within these categories, each fund is tabled under the following headings:

Fees - Expense ratio - RRSP - Volatility - 3mo - 6mo - 1 yr
2yr - 3yr - 5yr - 10yr - NAVPS - Assets (000s) - Telephone

- *Fees* refers to the sales charge or "load," if any, to purchase the fund. Sales charges and fees will be dealt with later in the chapter.

- *Expense ratio* is the cost of management fees and other expenses expressed as a percentage of the fund's assets.

- *RRSP* indicates whether the fund is eligible for your RRSP without resorting to the foreign content provision. The answer is shown as "Y" or "N" (for yes or no).

- *The volatility* of the fund is measured on a scale of 1 to 10, with 1 the lowest volatility and 10 the highest. Volatility (sometimes referred to as variability) is an indication of risk, as it reflects the degree of price fluctuation. High volatility funds are the big swingers that outperform the market on the upside, but fare worse than the market on the downside. Funds in the midrange are more sedate and tend to move parallel with the market. Those with low volatility ratings are the most stable, with consistent but relatively unexciting rates of return.

- The *figures in the monthly and yearly columns* are the fund's *compounded* rates of return for those periods. Remember that this is historical information, not a projection of future performance. These figures are, however, useful when comparing one fund with another. When screening funds, start with the near term figures and work back. But don't get carried away by a stunning one-year performance—it may have been a fluke. The three-year and five-year numbers are perhaps the most important, because they reveal the longer-term trend. The ten-year period is also worthwhile, but many of today's best funds haven't been around that long, and some seasoned funds have changed managers during the past decade. What you are looking for is a consistent return in good times and bad. Even then, before you buy the fund, check that the same management is at the helm.

- *NAVPS* stands for "net asset value per share" and indicates the fund's intrinsic value per unit. It is calculated by taking the fund's assets (cash and securities) and deducting the total liabilities. The balance is then divided by the number of shares in the fund. The resulting figure is the net asset value per share. Here's an example:

Value of securities	$57,000,000
Plus cash	+$ 3,500,000
Total	$60,500,000
Less liabilities	–$ 2,300,000
Net Assets	$58,200,000
Shares outstanding 4,850,000	
Divide 4,850,000 into $58,200,000	= $12
Net Asset Value Per Share	= $12

- *Assets* refers to the total assets of the fund in multiples of a thousand. Generally speaking, small funds—those with less than fifty million dollars in assets—have greater capital gain potential than large funds of, say, more than half a billion dollars. This is because of the limited number of Canadian securities, and the thinness of our markets. It doesn't mean that small is necessarily better, but it does suggest that "big" can be a limiting factor to performance.

FUND TYPES

Each of the fund categories is different and has its own characteristics. And each fills its own investment niche.

Balanced Funds

Balanced funds were the first to be offered to Canadian investors. This type of fund consists of a mix of securities—cash, short-term investments, bonds, preferred shares, and common stocks. The proportions of these investments is altered on an ongoing basis to suit the current economic situation. The key to running a successful balanced fund is to read the trends and structure your portfolio to take advantage of them. For instance, you can take advantage by overweighting the fixed-income portion when interest rates are high, by increasing the equity holdings when the stock market is low, or by accumulating a hefty cash position when the market is close to a peak. Balanced portfolios not only provide above-average returns, but also have strong defensive characteristics.

Recently a new and highly touted investment management concept—*asset allocation*—was introduced to mutual fund investors. Asset allocation means shifting the proportions of assets within a portfolio to achieve optimum performance. Its efficacy has been confirmed by several high-profile studies, which concluded that the asset class (bonds or stocks, for instance), rather than the specific security (such as BCE or Imperial Oil), is the more important ingredient for investment success.

I wouldn't dispute the theory of asset allocation, nor the findings of the studies for an instant. But I would suggest that asset allocation is not new, and that it is merely another name for balancing a portfolio. It's exactly the same concept, and balanced portfolios have been around for more than a century. In my opinion, asset allocation is a relatively harmless marketing ploy, and everybody has to earn a living. But what is absurd is that some firms in the fund business are now offering—for a fee—to manage your mutual funds by asset allocation. This is akin to paying somebody to manage your funds, which you are already paying to have managed. How droll.

Balancing or asset allocation, whatever you want to call it, is a proven method of portfolio management. The best way to achieve balance is to buy into a high-quality balanced fund. By doing so you'll not only keep things simple, but also avoid unnecessary expense. And you should have little difficulty in finding a good balanced fund—more than a hundred of them are listed in *The Globe and Mail.*

Equity Funds

Over a hundred Canadian equity funds are also listed in the *Globe.* These funds consist mainly of Canadian equities or common shares, and growth is their primary objective. Because most of the funds have a relatively small cash or cash equivalent component, and no bonds, they are volatile. If you're looking for capital gains, this type of fund is an excellent vehicle, but you must do your homework. Having isolated an equity fund with a good record, you should measure its performance with another yardstick, the Toronto Stock Exchange 300 Index. (If you don't do this additional step you may discover you've merely chosen the best of a bad lot.) The TSE 300 Index comprises three hundred of the stocks listed on the Toronto Stock Exchange. This group includes a grab bag of good, bad, and indifferent companies which, when taken together, fairly reflect the price level of stocks on the exchange. What you're looking for is confirmation that your prospective fund has, *at the very least,* matched the performance of the exchange. You may be surprised at how many funds—managed by highly paid experts—fail to pass this elementary test.

There are also U.S. and international equity funds, which invest in U.S. and offshore companies. The U.S. funds obviously focus on one country, but most of the international funds invest in a "basket" of countries. Although these funds are volatile, they are useful as a currency hedge and are suitable for the foreign content portion of many RRSP portfolios. Because they differ widely in their scope and investment philosophies, be sure to read the prospectus before making a commitment.

Bond Funds

Most bond funds are balanced in that they usually consist of short-, medium-, and long-term maturities. Some restrict themselves to government or government-guaranteed bonds, while others—the higher-yielding ones—buy securities with lower credit ratings. Income is paid out monthly or quarterly, while capital gains (if any) are paid out at the end of the year. Some bond funds structure their portfolios to produce capital gains rather than high income. This type of fund typically invests in low-coupon, long-term bonds, and is more volatile than income-oriented funds. But don't be misled—bond funds are essentially a defensive investment. If you want gross income, they'll provide it. But, if you're looking for dynamic growth, you're better off buying an equity fund.

U.S. and international bond funds offer diversification and a currency hedge. I prefer international to U.S. bond funds, because their managers invest all over the world, rather than in just one country. If you scan the globe, there are always countries that offer an interest rate play or a currency play—sometimes both. Also, because of the traditional interest rate spread between Canada and the United States, U.S. bond funds invariably yield *less* than Canadian funds.

Dividend Funds

Dividend funds are designed to provide good after-tax income with modest growth. To obtain the dividend tax credit, these funds normally invest in preferred shares and high-yielding common stocks. In recent years, however, some dividend funds have included interest income in their earnings, making them less "pure" from a tax credit point of view. Dividends are paid monthly or quarterly, with capital gains disbursed at year-end. To compare dividend income with interest income, multiply your dividends by a factor of 1.25. Thus $400 in dividends is roughly equal to $500 in interest, on an after-tax basis.

Real Estate Funds

Real estate funds, although their performance over the short, medium, and long term has been abysmal, continue to get good press. This is difficult to understand, as real estate funds were the worst-performing group in 1993, with a loss of 9.39 percent (versus a TSE gain of approximately 33 percent), a three-year return of *minus* 2.35 percent, a five-year return of 2.48 percent, and for ten years, an anemic return of 4 percent. By mid-1994, there were only half a dozen real estate funds left, the others being casualties of the recession. Some funds offer a tax break, by qualifying as REITs (real estate investment trusts), but this is a very expensive way to get tax relief. On balance, I can't think of any reason to buy a real estate fund. Then again, their performance has been so dreadful they might just be an interesting long-term speculation. But not for widows or orphans.

Mortgage Funds

Mortgage funds shouldn't be confused with real estate funds. These funds usually invest in first mortgages (often insured by CMHC) and are relatively safe. When interest rates are stable, they provide above average income with a modest potential for capital gain. You should be aware, however, that because rates have declined precipitously, advertised returns from previous years are not relevant today. Keep this in mind when shopping for a mortgage fund.

Segregated Funds

Segregated funds are issued by life insurance companies, and differ from standard equity and bond funds. (Segregated refers to the fact that the underlying securities are segregated from the insurance company's other assets—as are your securities when you leave them with a broker for safekeeping.) Segregated funds are sold by life insurance agents and are issued by the companies as insurance or annuity contracts. This allows the shares in segregated funds to be passed on to a beneficiary without probate, and has other legal ramifications. Some funds also insure from 75 to 100 percent of your original investment. One drawback to segregated funds is that they are a nuisance to track, as they are usually valued once a week, and some funds don't publish their prices—you have to phone the company. Because of the unusual terms of these funds, it is essential to read the fine print in the prospectus, or you could be in for a surprise. You must also compare their performances, because they range from very good to very indifferent.

Labour-Sponsored Funds

Labour-sponsored funds came into existence as a result of tax legislation to promote investment in Canadian business ventures. The best-known of these funds is the Working Ventures Canadian Fund, which is sponsored by the Canadian Federation of Labour. If a person in the top income tax bracket buys $5000 of this fund and then lodges it in their RRSP, the tax savings are enormous. The after-tax cost of the $5000 investment works out to something in the neighbourhood of $500. That's the good news. The bad news is that you must hold the shares for a *minimum* of five years. If you sell before that period has elapsed, you forfeit most of your tax credits. As venture capital is by definition high-risk and the Canadian Federation of Labour is not noted for its investment expertise, would you want to be locked in for five years? Three other provincial funds have even longer waiting periods that range from seven years to when you retire. The other thing to keep in mind is that when buying a tax "shelter," *always assess the quality of the underlying investment* before looking at the tax benefits. If the investment doesn't measure up, you should pass on the package.

Sector Equity Funds

Sector equity is the name for a diverse group of specialty funds. Most of these funds invest in a valuable commodity, such as gold or precious metals, a particular industry—like computers or telecommunications, or strategic resources (such as oil and gas). "Ethical funds" are also included in this group. Ethical funds have a political focus and won't invest in companies that do business with countries that have poor human rights records, of which there are many. Environmentally motivated ethical funds won't invest in companies that harm the environment (which rules out a large segment of Canada's forest products and mining industries). Notwithstanding their high-minded approach, ethical funds have an undistinguished investment record and appeal mainly to investors who wish to make a political statement. The other sector equity funds, because they target specific industries and commodities, are highly volatile, and not for the faint of heart.

Money Market Funds

Money market funds are just the opposite—safe and stable, and a comfortable place to park your money. This type of fund invests in Treasury Bills, bonds, commercial paper, and other short-term securities that usually mature within a year. Money market units normally have a par value of $10, and are *not* insured. In some cases the unit value will fluctuate with interest rates, and if rates are rising it's easy to suffer a capital loss. Because safety is your priority, *don't* buy a fund with with a fluctuating unit value. Most funds have a minimum purchase requirement of around a thousand dollars. But, as this figure varies, you should check it first.

There are two kinds of money market funds: one that invests only in Treasury Bills, and one that invests in a broader spectrum of securities. The T-Bill fund is the safer of the two, and yields less than the other one. But the question of safety, particularly if the fund is owned by a chartered bank is really academic (most chartered banks have both types of funds). Although their rates fluctuate from day to day, money market funds pay more than bank savings accounts. For this reason it makes sense to transfer the surplus in your savings account to a money market fund—and you won't even have to leave the bank to do it.

International money market funds invest throughout the world, and usually yield less than domestic funds. The main role of an international money market fund is to provide liquidity and a currency hedge.

The easiest way to shop for a fund is to look at the listings in the paper, and compare current yields. Ignore the "effective yield" because this is a nonsense figure based on a compounded fluctuating rate. Before you buy a fund, find out if there's any minimum period you must hold it, or if it can be redeemed on twenty-four hours' notice. And *don't, under any circumstances,* buy a money market fund that charges a commission. If you pay a commission you will decrease the yield, and you could even end up losing money. For instance, in the *Globe and Mail* March 1994 Report on Mutual Funds, the first money market fund listed charged a commission of 9 percent and its compounded rate of return for the previous year was 3.04 percent. Had you held the fund for those twelve months and then redeemed your units, you would have suffered a capital *loss* of nearly 6 percent!

COMMISSIONS

This brings us to the delicate subject of commissions. Some funds charge them, and some funds don't. Funds that charge commissions, or "loads" as they are called in the industry, do so in two ways: "front-end," which means you're charged at the time of purchase, or "rear-end," in which you pay at the time of sale. Loads are normally stated as a percentage of the net asset value. In the case of front-end loads, this can range from 9 percent to 2 percent, and is often on a sliding scale. The larger the purchase, the lower the sales charge. Here is a typical front-end load schedule:

Amount of Purchase	Sales Charge
up to $9,999	9%
$ 10,000 to $ 24,999	8%
$ 25,000 to $ 49,999	6.5%
$ 50,000 to $ 99,999	5%
$100,000 to $199,999	4%
$200,000 to $299,999	3%
$300,000 to $499,999	2%
over $500,000	Negotiable

The purchase of a load fund is a long-term investment. One compelling reason is that you will need a number of years to recoup the sales charge. If you pay, say, a 6 percent load, it's like entering a race with a handicap. If it's a short race, like the hundred-yard dash, you'll be six yards behind the starting line when the gun goes off. But on a long race, such as the mile, a six-yard handicap won't make much difference.

The length of time you hold your units is also relevant for back-end or "deferred" loads. Some funds charge a flat fee of from 4 to 6 percent, no matter how long you hold your shares. Other funds charge a back-end load on a sliding scale, which gets smaller with the passage of time. Here is an example of this type of charge:

Length of Ownership	Deferred Fee
less than one year	5%
two years	4½%
three years	4%
four years	3½%
five years	3%
six years	2½%
seven years and thereafter	2%

As a general rule, a rear-end load is preferable to a front-end load because with the former all your money is put to work at the outset, and you may hold the fund long enough to reduce or eliminate the sales charge. But you should check to see whether the rear-end load is levied as a percentage of your original *cost* price, or the current *market* price. It can make a great difference. For instance, if you bought $10,000 worth of a fund and three years later paid a 4 percent rear-end load on the cost price, you would be charged $400. But if the value of the fund had risen to $15,000 during the time you held it and the load was based on the market price, it would cost you $600.

Mutual funds are sold directly by the funds (some of whom have their own sales personnel) or indirectly by brokers, trust companies, banks, insurance agents, and money management companies. Normally a purchase is done on a lump sum basis, rather than by number of shares. Unlike stocks, there's no need or advantage to buying in board lots, and it's standard industry practice to issue fractional shares. In the case of a lump sum purchase, the sales charge is levied on the gross amount, which actually *increases* the effective rate of commission. Let's say you're going to buy five thousand dollars worth of a fund whose net asset value is $10 per share. The front-end load is 6 percent. You would think that this would be 60 cents per share, and your unit cost would be $10.60. But it doesn't work out that way. Here are the figures:

Cost of Purchase	$5000
Less 6%	–$ 300
Balance remaining to buy shares	
@ $10 per share buys 470 shares	$4700
(470 divided into $5000) = $10.63	
Effective commission rate is	6.3%

Is there any way to reduce your commissions? Yes, you can go to a discount house such as TD Green Line, which handles an immense number of funds. Or, if you're a good client, you can often negotiate a lower rate with your broker. With a little polite haggling, most money management firms and insurance agents will also give you a break. But trust companies, banks, discount houses, and funds with their own sales force will *not* budge from their published prices. (Investors Group, the largest mutual fund, which has own sales people, sometimes charges both a front-end *and* a rear-end load.)

Mutual funds purchased on a contractual basis—by signing up to pay so much a month for a period of years—carry the most onerous commissions charges of all. These commission fall into three categories: front-end load, level load, and rear-end load. Front-end load is assessed on your *total* commitment, which usually means that a large part of your first year's instalments will go towards paying commissions, rather than towards buying shares in the fund. Level load means that the commission— which is always at the highest end of the scale—will be distributed evenly over the term of the contract. Rear-end load (which is rarely found in instalment plans) means that you will pay your commission when the shares are redeemed. The most that can be said for contractual plans is that they are an expensive form of forced saving. If you have any other alternative, avoid them.

NO-LOAD FUNDS

Now for the good news. An increasing number of mutual funds offer their shares to the public with no sales charge. You might wonder how this is possible—if they don't charge a commission, how they can make money? Let me assure you that they do make money. There are two good reasons why no-load funds are profitable. First, the cost of selling no-load funds is relatively low, because no sales force is maintained, nor are commissions paid to third parties. Advertising—which is carefully controlled—is absorbed as an operating expense. Secondly, the bread and butter earnings of both load and no-load funds come from the annual management fees that are charged to shareholders.

These fees cover all the operating costs and provide the profit to the owners of the fund. Annual fee ratios run from about 1 percent to around 3 percent of total assets. Sector and specialty equity funds are at the top end of the scale, closely followed by foreign funds. Most foreign funds are run on a day-to-day basis by an overseas manager; for instance, a fund investing in the Pacific Rim might be managed from Hong Kong. This adds to the operating cost (the Canadian fund has to pay its foreign advisor), and this expense is passed on to the shareholders. Most domestic equity funds charge a fee in the 2 percent range, and bond funds fees are around half that amount. Money market funds charge the lowest fees. (And so they should; the average twelve-year-old, given a week's instruction, could competently run a money market fund.)

TRAILER COMMISSIONS

As an aside, some funds pay "trailer commissions" from their fees. Trailing commissions are disbursed to salespeople, on an annual basis, so long as their client holds units in the fund. They serve as an incentive to keep clients in the fund. This is important to the funds because their fees are levied as a percentage of the total assets under administration—and the larger the pool of assets, the bigger the fee. I mention this because, if you hold a fund that pays trailing fees (and you'll have to ask, or read the prospectus to find out), it could influence your broker's opinion of whether or not you should sell that fund.

THE LOAD VERSUS NO-LOAD ARGUMENT

Load funds defend themselves by saying that no-load funds charge much higher management fees. The truth is that management fees of some no-load funds are higher than the fees of some load funds—and vice versa. For example, let's look at two representative funds from the Balanced Funds section of the *Globe and Mail's* March 1994 Report on Mutual Funds. The Investors Group has the largest "family" of load funds in Canada, while the Altamira group runs a leading "family" of no-load funds. (The advantage of dealing with a fund family is that you can switch from one fund to another within the family at little or no cost.)

Fund	Fees	Expense Ratio
Altamira Growth & Income	NIL	1.41%
Investors Asset Allocation	F5% & R1%	2.3%

The other charge made by the load fraternity is that no-load funds don't perform as well, there by implying that they skimp on the quality of management. This is not true either. Of the eight Canadian mutual funds that advanced by 100 percent or more during 1993, four were no-load funds. The only real difference between load and no-load funds is how they are marketed. Load funds provide a cash incentive (paid for by the customer) to sell their product.

If you do buy a load fund, you shouldn't pay more than 5 percent commission. (As a point of interest, Green Line discount *all* their load funds to a flat fee of 2½ percent). Buying a load fund is justified under certain circumstances. For example, if you want to invest in a special niche in the market, reward your broker for good service, or help out a relative in the mutual funds business, load funds are acceptable. Otherwise, you should stick to no-load funds.

GENERAL BUYING AND SELLING TIPS

Whether they're load or no-load, don't buy too many funds. Overdiversification leads to mediocre performance. You don't need a portfolio of funds (although the industry would like you to have a whole raft of them). Each fund, with dozens and some- times hundreds of securities, is a portfolio within itself. If you buy balanced funds, you only need two or three, plus possibly a money market fund. And, if you buy these from within families of funds, you'll have all the mobility and selection you need. For instance, in the no-load field, Royal Bank/Royal Trust have more than twenty funds in their joint family, and there are several other companies with nearly as many.

Mutual funds make good sense for the small or the novice investor because they provide diversification and professional management. For the more sophisticated investor, mutual funds offer an excellent way to participate in foreign markets—an area where expert management is essential. In this connection, I would note that foreign markets have consistently outperformed the Canadian market.

It's best to approach mutual funds as a long-term invest- ment. Except for money market funds, plan on holding them for at least two years. If you try trading funds—even during markets swings—you risk getting whipsawed. And some companies, like the high-performance Altamira group, actively discourage jumping in and out of the same fund. Because funds are a good long-term investment, they are ideal for Registered Retirement Savings Plans.

The entire investment community—the banks, trust companies, money management firms, and insurance compa- nies, as well as the brokers—is well aware that mutual funds and RRSPs go together like ham and eggs. Indeed, each year the com- munity mounts a vigorous campaign to attract RRSP contribu- tions to mutual funds. It's invariably successful, and mutual fund sales soar during this period.

The campaign starts on the first of January. On that morning thousands of bleary-eyed Canadians wake up to the realization that the year is over, and they must do something about their Registered Retirement Savings Plan. If they don't make a contribution, they will pay more tax. Figuratively clutching as much as $15,000 in their hands, they frantically look around for a suitable investment.

The investment community is ready and waiting for them. Huge ads in the newspapers trumpet the virtues of various mutual funds. On the car radio, money management companies exhort their listeners to drop in for a chat, without obligation. At the bank, a smiling teller asks if you would like to talk to a mutual fund specialist. The trust company on the corner has taken down its sign in the window offering a "Merry Guaranteed Investment Certificate" (the ideal gift for a loved one) and replaced it with a sign offering mutual funds and *free* RRSP advice. Staid insurance companies also get into the act, shamelessly extolling their segregated funds as the ideal investment for a Registered Retirement Savings Plan.

Even the brokers, including those who cater to the carriage trade and usually shun small accounts, suddenly become enthusiastic about mutual funds. (The fact that 6 percent of $15,000 is $900 may be a contributing factor.) Brokers bombard their clients with RRSP literature and broadcast their message with extravagant newspaper ads. It's about the only time in the year that brokers spend this sort of money touting mutual funds. As a colleague in the business once said to me, "Little fish taste sweet."

Indeed, as the March 1st RRSP deadline approaches, the investment community's pursuit of mutual fund buyers reminds me of a bluefish "blitz." The bluefish is a powerful ocean fish with sharp teeth and a voracious appetite. Even after they've had their fill, they will continue to chomp through a school of baitfish. Bluefish are particularly fond of small herring, and when they encounter a school in shallow water all hell breaks loose. If you're standing on a beach, you'll suddenly notice little silver fish darting out of the water. Moments later, bluefish erupt in the middle of the school like hand grenades. The commotion attracts seagulls, who seem to appear from nowhere. The noisy gulls add to the pandemonium by wheeling and diving on the hapless herring. It's an awesome sight. The carnage ends as suddenly as it began, when the herring move out to deeper water. Which is what happens to the financial community on the first of March—on that day, their feeding spree ends.

But mutual funds, the source of all the excitement, continue to attract attention throughout the year. This is because mutual funds are an increasingly popular investment. And this trend is likely to continue for the forseeable future.

9

OPTIONS— A VERSATILE TOOL

Options can be very risky—some experts advise that you avoid them altogether. Leverage is what makes options dangerous, but paradoxically, it also makes them useful as defensive investments. Depending upon your strategy, options can be a pair of dice thrown against the wall, or a security blanket. It all depends on how you use them.

Options have been around for three centuries. In England, the first option transaction on a common stock took place in 1694. But it wasn't until 1973 that the Chicago Board Options Exchange became the first exchange in the world to list options for trading. In Canada, the Montreal Exchange began trading options in 1975, and the Toronto Stock Exchange followed suit a year later. The Vancouver Stock Exchange became a junior partner in the Canadian option market in 1984.

An option gives you the right to *buy* or *sell* something at a *fixed price* for a given period of time. Options are often used in the real estate business. If a person is interested in a property, he might offer the owner a fee for the right to buy that property at a specific price until a certain date. For example, he might pay the owner $2000 for an option on the property until the end of the year. Exactly the same principle applies to stock options.

There are two types of stock options: "call" options and "put" options. A call option gives you the right to *buy* shares at a fixed price for a fixed period of time, *regardless of the current market price*. A put option is the reverse of a call option. A put option gives you the right to *sell* shares on the same basis.

Locking in purchase and sale prices through options opens the door to a variety of investment strategies. Some of them are quite simple, while others are almost incomprehensible. Generally speaking, the simpler the strategy, the better. But before we get into strategies, let's look at the basics.

THE BASICS

Option leverage is caused, in part, by the multiplying factor. A *single* call or put represents the right to buy or sell *one hundred* shares of common stock. Thus, five calls represent the right to buy five hundred shares. The price at which the option may be exercised is known as the "strike price" or the "exercise price." The strike price is described simply by a number, for example, 25. The term or the length of time the option has to run is identified by the month (and in certain cases, the year) in which it expires. This may sound vague, but there is a precise date for each security, usually the third Friday in that month. The price you pay to buy a stock option, or the amount you receive when you sell one is known as the "premium."

The premium consists of *intrinsic* value and *time* value. Intrinsic refers to its actual value, based on the price of the underlying shares, while time is the value attributed to the period remaining before expiration of the option. When the shares of a company are trading below the strike price, a call option is said to be trading "out of the money." In this case, there's no intrinsic value, only time value. When the shares are trading at the strike price, the options are said to be "on the money." Here again the premium consists solely of time value. If, however, the shares are trading above the strike price of the calls, the options are described as being "in the money." An in-the-money option has both an intrinsic value and a time value. It's easy to determine each component of the premium (an essential exercise, because you want to know what you're paying for). Let's take a call option with a strike price of $20. The shares are trading at $21, and the options are trading at $3. Here's the calculation:

Current market value of shares	$21
Strike price of calls	–$20
Intrinsic value of option	$ 1

Cost of option minus intrinsic value ($3–$1) = $2 time value
Therefore, this option consists of an intrinsic value of $1 and a time value of $2.

As a general rule, the longer the term of the option, the higher the time value. This makes sense because the longer the term, the more time the underlying shares have to move, and the greater your opportunity for profit. For this reason, as an option approaches its expiration date, the time value dwindles and eventually disappears. So remember, as soon as you buy an option, the clock starts ticking (this can work in your favour if you've sold an option, but we'll go into that later).

The standard term for an option—either a put or a call—is nine months. There are also Long-Term Equity Anticipation options, which go by the farfetched acronym of LEAP. LEAPs are identical to standard options, except they have a term of one or two years. Standard options, which are much more popular than LEAPs, trade in nine-month cycles with no more than three expiry dates outstanding at any time. Each optioned stock or investment derivative (such as an option on an index) is assigned one of the following cycles:

Cycle 1: January	April	July	October
Cycle 2: February	May	August	November
Cycle 3: March	June	September	December

When an option series expires, a new nine-month series begins trading the following day. Thus when the January series expires, trading commences in the October options. Or when the

May options terminate, trading begins on a new series that will expire the following February. There is also a formula to introduce new strike prices into the series if the underlying stock has a sharp move up or down. As a result, a volatile stock might have five or six strike prices for the same month, as the gold-mining company American Barrick did in April 1994:

> July 30
> July 32½
> July 35
> July 37½
> July 40

In the same month, American Barrick also had LEAPs outstanding, and they were listed in a separate column below the standard options. You will note that these long-term options have wider spreads in the strike prices:

American Barrick LEAPs 1996

> Jan 25
> 30
> 35
> 40
> 45

Your newspaper—assuming it has a good financial section—will list options, but often will only tabulate those that have actually traded the previous day. So, if you're interested in a stock or a particular strike price, and you don't see it listed, you'll have to phone your broker. Because options are quoted differently than stocks, they can sometimes be confusing. On the opposite page is an example of an option table, taken from *The Globe and Mail*.

If you *buy* an option, you *acquire a right*; if you *sell* an option you *assume an obligation*. Suppose you buy 10 calls with a $40 strike price, and the stock doesn't go above $38; you can simply let them expire. But if you sell (write) 10 calls with a $40 strike price and the stock goes to $42, you must hand over the underlying shares for $40 (or buy the calls back) to complete the transaction.

Option Table

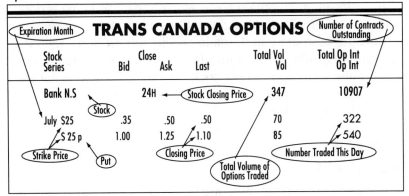

In practice, most option transactions are "closed out" (completed) before they reach the delivery stage. And most of the money is made by speculative trading in the interim.

Trading options is easy to do. You can buy 20 calls with no intention of taking delivery of 2000 shares and, regardless of the way the stock moves, you can sell the calls (hopefully for a profit). Or you can let them expire, if they're worthless. By the same token, if you write calls or puts and the underlying shares move in your favour, you can buy them back. You can do the same thing if the stock price moves against you, rather than taking or making delivery of the shares. (Buying them back can be an expensive solution, but it closes out the transaction.)

Because of the risk factor in options, there are stringent rules for both the broker and the client. To deal in options, a broker must take a special course and pass a licensing exam. The client must complete an options account application, an options trading agreement, and a margin agreement. After these forms are signed and accepted by a director of the firm, there is usually a twenty-four-hour cooling-off period before the client can make an option trade—"act in haste, repent at leisure." The main purpose of this tedious administrative process is to protect the client.

Options don't have any margin value, but they are traded through your margin account, and they may be margined, providing there's sufficient surplus in the account to cover the *full value* of the option transaction. And, even though they can be extremely risky, most institutions allow calls to be purchased and written on a covered basis (see p. 136) in self-directed RRSPs. Normally, there is no certificate in an option trade, electronic bookeeping is done by the custodians. Trans Canada Options Inc. is the main clearing house and custodian in Canada, while the Options Clearing Corporation performs the same functions in the United States. Options also differ from listed stocks in that settlement is not five business days, but the following day. This quick settlement is due to the volatility of options.

STRATEGIES
Puts or Calls

Only the strongest companies are permitted by the exchanges to have options traded on their common shares. One of the basic eligibility requirements is that the company's shares trade at a price of more than $5. This brings us to the favourite option game—buying calls in the hope that the stock will rise and the options will increase in value. Call options are attractive for several reasons. First off, they're easy to understand: if the stock goes up, so will the calls. When you buy calls, you get tremendous leverage. You also get quick action. Take, for example, a stock you like that's trading at $20. A thousand shares would cost you $20,000. But you can buy ten $2 calls for $2,000, and get the play off the same number of shares for one-tenth of the cost. Let's assume that the calls have a strike price of twenty; so, they're on the money, and your premium is purely time value. This is what happens if the stock goes to 24:

Cost of 1000 shares at $20	$20,000
Cost of 10 calls at $2 (x 100)	$ 2000
Price of shares rises to $24:	
1000 shares now worth $24,000	
10 calls now worth $ 4000	

Profit on shares $4000 or 20%
Profit on calls $2000 or 100%

In this example I've valued the calls at their intrinsic value and haven't added any time value to the premium. Even so, the leverage is dramatic. (This is a conservative calculation because these options could have a significant time value, depending on how long it is to expiry.)

Calls are a good way to speculate, if you can stomach the risk. Put another way, *whatever money you put into options you must be prepared to lose.* Options allow you to take a gamble on a blue chip stock, which is better than taking a flier on Old Moose Pasture Mines. At least the game is honest. The advantage of buying calls, rather than the underlying shares on margin, is that you get better leverage, and you don't have to put up more money if the stock goes down. But remember, it's easy to lose your entire investment—especially if you buy out-of-the-money calls (the cheapest, and the ones with the most zip).

A good rule is to restrict your first option investment to less than 10 percent of the total amount you are prepared to lose. That way, if you're wrong, you'll still have capital to play another day. And never commit *all* your assets at one time. If you decide to go for broke, there's a good chance that's the way you'll end up.

Before you buy a call, do your homework on the stock. Only after you're satisfied that the shares will move higher should you look at the options. Many people make the mistake of seizing upon a call option because they think it looks cheap. If you investigate further and do some elementary arithmetic, you'll usually discover why the calls are cheap. Often it's because the underlying shares have been anemic performers, or the stock has been in a long decline. At other times, the options are so far out of the money that they're fully priced. Sounds obvious, but you'd be surprised at how many investors don't look beyond the price.

Time is of prime importance when you buy a call. You should always choose an option that expires *after* the time that you estimate the stock will move. Ideally, the call should have five or six months left to run, and the time premium shouldn't be more than 10 percent of the value of the underlying shares. From your assessment of the stock, the calls should have a risk/reward ratio of at least one to two. This means the calls must have the potential to *double*, because you stand the chance of losing your entire investment.

If you're right, and the price of your calls doubles, what should you do? When I was a boy, we used to play marbles. If you won the first roll, your opponent had to give you his marble. You then pocketed your marble and played with his. The same principle applies to trading options—the first thing to do is get your marble back, and then play with your winnings. If you buy ten calls that double, here's one way to do it:

Cost of 10 calls at $3	$3000
Current price $6	
Sell 5 calls at $6	$3000
Retain 5 calls at cost of	0

A more aggressive strategy, but one that still allows you to get your marble back, is to "roll up" to a higher strike price. The risk is higher but so is the potential reward, as you retain the original number of calls. In practice the cost of the new calls may not work out to be exactly half the market price of the original ones, but here's the idea:

Cost of 10 November 30 calls is $3	$3000
Sell 10 calls at $6	$6000
Withdraw original investment	–$3000
Balance	$3000
Buy 10 February 35 calls at $3	= $3000

By rolling up to a higher strike price, you'll be further out of the money, but you'll have the same number of horses running for you. This tactic works well, providing the underlying stock is in a prolonged uptrend. Inevitably, however, there comes a day of reckoning.

About fifteen years ago, when there was a lot of drilling excitement in the Hibernia oil field off Newfoundland, I bought Mobil calls for my own account. After I got my original investment back, I commenced to roll up with the stock. Each time I went to a higher strike price I took more money out of the market. It all seemed so easy. Then I went off for the March break with my family to the Cayman Islands. Stupidly, I forgot to put in a stop loss order before I left town. When I got back to Ottawa, I learned that poor drilling results had been released and Mobil had plummeted. So had my calls, which were now worthless. I lost about $10,000, which was painful, but essentially paper profit. Having taken out several times my original investment as I went along, Mobil didn't owe me anything. Had I been less conservative, it would have been a very different story.

Which reminds me of Conrad, one of my clients who loved options. Conrad could pick winners, and he had nerves of steel. I remember phoning him on his birthday to tell him he had received a present from the market; his options had advanced $26,000 during the day. Conrad, however, had one serious fault— he insisted on being fully invested all the time. As with all types of investing (or gambling), timing is critical and, to paraphrase the country and western song, "You gotta know when to hold em, and know when to fold em." Because Conrad wouldn't fold, he would pyramid his winnings until the pyramid eventually collapsed, and then he'd have to start all over again. Within a year he ran out of money, and was forced to withdraw from the market—which was no surprise. *If you commit your entire option capital, and constantly trade it, you will inevitably be wiped out.* It's like playing double-or-nothing until you lose.

Failing to take a profit can also bring you to grief. Ron, another friend and client, is a case in point. Ron was a Member of Parliament, and an inveterate gambler. When he came to me, he had lost a lot of money (enough to jeopardize his marriage) and he wanted to win it back in a hurry. After a few false starts he bought Hudson's Bay Oil and Gas call options. At the time, Dome Petroleum was rumoured to be on the verge of making a takeover offer. Hudson's Bay stock soared and so did the calls. Ron rolled up his original strike price, but didn't take out any of his original investment. Instead, he borrowed money and bought more calls. I pleaded with him to take some profit, but a colleague on the Hill advised him to sit tight—the best was yet to come. What came was a denial by Dome of the takeover rumour, and the bubble burst. Ron couldn't afford to carry his calls and had to sell them at a loss. (Some months later. Dome actually did make a bid, but by then it was too late for Ron). The moral of this story is when you have a big profit in an option—*take it.*

Calls are usually bought for speculation, but they can also be useful as a hedge. For instance, you might be expecting money at a future date (from a bonus, an inheritance, or whatever) and intend to buy stocks when the money comes in. In fact, you can lock in the prices for the shares now, by buying call options with the appropriate expiry date.

Writing "covered" calls can also be used to increase your income. A call is said to be covered when you own the underlying stock. It's a case of writing (selling) calls on your holdings. If the stock doesn't trade above the strike price by the expiry date, you keep both the premium and your shares. Should the calls be exercised, the sale price of your shares will be increased by the amount of premium you received. Suppose you own 500 shares of Royal Bank, which is trading at $28 and you write five August 30 calls for a premium of $2. Your effective sale price is $30 plus the $2 you received, or $32 per share (less commission on both the calls and the shares).

Calls are useful, too, if you want to take a loss on a stock but still retain the shares. To do this, you buy the equivalent number of calls when you sell the shares. Then, at a later date, you exercise the calls to reinstate your position in the stock. If the underlying shares go up in the meantime, so will the value of your calls. (Because tax legislation is continually changing, check this out with your accountant before you do it.)

If you're worried about a particular stock you hold—you think it's fully priced, but it may go higher—you can write calls to provide some downside insurance. Using the previous example of selling Royal Bank calls with the stock trading at $28, the $2 premium offsets a $2 decline down to $26.

It only makes sense to write calls if you are confident the stock will remain stable or decline in price. (If you think the shares are going up, you should obviously hold them.) Otherwise, for the sake of a few dollars you could miss a major market move. It's also important when you write calls to get enough premium—say, 10 percent of the underlying share price—to make it worthwhile if your calls are exercised.

Dwight and Helen, two of my American clients, made it a practice to write calls on their stocks. This augmented their income (and mine, because commissions on options are fat). Some years ago, when the market was in decline, Dwight and Helen were comfortably invested in money market funds. When the market bottomed out, they asked me for stock suggestions and subsequently bought a nice selection of blue chips. At this juncture they were well positioned to benefit from the economic recovery. The market surged ahead, but then had a brief correction. Some observers, including the entire panel of experts on *Wall Street Week* prophesied that this was the beginning of another market debacle. Being devout followers of *Wall Street Week*, Dwight and Helen believed the panel.

Early Monday morning Dwight phoned and instructed me to write calls on all their stocks. I didn't think this was very wise, but had learned long ago the folly of trying to argue with a client— especially one with considerable experience. So I sold calls on their recently purchased stocks. The average premium they received was under $3. In the next six months the market rose about 30 percent. Dwight and Helen missed the entire move, and most of their calls were exercised at strike prices that later made us wince. I recount this poignant tale to illustrate the negative side of writing calls. If you misjudge the market, you get a little extra income; but the big money is made by the person who *buys* your calls.

You can also make some extra income by writing calls, even if you don't own the stock. This is known as "uncovered" or "naked" writing. It's similar to selling short but provides more leverage. I wouldn't recommend naked writing because you may be obliged to deliver stock at a much higher price than you sold it for. Also the risk/reward ratio is unattractive. On balance, it's a dangerous practice.

If you think a particular stock (or the whole market for that matter) is going to take a dive, it's a good idea to buy puts. Puts will limit your risk to the amount of premium you pay, and will give you good leverage on the downside. If the stock goes up, you get rid of your puts for whatever they'll fetch or simply let them expire. As I explained earlier, a put gives you the right to sell the stock at the strike price for the life of the option. It's the mirror image of a call. As the underlying shares decline in price, the price of the puts rises. Let me give you an example of a put transaction compared with a *short sale* (a short sale is the selling of borrowed stock with the intent of buying it back at a lower price). In this example the stock is trading at $28 when you sell it short, or buy ten puts with a strike price of $27½ at a cost of $1.

Here is what happens if the stock drops to $25:

Short Sale

Proceeds of 1000 shares sold short at $28	= $28,000
Repurchase 1000 shares at $25	= $25,000

Profit on short sale $3000 or 11%

Put Purchase

Cost of 10 puts with a strike of 27½ @ $1	= $ 1000
Underlying stock falls to $25	
Puts now worth $2½ (27½–25 = 2½)	or $ 2500

Profit on puts $1500 or 150%

The combination of leverage and limited risk makes puts the best and safest way to speculate on the downside. As with calls, the idea is that once you've made a good profit, retrieve your original investment. In the case of puts, you roll *down* in your strike price as the stock price declines. Taking the previous example, you might sell your 27½ puts and roll down to a series with a 22½ strike price.

For conservative investors, puts can be an effective—though sometimes expensive—form of insurance. To protect the value of your holdings, buy puts with a strike price close to the present market. If your shares subsequently go down in price, the increase in the value of your puts will largely offset your loss. Later, if you need to liquidate your holdings you have two choices: you can either exercise your puts or, if it is more advantageous, you can sell both your puts and your shares. (A third strategy, the goal of which is to reduce the cost price of the underlying shares, would be to sell only the puts.) Investors who would like to take a profit in a stock, but for tax reasons must wait until next year, can buy LEAPs to lock in their profit until the time is ripe.

Writing puts—which are always uncovered or "naked"—is one way to buy a stock at an advantageous price. You might, for instance, have your eyes on the shares of a certain company but feel that they're too expensive. If you write puts and they are exercised (against you), the effective cost of the shares will be reduced by the amount you received for the puts. Say you'd like to buy Alcan at around $20, but the stock is trading at $25. If you write April 22½ puts for $2 and the shares are subsequently put to you, your effective cost will be $22.50 minus your $2 premium, or $20.50. Should Alcan not decline to your strike price, your puts won't be exercised—and you keep the proceeds as a consolation prize.

This possibility—that puts that are written won't be exercised— appeals to some investors as a way to increase their income. In fact it's a high-risk, low-percentage gamble, and not recommended.

Straddles

So far we've only looked at transactions on one side of the market, either puts or calls. But there are also many combinations involving puts and calls on both sides of the market. The two most common combinations are "straddles" and "spreads." I'm not going to discuss spreads because I think the broker is the main winner, and I would probably confuse you in the process. In this connection, Alexander Gluskin, a former colleague of mine and author of *Confessions of an Options Strategist*, categorically states that "simple strategies work best." I heartily agree with Alex and suggest you ignore any complicated option tactics. Straddles, unlike spreads, are relatively straightforward and frequently profitable.

A straddle is a bet on the volatility of a stock. You don't care whether the stock goes up or down, all you want is a pronounced move in either direction. The ingredients of a straddle consist of a volatile stock, and *a call and a put with the same strike price and the same expiry date.* The total cost of the two options, the put and the call, should be as low as possible. A straddle will only be profitable after the stock has moved one way or the other far enough to cover the cost of *both* options. Here is an example of a straddle on a stock that is trading at $30. This straddle consists of a June 30 call and a June 30 put, which cost a total of $5:

Break-even point on upside	$35	(call worth $5)
Strike price	$30	
Break-even point on downside	$25	(put worth $5)

The only way you'll get wiped out on a straddle is if the stock fails to move in either direction. In that case, both the put and the call will be worthless on the expiry date. (If you chose this type of stock, you shouldn't have done a straddle in the first place.) An ideal situation for a straddle is when news is pending; such as a takeover offer, drilling results, or the decision on a major lawsuit. Whatever the outcome, it's reasonable to assume the news will move the stock.

American Securities and Futures Contracts

Although a fair number of Canadian companies meet the eligibility requirements, only about sixty have listed options. This means that in many promising Canadian situations you won't be able to use options. The United States, on the other hand, has a much broader option market—and a more liquid one (with tighter spreads between the bid and ask prices). For these reasons, if you're interested in options, you should include American securities. And you can also option many futures contracts; doing so tends to reduce the risk somewhat. (Trading options is dangerous, but less so than trading commodities.)

Index Options

This brings us to options on indices. It used to be said you couldn't buy or sell the market, only individual stocks. This is no longer true, because now you can place a bet on the direction of the market by trading options on the indices. Standard & Poor (S&P) is the most popular stock index in the United States. Actually there are a number of S&P indices, but the two that attract the most attention are the S&P 500, which is based on five hundred stocks, and the S&P 100, which tracks of one hundred stocks. Both the S&P 500 and the S&P 100 reflect the movement of the market throughout the day by means of a continualy updated index number. Put and call options are available on a wide range of S&P strike prices.

The underlying security of both S&P indices is a *futures contract* that represents a basket of stocks in each index. (Futures are covered in the next chapter, so I won't go into them now.)

What you should be aware of is that the value of the S&P 500 futures contract is five hundred times the number of the index. Therefore, if the S&P 500 index is trading at 450 the value is 500 x 450 or US$225,000. By the same token, the value of the S&P 100 contract is one hundred times the number of that index. If the S&P is trading at 425, the value would be 100 x 425 or US$42,500.

This is important to know, because when you buy an S&P 500 call option the price is *five hundred times* the cost of the premium (i.e., one call at 3½ would cost $1750). The S&P 100 option—which is the most popular—costs the same as a regular option (i.e., one hundred times the price of the premium). If you're looking for the fast track, the S&P 100 options are the hottest game in town and trade an incredible number of contracts. In Canada, the Toronto Futures Exchange has futures contracts on the TSE 300 Index and the TSE 35 Index which are optionable, but they're rather tame compared with the S&P indices. Also, Canadian option markets are thin, and the price spreads are often prohibitive.

Toronto also trades options on bonds, treasury bills, and the U.S. dollar, as well as silver and a variety of other TSE indices. Montreal is another Canadian trading centre for financial futures and currencies. And Vancouver, in addition to listing options on a number of stocks, trades options on gold. So there's a whole smorgasbord of optionable companies, financial futures, and commodities on both sides of the border. Bon appetit!

FINAL BITS OF ADVICE

To close this chapter let me repeat three bits of advice. First, when you start off investing in options, don't commit more than 10 percent of your assets at any one time. Second, remember that trading options is a game of opportunity, and you should only play when an opportunity presents itself. Third, don't hesitate to take a profit—your first priority is to get your marble back.

One other thing to remember about options: bulls make money and bears make money, but pigs make none.

10

COMMODITIES AND FINANCIAL FUTURES

Even if you have no interest in commodities, you should know something about them, because commodity prices can directly affect financial markets.

But first, a word of warning. If you find trading options a heady experience, playing commodities is like inhaling pure oxygen. Small–time speculators routinely get sheared like sheep in the commodity markets. Hillary Rodham Clinton is one of the few exceptions. She defied the odds and parlayed $1000 into $100,000. Even more extraordinary, the First Lady quit when she was ahead, and kept her winnings.

Futures are traded on eleven exchanges in the United States and on three exchanges in Canada. Trading in futures began on this continent around 1850, and was initially limited to agricultural products. Futures contracts were particularly useful to farmers who faced the problem of not knowing what they would receive for their crops when they were harvested. To ensure a profit, they resorted to selling their crops for delivery at a future date.

FUTURES CONTRACTS

A futures contract is a trading unit of a commodity (such as wheat) or a financial instrument (such as a Treasury Bill) for delivery on a specific date at a specific price. The term of the contract ranges from one month to two years. Unlike an option, which gives you the *right* to buy or sell something, a futures contract is a *binding agreement* to take or make delivery of the commodity or financial instrument.

Commodities' terminology differs from securities' terminology. When you *buy* a commodity you are said to be "long" the commodity, and when you *sell* it you are said to be "short" the commodity. So, if you're short five cocoa contracts, you have a legal obligation to deliver fifty metric tons of cocoa to the buyer. By the same token, if you're long two Treasury Bill contracts, you have agreed to buy two million dollars worth of T-Bills.

Fortunately, there's an easy way to cancel these obligations. All you have to do is make an offsetting purchase or sale of the same contract *before* the delivery date. For instance, if you had shorted five cocoa contracts, you would buy five contracts. To avoid delivery of the Treasury Bills, you would sell two contracts. Approximately 98 percent of all the contracts that are written are subsequently cancelled by offsetting contracts before the delivery date.

This may sound like an exercise in futility, but it has a valid commercial application. A futures market, as well as being a casino, allows *bona fide* commodity producers and users to reduce the risk of price fluctuations. This type of transaction is known as a "hedge."

HEDGES

The purpose of a hedge is to protect a market commitment by means of an offsetting futures contract. The factors to be considered in a hedge are the "cash" or "spot" price and the "forward" or futures price. Normally, the cash price is lower than the forward price due to the time element and the storage costs. Because the two prices tend to move in a parallel manner, and to converge at delivery date, a loss in one market usually means a profit in the other market. In other words, what you lose on the swings, you make on the roundabouts.

Let's take the example of a farmer who knows he'll have wheat to sell in the autumn, and wants to ensure that he'll get an acceptable price when it's harvested. The time is May, and even though his crop won't be ready for some months, he would like to get the current "cash" price of $3.50 per bushel. To do this, he places a hedge. He sells November futures contracts for the amount of his crop on the commodity exchange. He's now *short* x bushels of wheat, but he's also *long* the same amount (which is growing in his back forty). If the price of wheat is higher when he harvests his crop, he'll buy back (and thereby cancel) his futures contract, and sell his wheat on the cash market. The loss he takes on the repurchase of his futures contract will be offset by the additional profit he makes on the spot market. Here are the figures:

Cash Market	Futures Market
12 May	
long wheat @ $3.50 per bu.	sells wheat @$3.65 per bu.
29 Sept	
sells wheat @3.80 per bu.	buys wheat @ $3.95 per bu.
Profit .30	Loss .30

This hedge will protect him even if the price of wheat declines. In this case, the profit on the repurchase of his futures contract will offset the loss in the cash market at the time of delivery. It works this way:

Cash Market	Futures Market
12 May	
long wheat @ $3.50 per bu.	sells wheat @ $3.65 per bu.
29 Sept	
sells wheat @ $3.25 per bu.	buys wheat @ $3.40 per bu.
Loss .25	Profit .25

The foregoing is an example of a *selling* hedge, which protects the price to be received for a commodity. The same principle applies to a *buying* hedge, which puts a ceiling on the price to be paid for a commodity.

To illustrate, let's look at a manufacturer of jewellery who knows in March that he will have to buy five thousand ounces of gold during the summer to manufacture items for the Christmas trade. He is faced with a dilemma: if he buys the gold now he'll have to carry the cost for six months, but if he waits until August the price of gold may be much higher. He can't afford to speculate, because a rise in the price of gold could wipe out his profit. To protect his profit margin—which is based on the current price of gold—he buys futures contracts for five thousand ounces for delivery in September. In theory, he is now short gold in the spot market and long in the futures market. When August rolls around, he sells his futures contracts and buys gold in the cash market. Regardless of whether gold has risen or fallen, his cost will be approximately the same as if he'd bought it in March, and his margin will be intact. Here are the figures on his buying hedge:

Cash Market	Futures Market
17 Mar	
short gold @ $375 per oz.	buys gold @ $392 per oz.
15 Aug	
buys gold @ $395 per oz.	sells gold @ $412 per oz.
Loss $20	Profit $20

Had the price of gold declined, the effect would have been the same, because the loss in the futures market would have been offset by a profit in the cash market.

Having given you these nice tidy examples, I should confess that *a hedge doesn't always work out perfectly.* It does, however, eliminate the risk of drastic price fluctuations. Also, a hedge is not always a zero sum game—sometimes it produces a loss and sometime a profit. Even with these qualifications, a hedge is a useful form of insurance.

THE SPECULATOR

You may wonder why it's so easy for hedgers to buy and sell futures. Who is willing to take the risk on the other side of the contract? Most often, it's a speculator. The speculator plays a vital role by providing liquidity in the commodities markets. He is cheerfully willing to go long or short, greasing the wheels of commerce by betting against the hedger. Most of the time, he is wrong.

In the animal kingdom the speculator would probably be classed as a species that is eaten by more powerful animals. Indeed, in some respects the speculator is similar to the lemming. This little rodent is preyed upon by hawks and owls, as well as a number of valuable fur bearers. Periodically, lemmings are seized by an urge to rush headlong to their destruction. It's not clear what motivates this unfortunate practice, but we do know what motivates the speculator. The hope of a fat profit.

Very little money is needed to buy or sell a futures contract. The margin is often less than 5 percent of the contract and, because the margin is considered a performance bond or "earnest money," no interest is charged on the balance. This gives you a free carry and stupendous leverage. Commissions are also seductively low (much lower than for stocks), and only one commission is charged instead of two. Furthermore, the single commission—known as a "round turn"—is a back-end load that is charged when you close your position.

Speculators make money when they correctly judge the price movement of a commodity or financial future. Usually, they only play one side of the market. If they think the price is going to rise they go long, if they think it's going to fall they go short.

Suppose you think the price of soybeans will rise. The time is April, and you buy two November contracts at $6.95. As each contract represents 5000 bushels, you are now long 10,000 bushels of soybeans. The margin on this purchase is $2500 per contract for a total outlay of $10,000. The price of soybeans goes up, and in October you sell your contracts for $7.51 per bushel. Here are the figures:

10 April	bought 2 Nov soybeans	@ $6.95
7 September	sold 2 Nov soybeans	@ $7.51
Profit per bushel		.56
	10,000 bushels x .56	= $5600
	less commission	–$ 160
Net profit		$5440
Return on $5000 margin investment		109%

Speculators play the short side of the market as much as the long side, and it can be very lucrative. For instance, you think the price of pork will fall, and so, in June you short 3 February pork belly contracts at 63 cents per pound. As one pork belly contract represents 40,000 pounds, you are short 120,000 pounds of bacon. Because your margin is $1500 per contract, your total outlay is $4500. Bellies decline, and in December you decide to cover your short position. You buy back your 3 contracts at 55 cents per pound. Here's the profit on the transaction:

6 June	sold 3 Feb pork bellies	@ .63
21 December	bought 3 Feb pork bellies	@ .55
Profit per pound		.08
	120,000 pounds x .08	= $9600
	less commission	–$ 270
Net profit		$9330
Return on $4500 margin investment		207%

So far, all my examples have shown the bright side of speculating in futures. There is also a dark side to the game. Leverage can provide staggering *losses* as well as glorious profits. And far more amateur speculators lose than win. In this connection, with futures not only can you lose the shirt off your back, but also all the shirts in your drawer.

OPENING A FUTURES ACCOUNT

If you're going to get into the futures market you should choose a firm that specializes in commodity trading. There are relatively few

Canadian investment dealers in the business. The best-known are Nesbitt–Burns, Midland-Walwyn, and Richardson Greenshields. Burns and Midland tend to concentrate on financial futures, while Richardson competently handles both commodities and financial futures (not surprising, as Richardson started as grain merchants).

The individual you select to manage your account should be someone who devotes all or most of his time to the futures market. If your regular broker isn't licensed to deal in futures (you must pass a rigorous exam) or only trades futures as a sideline—open an account with a specialist.

To open a futures account you will have to complete and sign a number of forms. One of the crucial questions is the amount of your liquid assets. Liquid assets are cash and negotiable securities. Your house—even if it's fully paid for—isn't considered a liquid asset. The stress on liquid assets should tell you something: namely that the broker wants to be sure you can come up with the money *after* you've lost all or part of your margin deposit. Most brokers won't open an account unless there's at least fifty thousand dollars in liquid assets.

The minimum margin requirement for each commodity is set by the exchange on which it is traded. However, many brokers have house rules that call for a higher figure. Also, if a futures contract becomes very volatile, the margin can be raised without prior notice.

There are, in fact, *two* margin layers to consider. The top layer is the initial margin or "earnest money," which is the opening amount, and beneath it is the "maintenance margin." If the maintenance level is breached, your account must be topped up to the initial margin. For example, the initial margin for a contract of canola (a prudish Canadian name for a plant that is called rapeseed in the rest of the world) is three hundred dollars. The maintenance margin below it is two hundred dollars. This gives you a cushion of one hundred dollars. If the price of rapeseed moves against you by more than a hundred dollars per contract you will receive a margin call. When this happens, you must put up more money *immediately* or you'll be sold out.

TRADING FUTURES

Because the margin on commodities is a performance bond rather than a partial payment, you can pledge Treasury Bills instead of cash. This allows you to earn a modest return on your deposit. And remember, if you trade American futures all of your transactions including margin deposits, must be in U.S. funds. After you've cleared all the hurdles and opened an option account, there's quite a list of goodies you can trade. Here are some of them:

Aluminum	Municipal Bonds
Barley	Oats
Broilers	Orange Juice
Cattle	Palladium
Coconut Oil	Pig Iron
Coffee	Platinum
Copper	Plywood
Corn	Pork Bellies
Cotton	Potatoes
Crude Oil	Propane
Currencies	Rubber
Eggs	Rye
Eurodollars	Silver
Flaxseed	Soybeans
Gold	Stock Indices
Heating Oil	Sugar
Hogs	Treasury Bills
Lead	Wheat
Lumber	
Mortgage Rates	

Not all these commodities and financial instruments are active traders. For this reason, if you're a speculator you should restrict yourself to futures that have good volume and liquidity so you can get in and *out* easily. It is also wise to choose commodities that trade on the busier exchanges.

In Canada the Winnipeg Commodities Exchange dominates the market for agricultural products. Winnipeg was also the first commodity exchange in the world to trade gold (although it's now a minor player in the metal). Both the Toronto Futures Exchange and the Montreal Exchange are primarily concerned with financial futures and their option derivatives.

In the United States, which is the best place for speculators to play, the Chicago Board of Trade is the largest commodity exchange. The CBT is mainly a market for agricultural products, but also trades U.S. Treasury bonds. The Chicago Mercantile Exchange and its subsidiary, the International Monetary Market, also actively trade commodities and financial instruments. New York has four commodity exchanges including the Comex (*Commodity Exchange*), which is the busiest metals market in the world.

A commodity order is processed very much like a stock order. Instead of being wired or phoned to a stock exchange, it's routed to the appropriate commodity exchange. The order is then executed in a trading "pit" (a tiered recess in the floor of the exchange) by open outcry, and the confirmation is wired back to your broker.

When placing an order you should always double check the size of the contract because the size can vary with the exchange. For example, gold trades on the Winnipeg Exchange in 20-ounce contracts, while the Chicago Board of Trade has two gold contracts: one for 32.15 ounces (one kilo) and another more popular, 100-ounce contract.

Having established a speculative position, you can't just forget it. If you do, you could get an unpleasant surprise. I don't mean that you'll have ten tons of cocoa dumped on your doorstep, or find a herd of cattle lowing on your front lawn. If you let a long position go to the delivery date, you'll receive a warehouse notice stating that the commodity is being held for you. For a price, someone will buy the warehouse receipt and assume custody of the contract. If you're short futures at delivery date, for a modest fee you can usually buy your way out of your delivery obligation.

The only time you can't get someone to make delivery on your behalf is if the market has been "cornered." When a market is cornered, it means that someone has bought up all the floating supply, and if you are short, the only way to make delivery is by buying it at an exorbitant price from the person who has cornered the market. In the bad old days, when legislation was lax (or nonexistent), markets were frequently cornered by robber barons, to the intense discomfort of the shorts. The most recent example occurred in 1980, when Nelson Bunker Hunt and his family nearly cornered the market for silver. After quietly buying for months, Hunt and his partners demanded physical delivery of all the silver that had been shorted to them. This "short squeeze" caused the price of silver to skyrocket, and forced the shorts to the wall. Hunt would have succeeded in cornering the market if the authorities hadn't changed the rules and let the shorts off the hook. As soon as this happened, the price of silver collapsed. (In this instance I feel a certain sympathy for the Hunts, because the goalposts were moved on them.)

KEEPING TRACK

Aside from phoning your broker periodically, you can keep track of your commodity investments by checking the financial section of your newspaper. Only the larger papers cover commodities. So, if your paper doesn't have the information, I suggest you subscribe to *The Financial Post* or *The Globe and Mail*. These two dailies provide good commodity coverage, but tabulate the prices differently. I prefer the *Post's* format, because I think it contains a little more information and I find it easier to read. On page 153 is an example of a *Financial Post* commodity quote.

To value a move in a commodity, multiply the size of the contract by the change in its price. Taking cocoa as an example, the contract size is ten metric tons; therefore, a move of $17 per ton is equal to $170 per contract. To maintain an orderly market, and to prevent violent price fluctuations, the exchanges establish daily trading limits for each commodity. Once the commodity has moved the limit—in either direction—no further transactions are permitted outside the limit. If, say, orange juice futures close at $1.20 per pound and the limit is 5 cents no trades can take place the following day below $1.15 or above $1.25. This may sound like a comforting rule, but the limit can cause acute anxiety.

Taking orange juice as an example again, let's suppose that you've shorted OJ futures, and a sudden frost blankets Florida. This will kill much of the crop and drive up the price of orange juice. You decide you'd better cover your short position. However,

Pork Belly Commodity Quote

```
PORK BELLIES (CME)    40,000 lbs ← Contract Size         Where Traded i.e., Chicago Mercantile Exchange
US cents per lb.; 2½ cents per cwt. = $10 per contract
                                                          Minimum Price Move
Est. Vol. 1211, Prev. Vol. 1805, Prev. Open Int. 8447
                                                                             Number of Contracts Outstanding
Currency   Number of Contracts Traded this Day           Closing Price
Season
Price Range    Delivery Month        For The Day          Net
High   Low     Month   Open   High   Low    Settle  Change  Open Int
```

High	Low	Month	Open	High	Low	Settle	Net Change	Open Int
60.90	38.60	Mar	56.60	56.85	56.15	56.80	+.15	417
61.80	39.50	May	57.32	57.80	57.25	57.72	+.32	5,705
62.00	39.30	Jul	57.40	57.92	57.35	57.90	+.20	2,421
59.50	42.00	Aug	54.92	55.22	54.90	55.20	+.20	455

when the market opens, the bid immediately moves up to the limit, and no one is willing to sell at that price. You're "locked-in," and there's nothing you can do about it. The next day the same thing happens; at the opening, the bid moves up to the limit and still, no one is willing to sell. By this time, you're seriously worried and you wonder where it will end. On the third day, the exchange expands the limit by 50 percent, and you manage to cover your short position at a heavy loss.

You can get in an identical bind when you're long a commodity, and it makes "locked" limit moves on the downside for days in succession. Whereas, if you own a listed stock, and price is not an obstacle, you can normally bail out whenever you want. But trading commodities is *not* like trading stocks. Keep this in mind.

FACTORS INFLUENCING COMMODITY PRICES

What factors raise commodity prices? In answer to this question the Four Horsemen of the Apocalypse clatter onstage, because bad news is good news for commodities. Calamities such as war, drought, frost, and floods all create shortages, and when shortages occur, prices go up. The reverse is true during times of peace and prosperity—these conditions usually result in abundant supplies and lower prices.

When assessing these factors, commodity traders often break them down into three categories: economic, political, and acts of God. Let me give you an example of each.

The demand for copper is directly related to the state of the economy. Half of the world's copper production is consumed by the electrical industry, while much of the balance is used by the construction and automobile industries. As a result, both the demand for copper and its price rise when the economy is buoyant, and fall during periods of recession.

In North America the demand for wheat is influenced by global politics. Canada and the United States are the world's largest wheat exporters, and Russia, China, and the former Communist bloc countries are among the major importers. When North America exports a lot of wheat to these buyers, the domestic supply is reduced and prices rise. But when there's a diplomatic hassle, large export contracts may be delayed, or even cancelled, which has the opposite effect.

Acts of God encompass a variety of weather phenomena and other natural disasters. Frost in the Citrus Belt, drought on the Prairies, and floods in the Cotton Bowl, for example, are all fairly common. One of the most bizarre acts of God was the disappearance of the anchovy school off Peru some years ago, which was caused by a shift in the Humboldt Current. Soybean meal futures reacted immediately to the news. Soybean meal is used as a high-protein supplement for poultry and livestock. Peru also competes for this market with fish meal made from anchovies. As a result of the little fish failing to show up off Peru, soybean meal had the entire market, and the price soared. Similarly, in 1993, flooding of the soybean crop in the Mississippi Valley removed a large amount of edible vegetable oil from the market. Buyers then switched to rapeseed, a secondary source, and the price of rapeseed went through the roof.

PROGRAM TRADING AND FINANCIAL FUTURES

Physical commodities, such as grains, livestock, and other produce, are subject to many influences. Financial instruments—stocks, bonds, currencies, and indices—are a little more predictable in that acts of God are not a major factor. The main things to assess with financial futures are the economic and political factors. I should add that financial futures are often an important component in "program trading."

Program trading is a catch phrase for a variety of sophisticated trading strategies that are executed with the aid of computers. The role of the computers is to tabulate trends and to crunch numbers. Most of the programs are forms of arbitrage, designed to take advantage of discrepancies in the cash price and futures price of indices—such as the S&P 500 or the NYSE Composite Index. There are also computer programs, based on technical analysis, that trigger massive buy or sell orders when a certain trend is detected. Aside from a few institutions, most of the program traders are large investment firms (which is not surprising, as you need access to the floor of the exchanges, research facilities, and deep pockets).

Program trading is controversial—many think it increases the volatility of the securities and futures markets. Those engaged in program trading deny this, and say that it's relatively harmless. There's no doubt, however, that the huge buying and selling waves buffet the markets and exacerbate the swings—so much so that many small investors have been scared away, or have sought refuge in mutual funds. The Securities and Exchange Commission has instituted some controls on program trading—such as an automatic ban after the Dow moves fifty points in either direction—but it continues to be a problem.

FINAL WORDS OF ADVICE

I would suggest that if you want to speculate in commodities, start with financial futures. With financial futures you can bet on the direction of the American or Canadian stock markets, on interest rate trends, or on movements in the world's major currencies. Also, hedging and spreading techniques (that aren't applicable to physical commodities) can be used to reduce your potential loss. If you're already in the stock or bond markets, you'll find it easy to relate to financial futures and you'll be relatively comfortable with them.

On the other hand, if you start by trading physical commodities, you may be handicapped by a lack of knowledge. For instance, unless you're a pig farmer, or run an abattoir, it's unlikely you'll have an informed opinion on pork bellies. Whatever you choose to trade, you would be wise to follow some guidelines. Here are a few suggestions (not original, but well proven) that you might consider:

- Do your homework on a commodity *before* entering your order.
- Always go with the trend—don't try to outguess the market.
- Limit your involvement in any single trade to 10 percent of your speculative capital.
- Spread your risk over two or three commodities and watch them closely.
- Select contracts in the more distant maturities. These are less volatile and give you more time.
- When you open a trade, have a specific target in mind. If your target price is reached, close out your position.
- Protect yourself with stop-loss orders. If you are long and the price increases, move up the price of the stop loss. If you're short, and the price declines, move the stop down.
- Do *not* pyramid your winnings.
- When you get a margin call, close out your position. You are wrong, and if you put up more money the odds are that you will lose it.
- Don't average down. That is a sucker's game.
- When you're wrong, don't *reverse* your position. You can easily get "whipsawed" (lose in both directions).
- Take your losses quickly, but let your profits run. One big win can erase a lot of small losses.
- Don't feel compelled to be in the market all the time. Often the smartest thing is to stay on the sidelines.

These suggestions won't make you rich beyond the dreams of avarice, but they may keep you out of serious trouble. If you're a speculator and you can stay out of trouble, you're doing well. It's estimated that between 80 and 90 percent of speculators eventually lose *all* their money. I've been told by commodity brokers that they have to replace their clientele several times a year. This high turnover is caused by financial "burnout" (a term that needs no explanation).

So, if you get an urge to take a position in wheat or pork bellies, don't pick up the phone and call your broker. Instead, trot down to your neighbourhood store and buy a loaf of bread, or a pound of bacon. This is the best commodity tip I can give you.

11

GOLD

Gold. The word fires the imagination. Gold is a rare and precious element. Its scarcity and value give it a mystical quality that fascinates people. Since the days of the Pharaohs, gold has symbolized wealth, and until the close of the Middle Ages it was also believed to have magical properties. Today, many feel that gold represents the ultimate refuge against economic disaster.

Gold has a natural lustre, it resists corrosion, and it is highly malleable—so malleable that one ounce of the yellow metal can be drawn into a wire eighty kilometres long, or beaten into a sheet covering ten square metres. For centuries gold has been used to make jewellery, but it also has industrial applications. Because it is an excellent conductor of heat and electricity, and is highly reflective, it is used extensively in the computer and electronic industries. Gold's main role, however, is that of a medium of exchange. Unlike paper money, gold needs no one's signature to make it valuable.

Although no country is still on the gold standard, most of the world's strongest currencies are backed, to some extent, by gold. The largest gold reserve is held by the United States. In 1934 the

United States "pegged" or fixed the price of gold at $35 per ounce. This price held until 1968 when mounting economic pressures forced the seven–nation Gold Pool to establish a two-tier market. Under the two-tier system gold was traded between governments at $35 an ounce, but among everyone else at whatever the traffic would bear. In 1970 the United States increased the official price of gold to $38, and raised it again in 1973 to $42.22 per ounce. (In effect, these increases devalued the American dollar.) On January 1, 1974, for the first time in forty years, American citizens were allowed to own gold. The free market exploded, and the price of gold soared.

Those who fervently believe in gold are known as "gold bugs." I have a friend named Stan, who is a skilful and industrious landscape gardener. Stan also owns a small gold mine in the backwoods of Nova Scotia. To call it a mine may be an overstatement; there are no buildings—not even a shed—and the tumbledown shaft is only about thirty metres deep. Stan bought the abandoned mine after the former owner succumbed to carbon monoxide gas while attempting to dewater the shaft.

Whenever Stan has a free day, he spends it at his mine. Because the shaft is still flooded, he's been developing an open pit nearby. His mining method is to pick the quartz out of the vein with a crowbar. This is punishing, brutal work, and the pit is on the edge of a fly-ridden swamp. In the past four years Stan has spent countless solitary days there. During that time, he has recovered less than five ounces of gold. Yet he remains full of enthusiasm, and he's convinced that the mother lode is waiting to be revealed by a blow from his crowbar. Why is Stan—a sensible man in every other respect—so optimistic in the face of so little success? The answer is simple. Stan is a gold bug.

My first encounter with a gold bug was in 1968. Gold was trading at around $40 at that time, and few people took any notice of the precious metal. One of the few who did was Cecil, a nervous, bright-eyed little fellow with a bald head. Cecil was certain that gold was going to double or triple in value. To convince me, he was always quoting from the writings of zealots on the subject. Often he would get so excited the words would just tumble out of his mouth. I listened to Cecil politely, because I liked him and he was a good client. Privately, I suspected he didn't have both oars in the water, and I knew he was wrong.

As it turned out, Cecil was right. Not only was he right, but he was conservative in his price projections. Within the next five years the price of gold tripled and then quadrupled. In 1980, in the London market, it hit $850 an ounce. It has since settled back down, but in the spring of 1994, it was still ten times higher than it was in 1968.

What caused this astounding increase? One reason is that for years gold was kept at an unrealistically low price. Unpegging it allowed the price of gold to catch up with other commodities. Because fear is a principal motive for owning gold, political turmoil around the world frightened people into hoarding gold. Fear of currency devaluations (most of which subsequently happened) also drove people into gold to protect their assets. But what really fuelled the price rise was skyrocketing inflation, which was aggravated in the 1970s by the spiralling price of oil. Having been paid with paper currencies for their oil, Middle Eastern countries turned around and bought gold. Speculators saw the price of gold moving, and jumped aboard for the ride. The result was a runaway gold market.

The market collapsed in 1980 because of accumulated excesses, and a turn in the tide of inflation. Although there were political incidents—such as the war in the Falklands—and further currency devaluations, gold didn't rally with these events. This highlights the main reason for owning gold—as a hedge against inflation.

Gold is a hedge against inflation because it has retained its purchasing power over the centuries. Historians note that the same amount of gold will buy the same amount of wheat that it did three centuries ago. The same can't be said for paper money. Pick any currency you want. Now look back ten years, and remember how much it cost you to buy a loaf of bread. This illustrates how, in the space of just ten years, inflation has eroded the value of the dollar.

Inflation will continue to ravage the dollar so long as the federal government spends more than it receives in taxes. Deficits produce debt that the government services by turning on the printing presses and creating more money. When money is pumped into the system in this way it dilutes the existing currency. Eventually, *all the currency* in circulation loses some of its purchasing power or real value. Because of reckless spending, inflation is now deeply embedded in the economy. (Can you remember when Canada last had a balanced budget?) The only inflation variable is its rate of growth. It should also be mentioned that many countries with high rates of inflation have been forced to devalue their currencies. This happens without warning—frequently on the heels of an official denial—and everyone suffers from the consequences.

Radical gold bugs are quite certain that inflation will lead to the collapse of the economy. On the heels of the collapse, the government will fall. With people out of work and starving, law and order will break down. The result will be chaos. Radical gold bugs believe the only way to survive is to convert your paper money into gold. Having taken this precaution, you should fortify your basement and provision it for a long siege. In addition to food, water, and gold, your bunker should contain arms and ammunition to keep insurgents at bay. To buy provisions during the crisis, you should also stash away a few bags of "junk silver" coins (battered coins of recent vintage with genuine silver content). When order is finally restored, you convert some of your gold into hard currency and resume your normal lifestyle.

Although it may be uncharitable, I suggest that there are a few flaws in this recipe for survival. If anarchy prevails, do you think the insurgents—knowing you have *real* money—will let you spend your junk silver at the supermarket? And, under these conditions, do you think there will be a supermarket open? If the answer is no to either of these questions, what will you do with your junk silver? You can't eat it.

As you may have guessed, I'm not a radical, or even a garden variety, gold bug. But I do think it's prudent to have some of your assets in gold (even though bullion has traded in a narrow range for nearly fifteen years). The amount you invest in gold is up to you. Personally, I've never committed more than 5 percent of my assets to gold. Remember that equities, especially resource stocks, are also a good inflation hedge. So is your house or condominium.

Silver is another inflation hedge. It is much more plentiful than gold, and hence less valuable. There is no fixed ratio between gold and silver prices, but they are inclined to move in unison. Silver, like gold, is an excellent conductor of electricity—in fact, it's the most efficient conductor of any metal. In consequence, silver is widely used by the electrical industry as well as for jewellery, coins, and camera film. At present, the consumption of silver exceeds the annual world production of the metal.

A fundamental difference between gold and silver is that a high percentage of gold used in industry is recovered and recycled. Millions of ounces of silver are lost forever in camera film. Gold, on the other hand, is melted down and survives from generation to generation. A rather grisly example of gold recycling occurred in Toronto when a man brought in a box of dental fillings to sell to a precious metals dealer. When asked how he came into possession of the fillings the man was vague, but eventually admitted to being an undertaker.

WAYS TO INVEST IN GOLD AND SILVER

There are a number of ways you can invest in gold and silver as a long-term inflation hedge. And, because of the volatility of the two metals, they can also be put to good use for short-term speculation.

Let's start by ruling out jewellery. The markup on jewellery—whether it be gold, silver, or precious stones—is so high that you'll need a huge price move just to break even. When you sell jewellery, unless it's by auction, you'll be paid *nothing* for the workmanship of the article. The gold or silver content—its intrinsic value—will be assessed, and that's what the price will be based on. Because gold is very soft, it's usually alloyed with another metal to make jewellery. This affects the purity of the item, and hence, its value. For this reason, the gold content is measured in "carats." Pure gold contains 24 carats—thus a 10-carat piece contains $10/24$ths pure gold; an 18-carat item, $18/24$ths, and so on. Gold jewellery is nice to own, but you shouldn't kid yourself into thinking it's a good investment.

The same applies to rare gold coins. Here again you run into the problem of buying retail and selling wholesale. A large part of the cost of a rare coin is made up of its numismatic, rather than its intrinsic, value. During periods of recession, the numismatic value shrinks to almost nothing. This is one of the reasons so many coin dealers go belly-up when the economy contracts.

Common gold coins, such as the Maple Leaf or the Krugerrand are another matter, because they have little numismatic value. This makes them an interesting investment. The Krugerrand is larger in diameter than the Maple Leaf, but both coins contain exactly one ounce of gold. The Canadian coin, however, has a fractionally higher gold content and is .9999 pure gold. Both coins are recognized throughout the world and have excellent marketability. They are convenient to own, attractive to look at, and take up little room under your mattress.

You can buy Maple Leaf coins and Krugerrands from most coin dealers, several of the chartered banks, and a number of trust companies. Because prices vary widely, it will pay you to shop around before making your purchase. (When you shop, remember that the market price of gold is constantly changing—so a quote from one outlet in the morning shouldn't be compared with a quote from another source in the afternoon.) You should also check to see if there are any additional charges, and whether the price is in Canadian or U.S. funds. The currency can make a huge difference. Also, there can be commissions or handling charges added to the price (the Bank of Nova Scotia levies *both* on the purchase of coins). Tax is another thing to watch. There's no GST on coins, but a number of provinces charge provincial sales tax.

Tax is also a factor to be considered when buying gold or silver bullion, (the refined metal in bar or wafer form). Most of the provinces charge tax if you take physical delivery of bullion, but not if you buy a bullion certificate. A bullion certificate gives you clear title to whatever quantity of gold or silver you have bought, and the institution will hold it in safekeeping for you. A certificate thus eliminates safekeeping charges, as well as potential sales problems (for example, when you sell bullion, unless you take it back to the vendor with proof of purchase, you may have to go through the hassle and expense of having it assayed). You can buy bullion certificates from several chartered banks and trust companies, as well as through the Montreal Exchange. Unless you're a dyed-in-the-wool gold bug, who must have the metal stashed in your bunker, this is the sensible (and cheapest) way to buy bullion.

Before leaving the subject of coins and bullion, I must add that they are negative investments. They provide no income, and they may incur carrying charges for storage and insurance. To these you must add the "lost opportunity" cost. Finally, there's no leverage, because you must pay for coins and bullion in full.

There are, however, two highly leveraged ways you can play gold and silver. One is with futures, the other is with options.

Precious metal futures are traded in Canada in a limited way, but the best market for gold and silver is the Comex in New York. The contract size for gold on the Comex is 100 troy ounces. Thus a one-dollar move in gold means a one-hundred-dollar move in the price of the contract. The size of the Comex silver contract is 5000 ounces. Therefore, a one-cent move in silver means a fifty-dollar change in the value of the contract. Most people trade gold and silver futures for the short term, and try to catch the swings. This requires some agility and a good dollop of luck. But it's a fascinating game, because the prices are always shifting, and a small move can mean a big profit.

Options on gold and silver are traded in Canada (gold on the VSE, silver on the TFE). Precious metal options are traded exactly like regular stock options, except that all trades are in U.S. funds. Because of the volatility of gold and silver, the premiums are often very high. If you're thinking of getting into this game, let me give you a word of advice. No matter how fat and juicy the premium, *don't write naked calls*. It just isn't worth the risk.

The easiest and most popular way to invest in gold is to buy shares in a mine. Canada is the third largest gold producer in the world so there are plenty of mines to choose from. If you are investing (as opposed to speculating) you should restrict your choice to mines that meet the following criteria:

1. Substantial proven reserves
2. Low cost of production
3. Relatively little debt
4. Good management
5. Politically stable location

Let's look at each one in turn. Ore reserves relate directly to the life of the mine—it's no good buying a mine that's running out of ore. Cost of production is critical, because it determines the level of profitability. If it cost a mine $340 to produce an ounce of gold, and the prevailing price is $360, it will make a small profit. But if the price of gold falls below $340, it will lose money. Obviously, the lower the production cost, the better. The amount of debt is also a consideration, because this is a fixed cost, and also a potential problem if interest rates soar. Quality of management is as important in mining as in any other business. Some mines (like American Barrick) are adept at hedging the price they receive for their production by selling forward. What you are looking for is a mine that does well, even when the industry is in the doldrums. Finally, there's the question of location. It may sound xenophobic, but with all the mines in North America, there's no reason to go offshore. Why take the political risk? For instance, a mining company may be invited to a country in Latin America with all sorts of guarantees, but the guarantees can disappear overnight. All you need is a political coup.

For starters, here are a few investment-quality gold mines that you might consider. All are listed on the TSE, and most are listed on other exchanges as well. There's no point in trying to rank them in some sort of pecking order because relative values are constantly changing. If you're interested in comparing them and finding the current best buys, speak to your broker. This is by no means a definitive list, but all the companies have good gold reserves, and some (like Agnico-Eagle and Pegasus) also have silver:

Agnico-Eagle	Echo Bay	Pegasus
American Barrick	Franco-Nevada	Placer Dome
Dickenson Mines	Hemlo Gold	

And for variety, I'll add one more name: Freeport McMoran. This company, which is listed on the New York Stock Exchange, has two gold–denominated preferred share issues. Both series pay quarterly dividends based on the current price of gold, and both are convertible to $1/10$ of an ounce of gold. Series one expires in August 2003, while series two expires in February 2007. You might care to investigate them.

Are you better off buying gold bullion or shares in a gold mining company? If you're a devout gold bug, you'll undoubtedly be happier holding bullion. But if you want to make money from a rise in the price of gold, buy the shares of producing Canadian mines. As an example of how shares outperform the metal; in 1993 the price of gold bullion rose less than 18 percent, while the TSE gold index rose 104 percent—a ratio of more than five to one.

Shares of senior Canadian gold mines—relative to other mines—always look expensive. Normally they trade at high multiples and pay small dividends. Investors don't buy these companies for income, but for wealth in the ground. On the other hand, shares of South African gold mines trade at comparatively low multiples, and some pay generous dividends. South African mines don't command higher prices for a number of reasons. Production costs are rising, and further increases are expected. Some of the mines are running out of ore, and are mining less profitable ore. And there is also the risk that political unrest in South Africa could shut down the mines.

One of the best ways to play gold is to buy a package of Canadian gold mines, in the form of a mutual fund. There are two closed-end funds listed on the TSE: BGR Precious Metals and Central Fund of Canada. Both have been around for some time, and both usually trade at a discount to their net asset value. There are also a number of open-end gold funds, (which I prefer). Here are five that have been established for at least five years, and have a measurable track record.

Goldfund
Goldtrust
Dynamic Precious Metals Fund
Prudential Precious Metals Fund
Royal Trust Precious Metals Fund

During 1993, a vintage year for gold stocks, the first four on this list advanced by an average of around 100 percent. Royal Trust fared poorly in comparison, although it matched the advance of the TSE as a whole. Ironically, the reason for Royal Trust's poor performance was that the fund held a substantial amount of bullion, rather than being fully invested in stocks.

What's the outlook for gold? Nobody knows the answer to that question. Some people think that in this era of low inflation gold has had its day, and will eventually settle around $200 an ounce. Others say that the price of gold is about to take off, and look for it to hit $3000 an ounce in the next few years. Take your pick, depending upon whether you're a bull or a bear.

When should you buy gold? It makes sense to buy gold if you see serious inflation on the horizon. Or if you expect the stock market to crash (gold stocks usually withstand severe market breaks). Or if you're worried that there may be currency erosion, or a devaluation. Or if you believe that the G7 countries will return to the gold standard (which I do not). And, lastly, if you have a visceral urge to own gold, you might as well buy some.

When should you sell gold? Let me relate a personal experience. In the autumn of 1979, when gold started its meteoric rise, I thought it was just a flash in the pan. Although the price continued to climb, I was confident that it would soon tumble. But gold kept on going, and every morning on the news I was reminded of how wrong I was, and what I was missing. This went on, like a Chinese water torture, for weeks and weeks. Eventually, I capitulated and decided to make a token purchase of ten ounces of gold. This, I reasoned, would be enough to get the monkey off my back. The price of gold when I made this decision was about $730 an ounce (and silver was around $29 an ounce).

The next morning, bright and early, I went to the main branch of the Bank of Nova Scotia. There was a long line-up at the precious metals counter, and I had to take a ticket, like you do in a crowded bakery. As I waited in line, I couldn't help over-hearing some of the conversations going on around me. Every-one was buying, and nobody had ever invested before. This got me to thinking: gold had taken a huge run, and now inexperi-enced people were betting the grocery money on it. When this sunk in, it dawned on me that I was doing something very stu-pid. I gave my ticket to the person standing behind me, and fled from the bank. Gold continued up for a few more weeks, and then the bottom fell out of the market.

The moral of this story is that after gold has had a prolonged rise, and you see people lining up to buy it—that's the time to sell.

12

MINES AND OILS

If you're going to invest in Canada, you should know something about mines and oils. Not only are these core industries, but mining and oil stocks make up a hefty percentage of the equities on the Toronto Stock Exchange.

Canadian mines range from giant multinational companies with operating subsidiaries all over the world, to one-room speculative promotions that are only interested in mining the Vancouver Stock Exchange.

SPECULATIVE MINES

Let's take a look at mines, starting at the bottom of the heap. One definition of a speculative mine is a hole in the ground with a liar standing at the top. In some cases this is true, but it should also be noted that many of Canada's major mines came into existence because someone was willing to gamble. In the old days, the gamble might be taken by a storekeeper who would extend credit to a prospector in return for a share in any discovery. This practice was known as "grubstaking." Today there are very few freelance prospectors, and none as famous as Ben Hollinger or Sandy McIntyre (both of whom hit the mother lode, and had mines named after them). Prospecting nowadays is done by companies, rather than by individuals. Senior mining concerns finance themselves, but junior mines are often grubstaked by promoters.

This may suggest that mine promoters are an altruistic lot who risk their money to help the little fellow. Promoters do risk their own money (if there's no alternative), but they much prefer risking yours. Because most people buy junior mines as a result of a "hot tip," and most hot tips can be traced back to a promoter, it might be useful to review how promoters operate. The aim of a stock promotion is to increase the price of the shares. This is known in the trade as giving the stock a "run" (a term borrowed from the track).

If a stock is given a run merely to allow the promoter to unload his own shares onto the public, it serves no useful purpose. On the other hand, the sale of *treasury* shares through a promotion can raise money for exploration and development. So promoters—in the process of lining their pockets—sometimes raise much-needed risk capital. Indeed, were it not for promotions, the flow of funds for speculative ventures would dry up to a trickle, and the country's resource industries would suffer.

Having acknowledged the positive side of promotions, I hasten to add that *most promotions have nothing to do with raising capital: their sole object is to fleece the investor.*

If you know what to look for, you can recognize a promotion, and avoid being shorn. And, if you're nimble, quite often you can make a quick profit. A typical mining promotion is planned with care, and unfolds over a period of months or even years. First, the promoter buys control of an inactive or dormant company. He then sells the company some mining claims and is paid in treasury shares. The promoter now owns a company and a large block of stock, which have cost him next to nothing. Because most provinces have escrow rules (which prevent his treasury shares from being sold for a number of months) the promoter bides his time. As soon as his shares are out of escrow, the promoter alerts the public that his company is about to drill on the new property it has acquired. His publicity campaign is orchestrated through a network of telephone calls. If he's a big operator, this network will include brokers and other influential people all over the continent. Because of the hype, the stock becomes active and starts to creep up—although nothing has happened, and there's probably not even been a drill on the property.

When the stock price reaches a predetermined level, the promoter sells the public some shares from the treasury. As a rule, less than half the proceeds from the sale of treasury shares actually end up in the company's coffers—the rest is siphoned off by the promoter for services rendered, or to pay brokerage fees and "kickbacks." But enough goes into the treasury to pay for a drilling program. The period between the announcement of this program, and the announcement of its final results is when the promoter gets his payoff. Anticipation, fuelled by carefully planted rumours, can send the shares into orbit. Usually the promoter sells the balance of his shares into this euphoric market. He now has all his money back, plus a handsome profit. If the drilling is unsuccessful—and you won't know until it's too late—the stock collapses. In this case the promoter, having inside information, will not only have sold his shares, but will also have shorted many thousands. From start to finish, the promoter pulls the strings and controls the market.

Variations of the promotional cycle are repeated over and over again. Be suspicious of any speculative stock that suddenly becomes active; look for the pattern, and act accordingly. *Most people lose money because they buy too late in the cycle, and they hold their shares too long.* The best way to play a promotion is to buy early and ride the wave of anticipation. There's an old market adage that says "Buy on anticipation, sell on news." The odds will be even more in your favour if you don't wait for the news, but sell just *before* the drilling results are announced. A promotion is like a huge balloon being inflated—you don't want to be too close when it goes "bang."

Although chicanery is prevalent in the junior mining sector, not all mining plays are promotions. There are plenty of small companies run by honest people who are trying to find a commercial orebody, and there are also small companies with proven reserves struggling to raise funds to go into production. But because the shares of these companies aren't manipulated, they attract much less attention than promoted stocks.

For years most of the stock promoters were based in Toronto, and the TSE had the lion's share of speculative listings. However a royal commission investigation into the Windfall Oils and Mines scandal in 1964 forced the TSE to clean up its act. As a result of the royal commission's chilling recommendations, most of the promoters moved to Vancouver.

Viola MacMillan was the promoter behind Windfall Oils and Mines. Nicknamed the Queen Bee of Mining and the Petticoat Prospector, Viola was president of the Prospectors and Developers Association for more than twenty years. After the sensational base metal strike at Kidd Creek (near Timmins) by Texas Gulf in 1963, Viola acquired a piece of property adjacent to the Kidd Creek discovery. Drilling commenced but no ore was found. Nonetheless, Windfall was given an incredible run before the truth came out and the shares collapsed. Viola was subsequently convicted of stock manipulation, and served a short time in the slammer.

Viola MacMillan's conviction sent a clear message to Toronto's stock promoters that they were no longer welcome. After the promoters moved west, the Vancouver Stock Exchange became the busiest market for junior resource stocks in North America. This freewheeling exchange, combined with British Columbia's casual approach to securities regulation, make Vancouver a stock promoter's paradise.

The gaudiest rooster in Vancouver's financial barnyard is a gentleman by the name of Murray Pezim. To friend and foe he is known as "The Pez" and has often described himself as "the greatest mining promoter that ever lived." Pezim was one of the Toronto emigrés who moved to Vancouver in the '60s. During his checkered career he has made and lost fortunes, he has been tried (and acquitted) on fraud charges, and on at least one occasion he has declared personal bankruptcy. Today he has a string of fifty or sixty companies and measures his net worth in the tens of millions. What sets him apart from his fellow promoters—and eases the pain of his followers—is his willingness to risk his own money in some of his promotions. Many of his deals have caused catastrophic losses, but a few have resulted in valuable discoveries, the most notable being International Corona, the first company to make a major gold strike in the Hemlo area. The Pez is famous for his ability to move a stock, but before you board one of his high fliers, you would be wise to strap on a parachute.

Which brings us to some guidelines you might consider before buying *any* speculative mining stock. First, the stock should be listed. If it's not listed, forget it—unlisted stocks are pure poison. Next, find out who controls the company. You want people of integrity with a record of success. What does the company hope to find? Unless there's a base metals boom, when copper and nickel are in heavy demand, stick to precious metals.

Turning to the company's balance sheet, how many shares are outstanding? A company with three million shares is obviously more attractive than one with thirty million, because the fewer the shares, the greater the impact of a discovery. In this connection, you should always try to estimate the "float," which is the number of shares in the hands of the public. Many companies are controlled by a family or a syndicate. These shares normally won't be traded, so you can *deduct* them from the total. A company with a small float is attractive because it will take relatively little buying to move the stock. When looking at the capitalization, you should also check if there are warrants outstanding. Exercise of the warrants will dilute the existing shares. By the same token, if there are escrowed shares, find out when they will be released from escrow—and possibly dumped on the market. The amount of money in the treasury is another factor related to the number of shares. Is there enough money in the treasury to finance a drilling program, or will the company have to issue more shares? Additional shares will dilute the value of the existing stock.

The price of the shares is also a consideration. If the shares are trading near the top of their range for the past year, they may be in the terminal or "blow-off" phase of a promotional cycle. This is a tough one to call, because the price *may* be justified by recent drilling results. Ideally, you should buy shares trading at the lower end of their range for the previous twelve months.

Having done this preliminary investigation, you can look to the mining aspects of the deal. Location of the play is of prime importance. Is it near a proven orebody? If the answer is yes, this will improve the odds slightly, *but is no guarantee of success.* I stress this point because it's a favourite ploy of promoters to tout a stock near a proven orebody. And, the promoters imply, success is virtually guaranteed because the property usually has a huge anomaly. The truth is that an anomaly (which is an aberration in the geophysical survey) rarely reveals an orebody. One of the old jokes in the mining business is that the way to ruin a good anomaly is to drill it.

Now let's take a further look at location, but in a broader context. Assuming the prospect or discovery is in North America, how remote is it? If the location is far from civilization like Echo Bay's Lupin gold mine, which is fifty miles from the Arctic Circle, then the ore grade will have to be very rich to justify the extra costs involved. What about environmental considerations? Is mining allowed in the area, or would a mining complex clash with environmental regulations? If the prospect or discovery is in a foreign country, there can be significant political risk. In a banana republic, a guarantee is good only as long as the guarantor is alive. If there's a coup, and the guarantor ends up hanging by his heels in the town square, the guarantee won't be worth the paper it's written on.

Now, turning back to the prospect. Assuming the location is satisfactory, and it's a drilling play, how many holes is the company going to drill? You don't want to gamble on just a few holes. From a market standpoint, an extensive drilling program can be good for the stock (particularly if one of the early holes has been encouraging). Promoters love this type of situation because speculative fever mounts with each succeeding hole.

Unless you're a plunger, don't buy on the strength of the first hole. A lucky hole can produce totally misleading results. Wait for a "step-out" hole or some "fill-in" drilling. A step-out hole is one drilled some distance away, and its purpose is to delineate the size of the orebody. A fill-in hole is close to the original one, and its purpose is to determine the density of the orebody. Remember, a single hole can make a promotion, but it doesn't make a mine.

As a crude analogy, a drill hole is a blind probe, like a hollow needle pushed into a cake to find a cherry. The material in the core of the drill is brought to the surface, and assayed for its mineral content. Speculators often get carried away with the grade of ore, but this figure is meaningless unless you also take into account the *depth and width* of the intersection. As a rule of thumb, the width of the intersection should be at least six feet (so that it can be mined), and the length of the intersection should be at least two hundred feet (to assure a commercial quantity of ore). Base metal assays are given as percentages, while precious metal assays are usually stated in troy ounces per ton. Excluding low-grade, high-tonnage deposits, what are good grades of ore? From a *stock market point of view*, here are three boasting grades: .5 ounces of gold per ton, 200 ounces of silver per ton, and 4 percent copper per ton.

Even after an orebody has been outlined by a series of drill holes and the ore has been graded, there are still many questions to be answered. The crucial one is whether it's a commercial discovery. All sorts of things must be considered, including the rock structure, the depth of the deposit, and the substances in the ore, before this can be determined. If mining is feasible, could it cause environmental problems, such as the pollution of a lake or a river (arsenic is often present in conjunction with gold)? The bottom line is the cost of production. If you have a potential gold mine and the cost to produce gold will be US$500 per ounce, then it will only be feasible to bring the property into production if you are confident gold will *stay above* $500 per ounce. After you've done all your calculations, and taken everything into consideration, there remains the question of financing. And some mines have waited literally years for their financing. I mention these technical, administrative, and financial factors to make clear that there's more to a mine than simply discovering an orebody.

PRODUCING MINES

If you're lucky enough to buy speculative stock that subsequently becomes a producing mine, you may be surprised at the behaviour of your shares. They won't go straight up. The price will rise during the discovery period, settle back after drilling stops, recover to some extent with the production announcement, and then slump again until production commences. Interestingly enough, the highest price of the shares will probably be reached during the discovery phase.

Here is a diagram that shows the typical price pattern:

Price Pattern

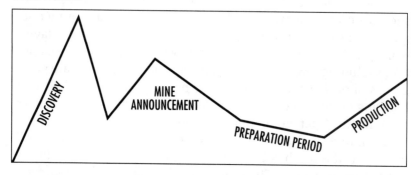

Producing mines are different from speculative mines. Unlike the "specs," many established mines earn large sums of money and are considered quality investments. Regardless of their quality, however, producing mines are subject to three strong influences: the economic cycle, metal prices, and the state of the stock market. These sometimes conflicting influences cause wide swings in the price of their shares. For this reason you shouldn't buy senior mining stocks and forget about them. What you should try to do is to play the swings—buy them when they're cheap and sell them when they're dear. Sounds obvious, but doing this successfully requires excellent judgement.

First, you must establish where the mines are in the economic cycle. There are three distinct phases to watch for. At the end of a recession, mining shares (along with most stocks) are bumping along the bottom. As soon as the market turns, senior mines start to recover—even though their earnings may be nonexistent. This is known as the "anticipation phase." Following this early surge, mining shares usually give up a third to a half of their gains. The next upward leg is propelled by a recovery in earnings, and is known as the "fundamental phase." Again, there's a substantial correction. The last and most exuberant move occurs at the end of the economic cycle, and is called the "speculative phase." This phase is followed by a prolonged decline that marks the end of the cycle. Ideally, the time to buy is at the beginning of the anticipation or fundamental phases, and the time to sell is during the speculative phase. Below is a diagram of the three phases.

The Mining Cycle

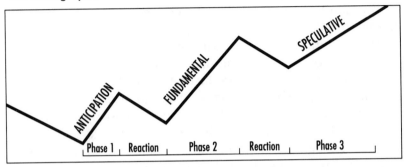

Having identified the stage of the mining cycle, your next task is to decide what metal to play. Ask your broker for a current report on metals (noting especially their outlook), check the commodity quotes (noting prices in relation to their seasonal range), and use your own common sense. Picking a metal to invest in is not too difficult. For example, if the outlook for copper is strong, and the price is rising, you might consider a copper stock. If auto production is picking up, look to lead and zinc stocks. The auto industry uses a lot of zinc for galvanizing, and lead is a major component of car batteries. The auto industry is also using an increasing amount of aluminum. If the economic recovery is gaining momentum, and capital spending is rising, the steel companies will be busy. Increased steel production, in turn, will be good for molybdenum and nickel, both of which are used in steel alloys.

After you have chosen a metal, look at mines that produce it as their primary source of income. (Most senior mines also produce other metals as by-products of the recovery process). In addition to the normal yardsticks, like price/earnings ratios and book values per share, there are a couple of other things you should consider. Because mines are major exporters, you should find out the effect of a one-cent change in the value of the Canadian dollar on the earnings per share. (Any good research report will include this figure.) It is also useful to have an informed opinion on the *direction* of the Canadian dollar—again, consult your broker. Book value per share and the current price of the stock in relation to its book value are two more considerations. Senior mines usually trade at a price of one to one and a half times their book value.

You should also check out the cost of production and the production per share. To find the production per share, simply divide the number of outstanding shares into the total amount of metal produced. For example, if a company has 2,000,000 shares outstanding, and it produces 40,000,000 pounds of nickel, production per share will be be 20 pounds. Cost of production varies from mine to mine. Those with low-cost operations are the safest investments—but they have very little leverage. A mine with a high cost of production is riskier, because of its high break-even point, but a small increase in the metal price can make a big difference to its earnings. Taking gold as an example, here's how metal price leverage works:

Cost of Production	Gold Price (per ounce)	Effect on Profit of $10 Increase
Mine A $155	$400	+ 4.1%
Mine B $380	$400	+50.0%

The life of a mine depends upon its ore reserves. This can be tricky to estimate because the managers of many mines, especially of gold mines, are content to find new reserves in the process of removing ore. Some gold mines have gone for decades reporting only two or three years worth of reserves, but have uncovered more ore each year. Ideally, when you buy mining stock you want to be assured of at least five to six years of reserves. Ten to fifteen would be even better.

Producing mines pay relatively small dividends, and the amount of their dividends is largely governed by metal prices. Normally, dividend yields range from nil to around 4 percent. If you spot a high-yielding mining stock, *don't buy it until you've checked it out.* What you will probably find is that the mine is running out of ore. Investors accept lower yields from mining stocks because they represent wealth in the ground, and are a hedge against inflation. Because mines are cyclical, their earnings are subject to wide swings. This means that when their earnings are low, the price/earnings ratio of their shares is unreasonably high, and when their earnings recover the P/E ratios can be unreasonably low. In normal times—the midpoint of the boom and bust cycle—senior base metal stocks usually trade at about ten times their earnings, and gold mines at close to twice that multiple.

Before leaving the subject of mines and turning to oil stocks, I'd like to offer one more word of advice. If you're considering several mining stocks, and you can't make up your mind which to buy—choose quality. Every time.

OIL STOCKS

Oil stocks are similar to mining stocks in that both are natural resource investments. They are also similar from a market point of view, because senior oil stocks are an inflation hedge, trading at relatively high price/earnings ratios with low, or nonexistent yields. Junior oils have much in common with junior mines, because drilling for oil has the same speculative potential as drilling for precious metals. Indeed, if they think they can make a buck, mining promoters will turn to an oil play without batting an eye.

This reminds me of a Vancouver oil stock called Bata Resources, which was promoted by Murray Pezim. Bata had all the ingredients of a classic promotion: a good story, a lengthy drilling program, several corporate mergers, and participation by an international all-star cast. With the skill of a conductor, maestro Pezim promoted Bata towards a magnificent crescendo. The performance lasted many months.

Although it was a promotion, Bata was a junior oil with genuine merit. I bought the stock for my own account at about $3, and later added to it. My average cost eventualy worked out to around $5 per share. Bata made it up to $13, and then began to retreat. I tried to find the reason for the reversal, but couldn't get a satisfactory answer. So I sold out. Bata recovered for a few weeks, faltered, and then began a steady descent. As the slide went on, it became obvious the promotion was in trouble. At this juncture, the "pros" moved in like sharks and began shorting Bata. Pezim marshalled all the buying power he could and even poured in some of his own money to stave off the shorts. But it proved a losing battle. The end for Bata came one fateful day when the shorts broke the stock from $3 to 30 cents. The Pez suffered grievous loss on this venture, as did his followers. A friend of mine, who at one stage had a paper profit of $800,000, ended up losing more than $100,000.

As this example shows, oil promotions are just as dangerous as mining promotions. So if you are going to gamble on an oil play you should screen it just as carefully as a mining speculation. The most important thing to find out is the track record and integrity of the people behind the deal. If they're honest and have been successful in the past, you'll probably get a fair shake for your money.

The oil and gas situation in Canada is peculiar in some ways, and I'll try to summarize it briefly. Canada is fortunate to have massive natural gas reserves and a good supply of oil. Most of the country's natural gas comes from the Prairie provinces, and most of the oil from Alberta.

Natural gas reserves are sufficient to last many years, and are large enough to justify sales to the United States. The oil picture, however, is not as bright, as Canada has to import a certain amount of oil, particularly in the East. Exports of natural gas south of the border will not only continue, but are likely to increase. The reason is that the United States is not discovering enough natural gas to offset its consumption of domestic reserves. At present, many Canadian natural gas wells are capped, waiting for export contracts (and new pipelines to distribute it). Capped wells don't produce any income, but they represent wealth in the ground.

The price of oil is influenced by two main forces: the world economy and the machinations of OPEC. When the economies of the industrialized nations are buoyant, both consumption and the price of oil increase. The reverse occurs when the economies contract, in other words, consumption and the price of oil decline. Actually there are two oil prices: Brent, which is North Sea oil, and West Texas Intermediate crude. Both are quoted at their current, or spot price. In Canada, West Texas Intermediate, or WTI, as it is known, is the most relevant indicator.

OPEC is the acronym for the Organization of Petroleum Exporting Countries. Established in 1961, OPEC is a cartel that fixes oil prices and production. The members of OPEC are:

Algeria, Ecuador, Gabon, Indonesia, Iran, Iraq, Kuwait, Libya, Nigeria, Qatar, Saudi Arabia, the United Arab Emirates, and Venezuela. OPEC's heyday was the early '70s, when its meetings created apprehension and price shocks around the globe. Since then, however, cheating on production quotas and prices have robbed the cartel of much of its effectiveness. Even so, it's prudent to keep a wary eye on OPEC—it still sets the benchmark price, and one day it may again get its act together.

Regardless of what the rest of the market is doing, oil stocks track the price of oil. This is also true for the stocks of companies that are primarily natural gas producers—because the price of natural gas is linked to the price of oil. The accompanying diagram of the WTI price and the TSE oil and gas index over a three-month period shows how closely the index shadows the oil price. The solid line represents the West Texas price, the dotted line the oil and gas index:

WTI & TSE Oil & Gas Index

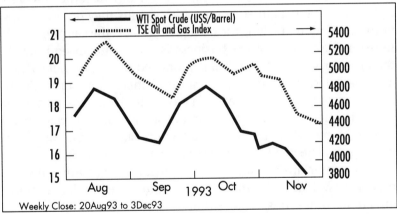

Weekly Close: 20Aug93 to 3Dec93

Canada has a good many promising junior and intermediate oil and gas companies. What you should look for are firms with a healthy balance sheet. This indicates good management. Don't rely on net asset values (which can be suspect) or try to compare earnings. Look at the *cash flow* of these companies. Cash flow is the sum of net income plus deferred taxes plus noncash charges (e.g., amortization, depreciation, and depletion). Cash flow is important because it shows what funds are available for exploration. Ideally, the exploration program should consist of low-risk drilling in western Canada, with a high-risk frontier play for a speculative boost. It might also include participation in an overseas project. Stocks with this type of profile have always outperformed the market, and there's no reason they won't continue to do so in the future.

Again, I must caution you not to get carried away by the discovery of a major oil well in Indonesia or some other remote place. No matter how sensational the find, it will be vulnerable to both political and war risks. An obvious political risk is the government of the host country arbitrarily confiscating the well. The Gulf War—and the consequential damage to Kuwait's and Iraq's oil production—is a prime example of war risk. Insurance coverage for war and political risks is rarely available, and it's often prohibitively expensive. For these reasons, except for Australia and the North Sea, oil and gas discoveries in North America are far more attractive investments than those overseas.

The heavyweights of the oil and gas industry are the integrated oils: Imperial, Petro-Canada, Shell, and Suncor. The term "integrated" refers to vertical integration, which means they do everything from exploration to selling the refined product at the gas pump. The most profitable part of the business is the upstream end, rather than the downstream end. (Oil is produced upstream, but refined and marketed downstream.) Because of increasing competition, the integrated companies see little growth in the downstream end, which is one of the reasons so many service stations have been closed in recent years. The production side of the business, however, is expected to continue to be a money spinner.

The senior oils are sound, if somewhat conservative, investments. As well as being influenced by the price of oil, they trade on an earnings basis the same way as industrial stocks. A reasonable price for an integrated oil stock would be fifteen to twenty times its earnings, with a yield of around 3 percent. Traditionally, senior oil companies reinvest a substantial portion of their earnings in exploration and development. Suncor Inc., because of the nature of its tar sands project, is a particularly interesting situation.

I would also strongly recommend Canadian natural gas stocks. Natural gas prices in the summer of 1994 are half of what they were in the early '80s. In the interim, there has been a continent-wide increase in the use of natural gas, because it's cleaner and more efficient than oil. During the same period, natural gas reserves in the United States have begun to dwindle. Canada, on the other hand, is increasing its reserves and has hundreds of capped wells. This combination—ample domestic supply and growing American demand—bodes well for Canada's gas producers.

Many investors, to hedge their bets, buy shares of companies that produce both oil and gas. This makes sense, because the outlook is bright for both commodities. After all, oil and gas generate energy, and there will always be a need for energy.

13

RRSPs

The best way to retire rich is to contribute as much as you can, for as long as you can, to a Registered Retirement Savings Plan. Sounds trite, but it's true. An RRSP is a super way to create a nest egg—your annual contributions are deductible, and both the income and capital gains in the RRSP are also exempt from tax.

THE BASICS

The purpose of an RRSP is to accumulate a sum of capital for your retirement. The Canadian government gives tax breaks to encourage this (so you won't, in later years, be a drain on the public treasury). From your point of view, it makes good sense to be financially independent. At the current rate of deficit spending, the government larder may be bare by the time you retire. So it's just as well to be prepared.

Anyone with earned income, up to the age of seventy-one, can contribute to a Registered Retirement Savings Plan. (The term "earned income" excludes pension or investment income.) There are strict limits on how much you can contribute each year. The amount is 18 percent of your earned income, on an ascending scale, to *maximums* of:

                1994 – $13,500
                1995 – $14,500
                1996 – $15,500

If you're a member of a registered pension plan or a deferred profit-sharing plan, the amount you contribute to either plan must be *deducted* from your RRSP allowance. The balance—after the RPP or DSP deduction—is the amount you may contribute to your RRSP. To find out what this amount is in your case, refer to your "pension adjustment," shown in box 52 on your T4 slip. You can carry forward any unused RRSP contributions, from as far back as 1991, for up to seven years. It pays to contribute the limit, and if you miss a year, you should do your best to make up the shortfall.

As I mentioned earlier, your RRSP contributions are deducted from your gross income. If you're in a high income bracket this can mean significant tax savings. For those in the top tax bracket in 1993, here are some samples of the amount saved per $1000 contribution:

                Ontario   – $523
                Quebec   – $529
                British Columbia – $511
                Nova Scotia   – $503

You can have more than one RRSP—in fact, you can have as many as you want. You can also transfer funds and securities from one RRSP to another, without being subject to tax. Having more than one RRSP is not necessarily a good thing, however. It leads to both additional paperwork and the hassle of administering scattered assets. (I'll come back to this subject later.) The deadline for contributions is sixty days after the end of the year—usually the first or second of March, depending on where the weekend falls, and on whether it's a leap year.

An RRSP can contain a wide range of investments. They include: savings accounts, term deposits, certain mortgages, bonds, listed (and some unlisted) stocks, call options, warrants, mutual funds, and special insurance plans. Among the investments that are *ineligible* for RRSPs are: most unlisted stocks, all commodities, gold bullion, and real estate. The last two categories can be circumvented, to some extent, by buying listed stocks or mutual funds that invest in precious metals or real estate.

Another important thing to note is that an RRSP can't have more than 20 percent of its assets in foreign securities. The 20 percent rule must be watched closely because it means foreign holdings as a percentage of the *book value* of the total portfolio. Book value can be difficult to figure out, especially after you've made a number of trades. In practice, if you have a self-directed RRSP with a broker, the broker will keep tabs on the foreign content. But you are still responsible, and *you* will pay the penalty if the percentage is exceeded. The 20 percent foreign content rule applies to *each* RRSP, and isn't a maximum applied to the total value of all your RRSPs. For instance, if you have two RRSPs, and each has a book value of $10,000, you can't put $1000 of foreign content in one and $3000 in the other—the limit for each is $2000.

You may also contribute to an RRSP for your spouse, and receive the full tax deduction. But you can only contribute to a spousal plan within your personal limit. If your limit is $14,500, the *total* you can contribute to your own and your spouse's RRSP is that amount; in other words, you could put $4500 in your RRSP and $10,000 in the spousal plan. And, while you get the tax deductions for your spousal contributions, your spouse *owns* the RRSP. This has two major ramifications. First, should your spouse withdraw funds from the RRSP within three years of your last contribution, you will be taxed on the withdrawal to the limit of your contributions. The other point to remember is that in the event of a break-up, your spouse owns the RRSP, even though you may have funded it entirely. The definition of "spouse," in this instance, includes common-law as well as married partners.

The purpose of a spousal plan is to create two income streams. Two smaller incomes—with two sets of deductions—attract less tax than a single large one. Income splitting is an excellent and a perfectly legal way to reduce tax. I need hardly add that it also involves a strong element of trust, and is best suited to those with stable, long-term relationships.

In 1992, more than 4.6 million Canadians contributed over $16 billion to Registered Retirement Savings Plans. Should you have an RRSP? For most people, the answer is yes. Even if you already have an adequate pension or deferred profit-sharing plan, an RRSP is a good way to accumulate savings (with tax breaks along the way).

Should you borrow to make your RRSP contribution? Conventional wisdom says that you should. This advice, however, assumes you'll receive a tax refund to repay all or part of the loan. It also assumes that you'll earn a higher return in your RRSP than the rate charged on your loan.

If you borrow to make your contribution, you will most certainly get a tax break. But what if you don't get a tax refund to repay the loan? And what if the interest rate on the loan rate is higher than the return in your RRSP? Ask yourself these questions before you run to the bank for a loan. My advice is to borrow *only if you can comfortably repay the loan within the calendar year.* There's no point in being saddled with debt—no matter how worthy the investment (or how attractive the tax deduction).

This brings us to another frequently asked question: should you buy a house or put your money into an RRSP? At the risk of being the devil's advocate, I would opt for the house. (You might also choose to pay down the mortgage, which I consider another priority.) In either case, you can use the carry-forward provision to catch up on your RRSP contributions. For most young people, retirement is a remote eventuality; their first priority is to buy a home. And a house or condominium is an excellent tax-sheltered investment. Not only can you enjoy living in it, but over the long term it will probably outperform your RRSP.

Current legislation allows home buyers to borrow up to $20,000 from their RRSP for the purchase of their first home. The withdrawal is an interest-free loan that must be repaid, in equal instalments, within fifteen years. Early repayment is permitted, but if you *miss* an instalment it's considered income, and you are taxed on it. Taking money out of your RRSP for this purpose obviously reduces the amount that is tax-sheltered. But the loss will be offset by the increase in value of your residence—which is also a tax shelter. On balance, it's an excellent arrangement.

On the opposite side of the ledger, you are allowed to *overcontribute* a maximum of $8000 to your RRSP. An overcontribution enjoys full tax shelter, but you're not allowed to deduct any portion of it. Should you withdraw all or part of the overcontribution, you'll be taxed at your marginal rate, which amounts to double taxation. The only way to work off an overcontribution is to wait it out and apply it to next year's instalment. There's little, if any advantage, to overcontributing—the sole purpose of the rule is to give you leeway in case you've inadvertently gone over the limit.

NAME A BENEFICIARY

When you fill out your RRSP form be sure to specify a beneficiary. If you die without naming a beneficiary, your RRSP will be liquidated and the proceeds will be added to your taxable income for that year. It is especially important to name a beneficiary if you're married, because an RRSP can be passed on to your spouse without any tax liability. I had a client named Bill, who was a busy surgeon. Bill always intended to make his wife the beneficiary of his self-directed RRSP, but he never got around to it, even though I sent him the papers to sign several times. Bill died suddenly, and his RRSP was liquidated and taxed at a rate of 53 percent. For the lack of a signature, his widow forfeited more than $100,000.

TYPES OF PLANS

There are two basic types of RRSPs: managed plans or self-directed plans. Managed plans are the simplest and most popular. Self-directed plans require some personal attention, but are the most versatile. Whichever plan you choose, only buy quality investments. Your RRSP is your nest egg, and the best way to protect it is to stick with quality. No junk stocks or bonds—and no rinky-dink schemes with big tax writeoffs.

Managed Plans

About 85 percent of the RRSPs purchased each year are managed plans. They are offered on a "package" basis by banks, trust companies, brokers, and other financial institutions, as well as by mutual funds and insurance companies. Buying a managed plan is a one-shot deal, where you plunk down your money, sign the appropriate forms, and the institution looks after the rest. Under the managed plan heading, there are several subcategories, most of which are income investments.

A savings account deposit is one of the most common RRSPs. If the institution is a member of the CDIC, the deposit will be guaranteed, making it virtually risk-free. Interest is calculated on the daily closing balance, and compounded monthly, quarterly, semi-annually, or annually. Some savings accounts have a tiered rate, whereby the interest rate increases with the amount of the deposit. About the only thing that can be said for a savings account RRSP is that it's safe. The interest rate is invariably low (often less than the rate of inflation), and there's no possibility of capital appreciation.

If you insist on this type of RRSP, you would be better off buying a money market mutual fund. These funds are not insured, but they invest in Treasury Bills and other high-quality short-term paper, so they are very safe (especially if sponsored by one of the major chartered banks or trust companies). Money market funds normally pay at least 2 percent more than savings accounts.

Savings institutions also offer a variety of term deposits and guaranteed investment certificates. They are usually insured by the Canadian Deposit Insurance Corporation, which has a maximum exposure per institution of $60,000. This means that if you have deposits or GICs (both RRSP and non-RRSP) with an institution, your *total* coverage will be $60,000, regardless of their value.

Term deposits bear a set rate of interest, and usually mature within 30 to 364 days. In some cases you can liquidate these deposits before they mature, but the terms vary. Quite often, if you want to liquidate or transfer the funds, you will forfeit the interest. Money market funds are more liquid, and generally provide a better yield. Whatever investment you choose, whether it be a term deposit or a money market fund, it pays to shop around for the best rate. *The Globe and Mail* and *The Financial Post*, as well as other major papers, publish comparative rate tables every week.

Next to savings accounts, Guaranteed Investment Certificates are the most popular RRSP investment. GICs have a fixed term of from six months to seven years, and usually a fixed rate of interest. Most GICs can't be cashed until they mature, which means that you can be locked-in for up to seven years. Cashable GICs pay a lower rate of interest, and there is often a rate reduction or a service charge for early withdrawal. Before buying a GIC, try to estimate the present stage of the interest rate cycle. When rates are high—in the double digits for five year terms—buy long-term maturities. Conversely, when rates are low, as they were in 1993, buy short-term maturities so that you can take advantage of a rise in rates down the road.

Recently, mutual funds, especially money market funds, have attracted a huge amount of RRSP contribution money. After rates declined in the early '90s, and the stock market began its recovery, many GIC investors became disenchanted with the low rates offered on renewals. As a result, they turned to money market mutual funds and to a lesser degree, to equity funds. Mutual funds are an excellent RRSP investment. Their purchase, however, requires some judgement. Stick to quality. Diversify to create a balanced portfolio—so much in money market funds, so much in fixed income, a percentage in Canadian equities, and the maximum amount of foreign content. Depending on your age and financial position, foreign content can be anything from a U.S. money market fund to a fund that invests in the Pacific Rim. If you really want to simplify things, there are a number of good balanced funds available. Some of these funds even have 20 percent of their assets in foreign securities.

Self-Directed Plans

Now let's turn to the other type of RRSP: the self-directed one. Self-directed plans allow you to manage your own RRSP investments under a single umbrella. Unlike managed plans that consist of only one security, self-directed plans can hold any number of eligible investments. This provides flexibility, and permits you to run your RRSP like your regular portfolio.

Self-directed (also called self-administered) RRSPs are offered by brokers, trust companies, banks, and some mutual funds. Most institutions charge an annual fee, and there can also be transaction fees, in addition to regular brokerage commissions. Annual fees range from about $100 to $250, and are tax-deductible if paid with outside funds. (If the fee is paid with funds in your RRSP, there's no deduction.) Although the fee is inconsequential, you should have an RRSP worth at least $15,000 to justify the expense of a self-directed plan.

There are advantages and disadvantages to having a self-directed RRSP. The bad news is that you must play a role in the management of your assets—and if you're incompetent, ill-advised, or just plain unlucky, you could lose a bundle. Having said that, you don't need to be a mental giant to run an RRSP. If you are prudent and you use common sense, you should do just fine. Indeed, most brokerage firms only offer self-directed plans to their clients, regardless of their level of sophistication (a policy that may be influenced by the trading potential of self-directed plans).

The basic advantage of having a self-directed RRSP is that you are in charge of your financial destiny. By consolidating your assets, you make them easier to manage. The single statement you receive is also a benefit because it provides an overall picture—including asset allocation and foreign content—at a glance. Self-directed plans are much more flexible than managed plans. For example, if you're short of cash, you can contribute eligible securities to your RRSP. You might contribute $10,000 in Canada Savings Bonds, or several hundred shares of a listed stock. When securities are transferred to your RRSP, they are deemed, for tax purposes, to have been sold. In this instance, *you can't claim capital losses, but you must report capital gains.* Being able to transfer securities into your RRSP is also useful when you want to shelter a high-income investment. As a policy, you should hold high-tax investments, like bonds and GICs, inside your RRSP, and low-yielding growth stocks and equity funds outside it.

Among the income investments that self-directed plans can hold are T-Bills, CSBs, GICs, regular bonds, foreign bonds, Canadian bonds denominated in foreign currencies (an excellent way to hedge the Canadian dollar), strip bonds, and mortgages—including your own mortgage. Holding your own mortgage in your RRSP may sound like a swell idea. After all, you'll be paying yourself all that interest. But think it through.

First of all, you won't get a deal; you'll have to pay the going rate, and there will be an impressive array of expenses, such as:

1. A set-up fee ($150–$250)
2. An appraisal fee ($200–$250)
3. An administration fee ($175–$225)
4. A lawyer's fee ($500–$1000)
5. Mortgage insurance (.5%–2.5%)

In most cases, it would be cheaper to obtain a mortgage in the normal way. If, however, you decide to go ahead and take on your own mortgage, you'll undoubtedly have to liquidate more appropriate RRSP investments to raise the money. By failing to be objective, and downgrading the quality of your investments, you will break not one, but two investment rules. But let's assume you ignore these trivialities and pay all the fees and sign all the papers. The mortgage on your home is now safely lodged in your RRSP. What happens if you sell your home? Do you want to be holding some stranger's mortgage? Is it the best investment you can buy?

This is not to say that mortgages are unsuitable for an RRSP. But you should be wary of a mortgage with an unusually high yield—there's always a reason for it. And even the best mortgages are "messy," in that the principal and interest instalments are an ongoing reinvestment chore. If you want to invest in mortgages, you're better off buying a good mortgage mutual fund. Mortgage funds are diversified (both by term and geography) and provide competitive yields, as well as a modest opportunity for capital gain.

The other word of caution concerns venture capital funds. Recently, labour-sponsored venture capital funds have been touted as a wonderful RRSP investment. From a tax point of view, they are. In addition to a 20 percent federal tax credit (to a maximum of $1000), Ontario and some of the other provinces allow purchasers of these funds an additional 20 percent tax credit. Furthermore, you can take the tax credits and then contribute the shares to your RRSP at full face value. If you're in a high tax bracket, the net cost of these funds is very low. But you must hold them from *five to seven years*, otherwise you'll forfeit the tax credits.

From an investment point of view, the outlook is not quite so bright. Venture capital companies provide equity capital to business concerns that are unable to obtain money from conventional sources (banks and other lending institutions). If they back a winner, the payoff can be glorious. That's the good news. The bad news is that venture capital is an extremely risky business. When a venture capital investment goes sour—and many of them do—you are looking at a 100 percent loss. For this reason, the venture capital sector is the graveyard of the financial business. And that is why the federal and provincial governments are giving away those lovely tax credits—to induce you to risk your money.

The acid test of a tax shelter is whether you would buy it *without* the tax breaks. And the golden rule for RRSP investing is "stick to quality." On either count, labour-sponsored venture capital funds have no place in your RRSP. Don't be blinded by the tax writeoffs; the object of an RRSP isn't to reduce tax today, it's to build a nest egg for tomorrow.

To this end, you shouldn't speculate with junk, but strive for a balanced portfolio. Decide on the mix you want of income and growth, and then assemble the securities. If you're going to err, err on the conservative side. This means a healthy proportion of defensive investments, such as bonds and money market funds. Remember, there's no tax on RRSP investments, so you can ignore tax credits and after-tax returns, and concentrate on *gross* yields. In this connection, strip bonds or strip coupons are ideal for RRSPs. You buy them at a discount—so you get a big bang for your buck—and there's no need to reinvest interest.

High-yielding investments in an RRSP can compound over the years at an astonishing rate. I have in my hand a TD bank brochure titled *The Facts from the RSP Shoppe*. While I'm a little curious about the Olde Englishe twist (possibly the TD was being whimsical, although banks are not noted for this trait), the brochure contains some interesting information. One page says, "Contribute to a TD RSP today ... you could be a millionaire at retirement ..." Below this exhortation is a graph that shows that $5000 invested every year for 40 years, compounded at 8 percent, would produce a grand total of $1,398,905.

Compound interest is all very well, but you should also take into account the ravages of inflation. Because inflation is endemic in

North America, some of your RRSP portfolio must be in equities. The proportion of defensive securities to equities you should hold will vary with your age, your circumstances, and the state of the economy. So it's impossible to make any flat statements. But the rule is: the younger you are, the lower your proportion of defensive investments. To roughly illustrate this principle, let your age represent the percentage of defensive investments. On this basis, when you are 25, only 25 percent of your portfolio will be in income securities, and the balance will be in equities. But by the time you reach 70, you will have 70 percent in defensive investments. The reason for shifting the weightings is that the younger you are, the more risk you can take, while the nearer you get to retirement, the less risk you can afford.

If you're uncertain about the allocation of your assets, buy some *balanced* mutual funds. These funds normally hold cash, income securities, and equities. As the fund managers monitor and continually rebalance their holdings, the problem of asset allocation will be automatically looked after for you. If you choose this approach, you can assemble a sound RRSP with only three components—a money market fund, one or more balanced funds, and an offshore fund (for foreign content). This simple strategy will remove much of the worry, and it will work.

Before leaving the subject of RRSPs, if you'd like more detailed information, I recommend two annual publications. One is Gordon Pape's *Buyer's Guide to RRSPs*, published by Prentice-Hall Canada. The other is Steven Kelman's *RRSPs—Everything You Need to Make the Right Choice*, published by The Financial Times of Canada.

CASHING IN

Now let's turn to the payoff of a Registered Retirement Savings Plan. You can cash in your RRSP at any age, but you *must* collapse it by the end of the year you reach 71. When you collapse your plan, you have three options:

1. You can roll it into an annuity.
2. You can roll it into a Registered Retirement Income Fund (RRIF).
3. You can take the money and run.

Annuities

If you buy an annuity you can roll the proceeds of your RRSP into it without attracting tax. The annual income, however, will be taxed. You can also roll your RRSP tax-free into a Registered Retirement Income Fund. The proceeds of the RRIF will be paid out on a sliding scale, and taxed in the same way as an annuity. Should you opt for cash, the total will be included in your gross income for the year, and taxed at your marginal rate. If you do nothing, your RRSP will be liquidated and treated for tax purposes as though you had cashed it.

A "locked-in" RRSP is an exception to these rules. This type of RRSP usually comes about as the result of a pension transfer from a former place of employment. You manage a locked-in RRSP the same way as a regular RRSP, but you can't withdraw money from it, and it normally can't be collapsed until retirement age. When a locked-in RRSP is collapsed, you can't take the cash, nor can you roll it into a RRIF. *You must buy a life annuity.* (In some provinces, you also have the choice of buying a life income fund.)

An annuity—whether it be for life or to age 90—is safe, and it provides a steady stream of income. Although you have no control over your annuity, it requires no management. Most annuities pay a level amount from start to finish—there's no protection against inflation. Also, when you sign on to an annuity, you're usually locked-in for the full term. There are, however, a wide variety of annuities, and it's possible to get around these drawbacks. But you must realize that the more bells and whistles—such as indexed payments—you want, the less income you'll get.

Two annuity options that I consider essential are: term certainty and joint survivorship. Term certainty guarantees payments for a given number of years. If you have a term certainty of ten years and you die after three, your estate will receive payments for seven more years. The rule of thumb for this option is to select a long enough period to recover your original investment. Ten years will usually do the trick, and is a good minimum figure. (Remember, this is an *option*, and the longer the period, the lower the annual payout.) If you have a joint survivor clause and you die, your spouse will inherit your annuity tax-free. If your annuity also has a term certainty clause, your spouse will inherit the remaining portion of the guaranteed period.

For those who don't want to take any risks (except the risk of inflation), an annuity is the logical way to fund your retirement. If you want the best value, don't buy your annuity from your friendly insurance company agent—go to an annuity broker. An annuity broker will shop the entire market, and may check fifty or sixty companies to get you the best rate.

Now let's move on to the other two retirement options: cashing in your RRSP, or rolling it into a RRIF. Except in unusual circumstances (and I can't think of any), it doesn't make sense to cash-in your RRSP. The tax bite is too severe. This leaves us with the RRIF or Registered Retirement Income Fund.

Registered Retirement Income Funds (RRIFs)

A RRIF is the opposite of an RRSP. Instead of being a vehicle to accumulate capital, it disburses the proceeds of your RRSP in instalments. Income and capital gains within a RRIF are tax-sheltered, as with an RRSP. Annual payments are fully taxable, as with an annuity. You stipulate the amount of these payments. There's no upper limit, but there's a minimum amount—depending on your age—you must disburse each year. Stated as a percentage of the value of your RRIF, the minimum amounts are as follows:

Age	Minimum Payout (%)
71	7.38
72	7.48
73	7.59
74	7.71
75	7.85
76	7.99
77	8.15
78	8.33
79	8.53
80	8.75
81	8.99
82	9.27

| | Minimum Payout |
Age	(%)
83	9.58
84	9.93
85	10.3
86	10.8
87	11.3
88	12.0
89	12.7
90	13.6
91	14.7
92	16.1
93	17.9
94	20.0
95	20.0

A RRIF, like an RRSP, can be bequeathed to your spouse, and you can have more than one RRIF. Furthermore, if your spouse is younger than you are, you can use your spouse's age to reduce the payout percentages of your RRIF.

RRIFs: Self-Directed or Managed?

You can buy RRIFs at all the same sources at which you buy RRSPs. Indeed, if you have a self-directed RRSP, it's logical to stay with the same institution and roll it into a RRIF. This brings up the question of whether you should have a self-directed or a managed RRIF. Because you're obviously older when you take on a RRIF, your age and state of health must be taken into consideration. Age and infirmity can affect your competence. Also, even if you're an experienced investor, do you really want to go on monitoring your investments? After they retire, some people like to keep in touch with the market, while others prefer to think about their golf scores. The conservative choice, and the one I recommend, is a managed RRIF.

If you decide on a self-directed RRIF (if you want, you can switch to a managed RRIF later on), give serious thought to the contents of your portfolio. As a strategy, try to make your annual withdrawals from income for as long as possible. To do this, you need a high proportion of income–producing investments. By paying out income, this will allow your capital to grow. Capital growth is essential because of inflation. At a rate of only 4 percent inflation will double your income requirement in fifteen years. So, you will also have to have some equities in your RRIF.

Some investments are more suitable for RRIFs than others. First off, your securities must be *marketable*, because eventually they'll all be sold. This rules out such things as personal mortgages (even though they're insured). And it also eliminates strip coupons or strip bonds, because they pay no income and are unwieldy to sell, especially in odd lots. In this connection, sales of odd lots of listed stocks, such as 37 shares of Bank of Nova Scotia or 18 shares of BCE, are also very expensive. But I should quickly add that high-yielding common stocks, especially those of banks and utilities, are excellent RRIF investments. GICs with staggered maturities work well in RRIFs, as do "packages" of high-grade bonds with staggered maturities. (The purpose of staggered maturities is to prevent you from being locked-in, and to give you an opportunity to reinvest at current rates.)

Mutual funds with low volatility are particularly well suited to RRIFs. (Low-volatility securities are solid performers, never hitting the peaks or plumbing the depths.) This type of fund, like all mutual funds, also provides safety through diversification. There's a huge variety of funds for you to choose from—whether you're looking for income from a bond or mortgage fund, a currency hedge from an international bond fund, or professional asset allocation through a balanced fund. Equally important, you can buy top-quality, no-load funds in every category, and most can be liquidated in small amounts at no cost.

RRIFs or Annuities?

Which should you choose, a RRIF or an annuity? A RRIF is more flexible (you can roll it into an annuity any time you want) and it gives you a chance to offset the erosion of your capital with a measure of growth. If you die before your capital runs out, the balance of your RRIF goes either to your beneficiary, or to your estate. Either way, there is a residue. There's also the risk with a

RRIF that your money will run out (unless it's guaranteed, as some managed plans are), and you can't predict values in future years.

An annuity offers a guaranteed sum that you can count on for life, or until you reach 90. In most cases, however, it doesn't provide any protection against inflation—and if you buy an indexed annuity, the payout is reduced dramatically. When you die, there's usually no residual value (unless you have a term certainty clause, and it's within that period). On balance, the most appealing feature about an annuity is that you'll never run out of money. There'll always be a cheque coming in—though the amount may be inadequate.

If you have a reasonable pension, I would choose a RRIF rather than an annuity to supplement it. If you don't have a pension, and you don't want to take unnecessary risk, why not start out with an annuity *and* a RRIF? You can split the proceeds of your RRSP any way you want, and down the road, if you're uncomfortable with your RRIF, you can roll it into an annuity. Nothing ventured, nothing gained. And, if you have substantial investments—either in your RRSP or outside it—I would definitely go for a RRIF.

Don't do anything in haste. Sit down with a professional advisor several years *before* you collapse your RRSP. Go over the pros and cons with him, and then think about it for a while before making your decision. Like marriage, planning for retirement shouldn't be entered into lightly.

Remember—the steps you take today will determine your financial situation tomorrow.

14

FORECASTING PRICES

It's easier to forecast the weather than to predict stock market prices. This, despite the fact that millions of computer hours have been spent trying to unlock the secret to prophesying market moves. The reason forecasting can't be reduced to a science is because the market is largely influenced by human emotions. You can't program emotions, such as greed and fear, into a computer. In a way, this is a comfort. If we knew exactly what was going to happen, it would take the fun out of the game.

Some market savants have been incredibly accurate for brief periods of time, while others have made brilliant but isolated calls. So far, no one has been right all the time. This shouldn't discourage you from trying to predict market moves, but it does indicate that forecasting is a formidable challenge.

Forecasting applies to both buying and selling decisions. Which brings to mind the old market saying "timing is everything." I mention this because forecasting encompasses not only *what* to buy, but also *when* to buy and when to *sell*. Recently an old friend complained to me that brokers were great at telling you when to buy, but they never seemed to tell clients when to sell. This was true to some extent in the past, but today most analysts will jump on a sell recommendation as quickly as a buy recommendation.

If you're an investor—or planning to invest—you should know the rudiments of market forecasting. If nothing else, it will help you to understand stock charts and research reports. To this end, I'll try to outline the main methods used to predict price movements, which may lift the veil of mystery that surrounds the investment business. Who knows, you may decide to try your own hand at forecasting. When you're right, it's wonderfully satisfying (and when you're wrong, it can be painfully expensive).

The first thing an analyst must do is assess the stage of the economic cycle. This is crucial to any decision, because the *market leads the economy by six months to a year*—sometimes longer. In other words, stock prices today reflect earnings and other developments far down the road. What this means is that you must anticipate the future to establish fair value today. You can't simply base your assumptions on the present. If you fail to look ahead, you could miss a golden opportunity—or get a nasty surprise.

Investment forecasters study all sorts of economic and political cycles. Here's an assortment of well-known cycles, with their average durations:

Kitchin cycle:	4 years
Juglar cycle:	8 - 11 years
Wardwell cycle:	11 - 16 years
Kuznet cycle:	22 years
Kondratieff cycle:	50 - 60 years

There's no need for the average investor to get involved in the study of cycles, except to establish where one is in the current business cycle. As a point of interest, the Kondratieff cycle (or Kondratieff wave) correctly foretold the Great Depression. It was devised by Nikolai Kondratieff, a Russian economist, who was dispatched to a Siberian labour camp in 1930 for his political views. According to Kondratieff's theory, North America will enter a terminal economic phase by the end of this century. (Some gold bugs believe we're already in it.)

There are also several frivolous cycles. One is that hemlines reflect the state of the economy; in the '20s both the stockmarket and hemlines were high, but during the Depression hemlines fell with the market. Another is that the winner of the Super Bowl in January will determine the direction of the market for the rest of the year. If one of the original NFL teams wins, it will be an up year, but if a former AFL team wins it will be a down market. (Or is it vice versa?)

As well as studying cycles, economists and forecasters use other methods to prophesy the future. Most, if not all of these methods, are based on assumptions that make them highly susceptible to human error.

One of the favourites is the "Old Grey Mare" theory, which compares the present situation with a past period, and then projects a similar outcome. The flaw in this method is that, while history repeats itself, forecasters often jump to a conclusion *first* and then twist the facts to justify it—a case of comparing apples with oranges. On the fiftieth anniversary of the 1929 stock market crash, many pundits wrote scare articles comparing 1979 with 1929, and projected another market debacle. As the two periods weren't comparable, these articles were rubbish.

Consensus forecasting is a popular and pleasant way to predict the economy. In this method like-minded analysts confer with each other and reach a joint conclusion. If it's wrong, nobody blames the other fellow, because they're all in the same boat.

Then we have "Econometric Model" or "Ivory Tower" forecasting, which is extremely complex and fraught with peril. In this method an immense amount of data is poured through computers to project the state of the economy at a future date. Both the Bank of Canada and the Conference Board of Canada use econometric models. The problems and variables with this type of exercise are staggering, and may be summed up with the phrase "garbage in, garbage out."

However, some of the economic indicators fed to the computers can, by themselves, provide valuable information. They include such things as the number of housing starts, new car sales, unemployment, excess plant capacity, the rate of inflation, consumer confidence, and other significant figures. If you watch these indicators (which are published in the press), you can judge for yourself where the economy is heading.

INTEREST RATES AND THE MONEY SUPPLY

Two key indicators to note are the prevailing interest rate and the money supply. The interest rate establishes the *cost* of money, while the money supply determines its *availability*. To get a handle on the money supply look at the "M-1" figure, which reflects the amount of demand deposits and currency in circulation. This figure is published weekly in the papers, or you can get it from your broker. The interest rate is established each Tuesday, following the Treasury Bill auction. Money becomes more expensive as the interest rate rises, and cheaper as the rate falls. Money becomes more available as the supply increases, but "tighter" as the supply decreases. The best scenario for business is a declining interest rate and an expanding money supply. The worst is a rising rate and a declining supply.

Because money is the lifeblood of the economy, interest rates have a tremendous effect upon the financial markets. During an expansionary phase, inflation forces rates higher due to competition by business and government for funds. At some stage in the inflationary cycle the government usually steps in to check inflation by manipulating rates even higher. This stops the inflationary cycle by inducing an economic recession. It's a harsh measure, akin to burning a firebreak to contain a forest fire. On the opposite page is a diagram that shows how, over a recent thirty-year period, rising interest rates have precipitated every recession.

This diagram reveals how sensitive the economy is to interest rates. It also shows how rates trended higher, because the peaks and valleys are rising—a rate of 5½ percent triggered a recession in 1958, but it took more than twice that rate to achieve a recession in 1974, and rates of more than 16 percent to cause a recession in 1979. This suggests that the economy, over a period of time, can accommodate higher interest rates. The danger signal, and what you have to watch out for, is an *inverted* yield curve—when short-term rates are higher than long-term rates. *Invariably, this spells trouble for the financial markets.*

Commercial Paper Rates

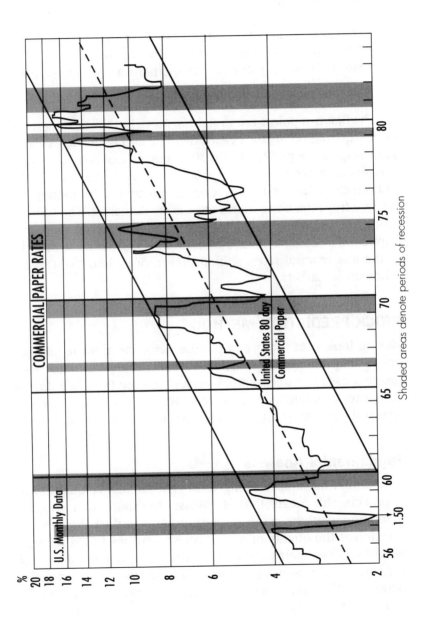

Shaded areas denote periods of recession

Before leaving the subject of money and interest rates, remember these three points:

- Money is always invested (unless it's in transit).
- All the financial markets are interconnected.
- Money inevitably flows to where there is the highest rate of return with the lowest perceived risk.

The first two points are straightforward, but the third deserves some explanation. If stock yields dwindle and bond yields rise, at some stage money will leave the stock market and be reinvested in fixed-income securities. As a result, the stock market will fall. Conversely, if interest rates decline precipitously, money will migrate from the bond market to the stock market. The influx of funds then fuels a surge in stock prices. This phenomenon happened in Canada in 1993 when many GIC investors, horrified at the low renewal rates, shifted their money into the TSE and other stock markets.

STOCK PREDICTION METHODS

Having looked at the broad picture, we'll move on to see how prices are predicted for individual stocks. There are hundreds of systems used to forecast stock prices, ranging from astrology to computer programs. For simplicity, we can divide security analysts into two camps: fundamentalists and technicians.

Fundamental Analysis

A fundamentalist takes a long-term view and uses a quantitative approach. This means that he assesses the shares of a company in relation to others in the industry, pores over the balance sheet, scrutinizes the quality of management, and measures its products or services against the competition. A fundamentalist is also concerned with earnings ratios, book values, dividend yields, plant capacity, and business in general. In short, a fundamentalist turns over every rock in sight. Only after an in-depth study of the company does he come to a decision on whether the shares should be bought or sold.

Most investors unconsciously rely upon fundamental analysis to come to their decisions. This reminds me of Olivia, one of my first clients. Olivia was a delightfully eccentric woman who used the quirkiest form of fundamental analysis to pick a good many winners. One day she phoned me and gave me a large order to buy Dupont. I was a little surprised, because Dupont's earnings were sliding; so I asked her why she liked the stock. Olivia replied that she was bullish on Dupont becase of the hula hoop craze, and she expected the company to sell millions of tons of plastic to make hula hoops. As it turned out, Dupont didn't cash in on the hula hoop boom—but Olivia made money because the stock went up for other reasons.

Technical Analysis

The technician, unlike the fundamentalist, usually takes a short-term view, and his approach is different. He couldn't care less about dividend yields, price/earnings ratios, or the nuts and bolts of a company. A technician believes all this information is distilled into the current price of the stock. He studies such things as advance/decline ratios, short interest numbers, odd lot figures, and moving averages (all of which are discussed below) to project future prices. His primary tool is a chart on graph paper that shows the price movement of the stock. So important is the chart to a technician, that so long as he can study the pattern, he doesn't even need to know the name of the company to pass judgement on it.

Because of the mumbo jumbo and the tea leaf reading aspect of technical analysis, it's easy to criticize. (One definition of a technician is a fundamentalist who's lost money.) But you shouldn't ignore technical analysis. For one thing, a great many investors follow charts, and believe in them. This means that when certain price movements occur, a lot of investors react in the same way. These investors may be misguided, but stock prices change as a result of their mass buying and selling. As an analogy, suppose everyone believed that if three seagulls and a crow flew over the Statue of Liberty at the stroke of noon on a certain Tuesday, the Dow average would go up one hundred points. This might be absurd, but if enough folks believed it, and three seagulls and a crow floated over the statue at noon on that Tuesday, the Dow would soar. The other reason you can't afford to ignore technical analysis is that quite often, it works.

The guru of technical analysis was Charles H. Dow, who from 1889 to 1902 was editor of *The Wall Street Journal*. It was he who developed the averages on the New York Stock Exchange that bear his name. The most famous of these averages is the Dow Jones industrial average, which is composed of thirty widely held stocks. When a client rings a broker to ask what the market is doing and is told the market is "up twelve points," the broker is referring to the Dow Jones industrial average on the NYSE or "Big Board." The Canadian equivalent of the Dow is the Toronto Stock Exchange composite index, which is made up of three hundred stocks.

Charles Dow developed the Dow theory, which projects market trends based on the correlation in price movements of the Dow Jones industrial, transportation, and utility averages. In recent years, because rail (and airline) stocks represent less than 3 percent of the value of NYSE listed stocks, the transportation average has lost importance, and the relative significance of the utilities average has also been questioned. The Dow Jones industrial average is also considered a poor market barometer because it is based on staid blue chips, and they're so few in number. As a result of these changes in status, many people regard the Dow theory as suspect. (Both the Standard & Poor's indices and the Valueline Index, because they consist of so many more securities, are truer reflections of the market's overall behaviour.) Nevertheless, a lot of investors still follow the Dow theory, and the Dow Jones industrial index consistently tracks the broader-based averages.

In the mid-'30s another American, Ralph N. Elliot, developed a market theory known as the Elliot wave principle. This is a complex theory that's difficult to master, and once grasped requires sound judgement to interpret. It might be described as a refinement of the Dow theory. Some analysts have had notable success using the Elliot wave principle.

Technical Indicators

Even if you have no interest in theories, you might like to keep your eye on a few of the more widely followed technical indicators. With this in mind, I'll mention some of the more popular ones, and explain their use.

The simplest is "volume," which is the number of shares traded in a particular stock (or the whole market) on a given day. An upward movement without a corresponding increase in volume is considered a weak signal, while an upward movement on heavy volume is very bullish. A downward move on low volume is a bad sign (because it indicates an absence of buyers) and a downward movement on heavy volume is very bearish.

"Insider trading reports" (which are published in the press) reveal what the informed players are doing. Officers and directors of listed companies are classified as "insiders." Due to their senior positions, insiders have a very good batting average, regardless of whether they are buying or selling. Insider reports can provide a tip-off, but you must view isolated sales with caution. The company might be in trouble, but then again, the officer or director may just have needed money.

The "ten most active stocks" on the major exchanges are listed each day in the financial pages (and usually mentioned in the market reports). These show where the action is, and can reveal a potential opportunity. If you hold common stocks, it's wise to keep an eye on the most active list—and if one of yours appears, you should find out why.

On the same page as the most active stocks you will see two columns: one is headed "New Highs," the other "New Lows." These report movements of individual stocks out of their 52-week price range. If you've been thinking of buying a certain stock, and it appears in the new lows column, it might be time to buy—but only *after* you've checked the company's current status. Conversely, if you hold a stock and it appears on the new highs, you might review its position. (I didn't say sell, I said review).

The size of "option premiums," and the "ratio of puts to calls" are two sentiment indicators. The average size of option premiums reveals how much enthusiasm is behind the market. While the ratio of puts to calls indicates whether the public is bullish or bearish—normally, call options are much more popular than put options, because people would rather bet on stocks going up than down.

The "short interest ratio" is interesting, because it indicates the amount of short selling. Normally, the *higher* the short interest, the more bullish it is for the market. The reason for this is that all the shares that have been shorted must eventually be bought back—which means there's a buying reserve in the wings. Also, if the market suddenly turns up, and there's a heavy short position, the combination can cause a buying panic.

The "odd lot" indices show what the little investor (the person who can't afford to buy "board lots") is doing. It's a cynical indicator predicated on the assumption that the small investor is usually wrong. Professional traders, by doing the *opposite* of what the odd lotters are doing, consistently make money.

"Market breadth" figures give the number of stocks traded, and break down the number of advancing and declining issues. Quite often the market averages will point in one direction and the breadth figures in the opposite direction. Breadth reveals the true undertone of the market.

A growing number of people are embracing the "contrarian theory." A contrarian believes that the crowd is usually wrong. Contrarians reason that if everyone is bullish about a stock, the buying will eventually be exhausted, and the stock will become a good short sale. By the same token, if everyone is dumping a stock, the selling will eventually dry up, and the stocks will become an excellent buy. To learn what the crowd is thinking contrarians watch the Barron's Confidence Index closely, and read publications that poll the recommendations of investment advisors.

Traditionally—but not so much in the last five years—General Motors and IBM have been considered bellwether stocks. How GM and IBM go, so goes the market. Merrill Lynch is also regarded as a bellwether stock on the premise that if the market goes up, so do the earnings of the "Thundering Herd" (and vice versa). The price of gold is another barometer, because historically the price of the yellow metal has moved opposite to the stock market (which is why it's a good idea to have a little gold, as a sheet anchor, in your portfolio).

Moving Averages

Most technicians keep "moving averages" of individual stocks and various market indices. A moving average is compiled by taking the average price over a period of weeks—the shorter the period, the more sensitive the average. The most common terms for moving averages are 13, 26, and 52 weeks. A moving average is charted as a line on graph paper, and indicates a change in the direction of the stock when the daily price goes above or below that line. The problem with moving averages is that they can give false signals. Should the current price cross back again, you'll be whipsawed if you bought or sold when the stock first broke through the line.

Having explained some of the indicator terms, let me define the various time periods for you. I should probably say *try* to define, because nothing is written in stone. (I had a gunslinger client who considered a stock bought and sold before lunch to be a "short-term" trade and one held overnight to be a "long-term" hold.) Excluding bonds, in the investment business "long-term" usually means more than one year, "intermediate-term" means three months to a year, and "short-term" is from one month to three months.

A chart provides the price history of a stock in the form of a jagged line. Technicians study this jagged line and, from it, project the probable future course of the stock. Two assumptions are made when interpreting a chart:

1. Prices move in trends.
2. A change in trend is usually signalled in advance by a characteristic formation.

Reading a stock chart has been likened to making a medical diagnosis. If you miss one symptom or misread the pattern, you'll arrive at the wrong conclusion. An oft-heard lament of technicians is that their chart was right, but they misread it. To help you understand what charting is all about, I'll explain a few of the basics and some of the jargon used in this form of technical analysis.

As I mentioned earlier, charts are plotted on graph paper. There are two ways of recording price changes: one is by "point and figure" the other is by "bar" charting. A point and figure chart records the price movements throughout the day in proper sequence. From this chronological pattern, it's possible to accurately predict short-term movements. Prices are recorded with noughts and crosses, one symbol being used exclusively for "upticks" and the other for "downticks." (You can use whichever symbol you wish, providing you're consistent.) The first diagram on the following page shows the way a point and figure chart is plotted—in this example, the noughts represent downticks, the crosses upticks.

A bar chart, which is easier to read, and much more widely used, employs a single vertical line to cover the day's trading range. The bottom of the line corresponds to the stock's low, the top of the line to its highest price. A horizontal line marks the price at which the stock (or index) closed for the day. At the bottom of a bar chart are vertical lines that indicate the trading volume each day. The second diagram on the page shows a section of a bar chart.

Earlier, I mentioned that stocks move in trends. These trends can be easily identified, and last for an appreciable length of time. Chartists usually highlight the trend with a line and an arrow to mark their channel. The third diagram shows an uptrend and a downtrend.

When a stock has no definite trend, but "backs and fills" in a sawtoothed pattern, it is said to be in a "congestion area." This formation occurs when the buying and selling pressures are roughly equal, and a tug-of-war is in progress. Eventually, the stock price will break out of the congestion area on the upside or the downside. Depending upon the direction, the congestion area becomes a "resistance level" or a "support level."

If the stock breaks to the downside, the bottom of the congestion area becomes a resistance level. This is caused by investors who bought the shares while they were in the congestion area and will sell "if it ever gets back to what I paid for it." This supply overhanging the market will make it difficult for the stock to move higher. Hence the term "resistance level."

Should the stock chew through the supply and move above the resistance level, it will magically become a support level (rather like the ceiling of a room becoming the floor of the next story of a house). The logic behind this is that many people who sold the stock—and then saw it move higher—will be waiting to buy it back if it comes down to the price at which they sold. These buyers will act as a barrier to a further decline, and will create a support level.

Point & Figure Chart

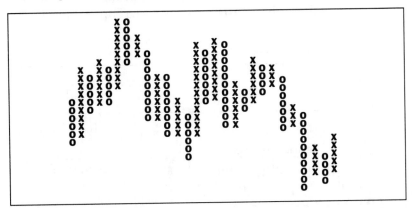

Sample Bar Chart

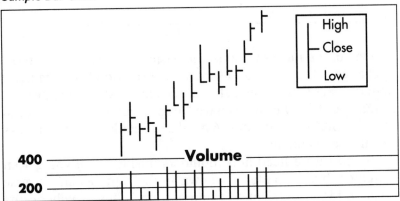

Uptrend & Downtrend

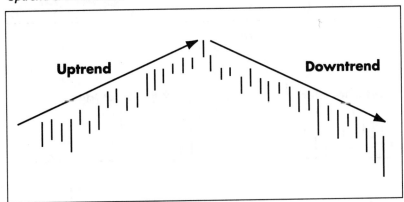

The following diagram shows the congestion area, with a stock moving through its resistance level to a support level.

Resistance & Support Levels

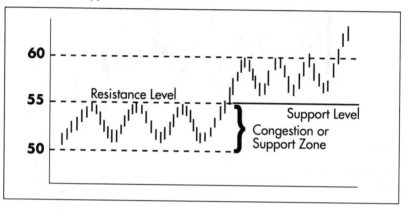

One of the most ominous and easiest to recognize patterns of change is the "head and shoulders formation." It's a reversal pattern that's usually seen after a stock has had a good advance. It indicates that the shares have "topped out" and are about to go into a prolonged decline. A head and shoulders pattern looks exactly like its name.

If you turn a head and shoulders upside down you get an extremely bullish pattern—known in the trade as an "inverse head and shoulders" or a "triple bottom." This usually occurs

Head & Shoulders

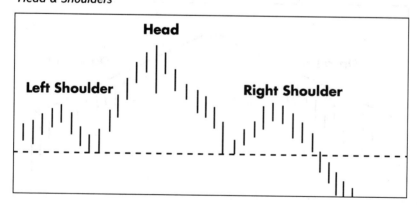

after a long sell-off and signals that the stock is about to move
up again.

A "double top" is another warning pattern. It signifies a
downtrend and has the same connotation as a head and shoulders formation. The opposite of a double top, quite logically, is a
"double bottom." This indicates that the selling has been
exhausted, and the line of least resistance for the stock is up.
This is what a double bottom looks like:

Double Bottom

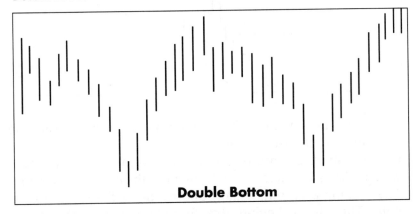

Double Bottom

Triangular formations can also signal a breakout. The direction of the breakout depends upon whether the horizontal side
is on the top or the bottom of the triangle. An "ascending
triangle," which has its horizontal side on the top, is formed by
the stock reaching a similar limit on each upward move, with
successively higher low points. On the chart it looks like a coiled
spring—and the breakout is to higher levels. A "descending
triangle" is the reverse of an ascending triangle, with the
horizontal side on the bottom. A descending triangle indicates a
move to lower levels.

This is what an ascending triangle looks like (note the horizontal side):

Ascending Triangle

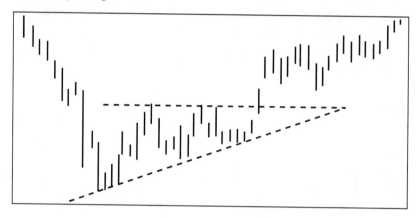

"Flags" are small but dynamic formations that indicate the continuation of a trend. They consist of a pole and a flag. The pole is a sharp upward or downward movement, and the flag, which follows it, is a minor movement in the *opposite* direction. The ensuing breakout, usually approximates the length of the pole. The theory behind this formation is that the minor fluctuations in the flag imply that reactionary buying or selling is contained and the original trend will reassert itself. Here is an upward flag:

Flag

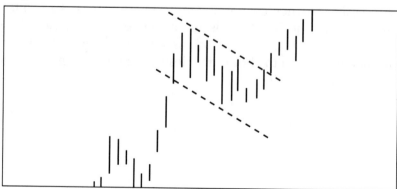

A "gap" occurs when a stock trades in a range above or below the previous day's range and leaves a *clear space* in the chart. This is a strong signal that can happen when there's a sharp upward or downward move. It's often caused by overnight news that causes a wave of buying or selling. As long as the gap is not filled in, the trend will continue. However, if the stock retraces its price and trades in the level of the gap, this means that the market has now fully discounted the news. Here is an diagram showing two gaps:

Gap

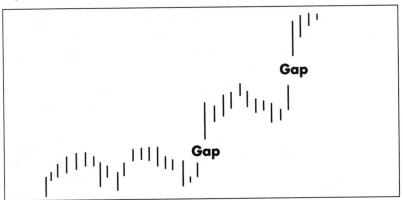

And now, for review purposes, here's a larger section of a chart that shows several of the formations I've mentioned:

The Whole 9 Yards

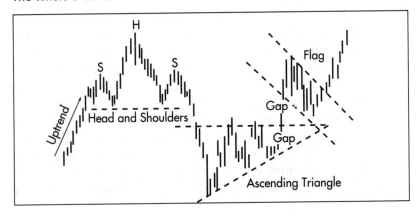

COMBINING APPROACHES FOR BEST RESULTS

What I like about technical indicators and charts is that they can identify short-term trading opportunities. Equally important, they can flash a warning signal. However, I wouldn't recommend that you rely solely on technical analysis to make your investment decisions. This is a personal opinion, but one shared with a good many successful investors.

The main drawback with technical analysis is that it's based on the law of probability—which means that even the most astute technician can be misled. This is also true of fundamental analysis, but a good fundamentalist will make less horrendous errors (and there's usually time to take evasive action). For this reason, I place more faith in the fundamental approach. Having said that, when I'm checking out a possible investment I always look at the technical side too. If the fundamentals and the technical picture disagree, I go back to the drawing board. But when they coincide, I can proceed with confidence.

If you want to learn more about fundamental analysis, I suggest that you read *Security Analysis* by Graham and Dodd, which is published by McGraw-Hill. This book was written ages ago, but it's still the bible on the subject.

Should you wish to delve deeper into the technical side of the game, I'd recommend *Technical Analysis of Stock Trends*, by Edwards and Magee, which is published by John Magee Inc. It, too, is an oldie but a goody. For those of you who are interested in charts, you can make them yourself (a lot of work) or you can buy them ready-made from a number of American and Canadian services. I like the charts produced by the Graphoscope ®, a long established Canadian service, published every two months by The Canadian Analyst Limited, 30 Duncan Street, Toronto, Ontario, M5J 2C3. They provide the jagged lines on graph paper—but interpreting them is up to you. Check the ads in the financial press for other sources, or ask your broker.

To close the chapter I'd like to share with you the most memorable market forecast that I was ever given. It was in 1958, and I was a sales trainee with Royal Securities at their head office on St. James Street in Montreal. At that time the senior executives were on the fifth floor of the building, while the sales staff occupied the ground floor. One day I got into the elevator to go to the fifth floor on an errand. I was joined by a very old and immensely rich senior partner who was reputed to have made millions in the market. Being the youngest and most junior salesman in the firm, I was in awe of my companion. The ancient elevator, which was lit by a single electric bulb, creaked slowly upward as the two of us stood together in silence.

Although I was nervous, I felt this was a heaven-sent opportunity to cadge a pearl of wisdom. Screwing up my courage, I said; "Sir, what do you think the market's going to do?"

The old gentleman obviously heard my question, but didn't answer. Finally, when we reached the top floor, he turned and slowly waved a mottled hand up and down in front of me, and, as he made this motion, he said in a dusty whisper, "Young man, the market will continue to fluctuate."

15

STRATEGIES
AND PITFALLS

The obvious investment strategy is to buy low and sell high. This is easier said than done, but there are ways to increase your profits and to avoid the hazards. In this chapter I'll mention some of the strategies that have helped me and my clients, and may be useful to you.

When I was a little boy, my grandmother used to take us on four-leaf clover hunts. The object of the game was to see who could pick the most four-leaf clovers. Although they're very hard to find, Granny could spot a four-leaf clover at thirty paces. I had keen eyesight and was closer to the ground than my two older brothers, but they often snatched clovers from under my nose. The reason they were able to do so was that they focused on the task at hand, while I was distracted by other flora and fauna (such as a dandelion or a wandering beetle). Had I concentrated on finding four-leaf clovers, I too might have been a winner.

I make this confession to illustrate a fundamental investment principle: to be successful, you must have a goal—and you must stick to it. If your investment objective is capital gain, don't be distracted by income securities; concentrate on equities. If your goal is income, don't get sidetracked by speculative situations; stay with high-yielding securities. If you decide you want a combination of both, build a balanced portfolio, and keep it balanced.

This may sound elementary, but I had many people come to me over the years who had no idea of what they wanted from their investments. In most cases, their holdings had simply drifted with the market, rising and falling with the economic tide. I repeat, if you want above-average performance from your portfolio, you must identify your goal and steadfastly pursue it.

NEW ISSUES

Buying new issues *indiscriminately* is a good way to turn a portfolio into a hodgepodge. Every new issue—at least in the eyes of the underwriter—has some good points. But what you must ask yourself is whether this particular new issue fits into your overall investment plan. For instance, if you're only interested in capital gain, you don't want a retractable preferred or a high-coupon bond, no matter how attractive their yields. By the same token, if your goal is income, a concept stock wouldn't be appropriate for you. Even if you have a balanced portfolio (one that combines growth and income), a new issue may not be suitable for you, because it may overweight a sector, or duplicate one of your present holdings.

Ideally, your broker should screen new issues, and only offer those that suit your needs. Now that I'm on the other side of the desk—as a customer rather than a broker—I'm surprised at the indiscriminate offering of new issues. Even when an issue appears to be suitable, you must exercise good judgement in deciding whether to buy it. If you have a good business relationship with your broker, it won't hurt to decline from time to time. (But if you turn him down too often, he may stop phoning you— at least on new issues).

Should you get a call from a broker you don't know offering a new issue, be on your guard. Normally, if it's a *good* issue, it's *always* sold to existing clients—not to telephone prospects. The only exception is if a broker knows you're a big account, and he's offering you a "hot issue" to induce you to become a client. (A "hot issue" is one that is in heavy demand and trading at a premium.) In most cases, however, this kind of approach means the new issue isn't selling well, and the broker is trying to unload it by "cold calling" (a practice prohibited by many securities commissions). In this connection, if you're offered new Canada bonds after 10:00 a.m. by *any* broker, you should probably pass them up. The reason is that Canada bonds are priced before 9:00 a.m. and if the issue is hot (or even lukewarm), the entire issue will be sold in the next fifteen minutes. Unless you told your broker you wanted some Canada bonds, and he's set some of his allotment aside for you, an offering after 10:00 a.m. is a sure sign that the issue is going slowly—and may already be trading in the aftermarket *below* the issue price.

Some folks buy new issues with no intention of paying for them. They hope to realize a profit between the issue date and the settlement date (the day you have to pay for the securities). This practice is called "riding" and is severely frowned on in the business, because the underwriters must remarket the shares that are thrown back at them. Having said that, I must add that some salesmen, to generate commissions, encourage clients to ride new issues. I don't recommend riding—although it can *sometimes* be an easy way to make a buck—but I can tell you how to use riders to your advantage. If you want to buy a new issue as an investment and you can't get any shares from your broker, the time to buy it in the aftermarket is *just before the settlement date*. During the last hectic days before settlement, most riders dump their shares to avoid paying for them. This selling wave temporarily depresses the price—allowing you to buy at an artificially low level.

SECONDARY ISSUES

I would also caution you about secondary issues. The first thing you must find out is *why* the offering is being made. Are insiders cashing in on their investment, or is there a valid reason—such as a court-ordered divestiture, or a cash flow shortage? Regardless of the motive, *the price of the shares will probably decline after the issue*. The reason for the subsequent drop in price is that the offering will likely sop up all the short-term buying interest. This doesn't always happen, but it happens quite often. You should only buy a secondary offering if you've had your eye on the stock for some time, and the price is right.

MUTUAL FUNDS

Never buy a mutual fund without first reading the prospectus. Study the prospectus and find out how long the management team has been running the show. If the same team have been with the fund for some years, they're obviously responsible for the fund's past performance. On the other hand, if a new management group has just taken over, you have no assurance that the past performance will continue—and you'll be buying a pig in a poke. You should also check how long it takes for the fund to redeem its shares and whether they can be exchanged within a "family" of funds. (The banks, several trust companies, and fund companies such as AGF, Altamira, Guardian, Investors, Mackenzie, and Trimark all have families of funds.) The right to transfer shares from one fund to another, at *minimal cost*, is a valuable option. When looking over a prospectus, you'll reach a more informed decision if you compare several funds.

CONSTRUCTING A PORTFOLIO

Building a balanced portfolio is akin to building a house. First, you must have a solid foundation. For most investors, the foundation should be something safe and liquid such as Canada Savings Bonds, Treasury Bills, or a money market fund. All three will provide a cash reserve for future investment purchases (or for emergencies). Having established a secure foundation, you might then buy some convertible bonds or convertible preferreds, or a fixed income fund with an element of growth. This combination of securities will provide safety, some income, and equity exposure.

After you've acquired these investments, you might buy some common stocks, or equity mutual funds. Because risk is now a factor, I would stick to proven companies and be extremely selective. On the principle of not putting all your eggs in one basket, you can reduce the risk by buying into several industries. But don't overdiversify—buy one, or at the most two, companies in a given industry. If you choose to go the mutual fund route, you won't need more than three equity funds (and one *good* one will do in a pinch). You might also consider buying an equity fund that invests overseas—in Europe, Asia, South America, or on a global basis. Mutual funds are the easiest and most logical way to invest offshore. After you have a reasonable equity representation, add to your *existing* holdings rather than buying new ones. The secret to dynamic performance is to have meaningful holdings in the leading companies of each industry. If you have a grab bag of a little of this and a little of that, your results will be mediocre at best.

OVERDIVERSIFICATION

Speaking of overdiversification reminds me of one of my favourite clients, an elderly lady named Florence. When she first came to see me, I explained that I could only be of help if she would give me a list of her holdings. Florence didn't have a list, but said she'd get her securities out of the bank and bring them in to me. The next day Florence tottered into the office with a huge Loblaws shopping bag. I assumed that she'd just bought her week's groceries, but I was wrong—the bag was filled with certificates. There wasn't enough room on my desk, so I emptied the bag on the floor, got down on my hands and knees, and ploughed through the contents. I found all sorts of things including: certificates for companies that were no longer in existence, companies that had changed their names, companies that had split their shares, a few that had offered to redeem their shares, and a number that had been taken over by other companies. The certificates in the pile represented everything from a fraction of one share, to more than six hundred shares.

After getting opinions from our research department, I set aside her best stocks and sold everything else. The proceeds from these sales were used to bolster and to round out her remaining holdings. Florence ended up with a fixed-income reserve and significant positions in ten companies. Streamlining her portfolio improved its performance—and for the first time in years, she was able to keep track of her investments.

DOLLAR AVERAGING AND DIVIDEND REINVESTING

There are two ways to systematically add to your stock holdings. One is by "dollar averaging," the other is by subscribing to a dividend reinvestment plan. Both methods are simple and effective.

To dollar average, set aside a fixed sum on a regular basis, say every quarter or every year, and use the sum to buy shares in the company. Because it's a fixed amount, you automatically buy more shares when the stock price is low, and fewer when it's high. Over a period of time, you will accumulate stock at a relatively low *average* price. Here's an example of how dollar averaging works, using $1000 instalments:

	Stock Price	Number of Shares Bought
1st purchase	$22	($1000 ÷ $22) = 45 shares
2nd purchase	$27	($1000 ÷ $27) = 37 shares
3rd purchase	$33	($1000 ÷ $33) = 30 shares
4th purchase	$30	($1000 ÷ $30) = 33 shares

Average purchase price $27½

Dividend reinvestment plans work on the same principle. Each quarter, instead of sending you a cheque, the company buys more shares for you. Normally, you'll save money on the purchase, either through lower commission fees, or by buying treasury shares at a discount. Many blue chip companies, including most of the banks and utilities, have dividend rein-vestment plans. My only caveat—and one that I hardly need add—is if you need income, you shouldn't subscribe to this type of plan, no matter how attractive the terms.

INVESTMENT CASHFLOW

For those who depend upon their investments for income, you can smooth out your cash flow by noting the dividend and inter-est payment dates. Common and preferred shares normally pay their dividends quarterly, while bonds usually pay interest twice a year. (Canada Savings Bonds pay interest once a year, in November.) With this knowledge, and a little planning, you can arrange to receive a similar amount each month. As a simple example, let's say that your portfolio consists of:

$20,000 money market fund, paying 5% (average) monthly
$20,000 Canada Savings Bonds paying 7% annually (in November)

1000 shs Noranda Convertible Preferred "B"
500　shs BCE Inc common
1000 shs Canadian Utilities common
3000 shs Nova Scotia Power common
1000 shs Royal Bank common
1500 shs TransCanada PipeLines common

Here's a dividend and interest schedule:

MM fund interest Every month (approx.)	$　85
Noranda Preferred and BCE Inc January, April, July, and October	$ 790
Nova Scotia Power and Royal Bank February, May, August, and November	$ 686
Canadian Utilities and TransCanada PipeLines March, June, September, and December	$ 705
Canada Savings Bonds interest November	$1400

In this example,(which contains bona fide income stocks), dividend and interest payments have been scheduled to provide a reasonably level monthly income. With money market funds you can let your interest compound or withdraw it—in this case, we've opted for automatic monthly withdrawals. The Canada Savings Bonds pay interest only once a year, but at a time when it's most needed, just before Christmas.

WAYS TO PROTECT YOUR HOLDINGS

Writing or Buying Options

If you're an income investor, and you're worried the market's about to fall, there's no need to sell your holdings. You can protect the value of your portfolio and maintain your income by writing or buying options. This may sound risky, but it's not. If you write (sell) covered call options, the money you receive will, to some extent, offset a decline in the value of your shares. Writing calls, however, won't compensate you for a *severe* price drop. Also, if you judge the market incorrectly and it goes up instead of down, your calls will be exercised and you'll lose your shares. Therefore, when writing calls you should strive for the highest strike price combined with the shortest maturity. You want as large a premium as possible for your option, and you want the buyer to have as little time as possible to exercise it. Ideally, you should sell your calls for at least 10 percent of the strike price; in other words, if the strike price is $25, you should get at least $2.50 for your calls. And don't write any calls unless you're prepared to lose the stock at the strike price (plus the option premium).

Put options provide better protection than call options, but they're much more expensive. Buying puts is exactly like buying insurance, even to the cost of the premium. Like insurance, there's no payoff unless your stock goes down in price. If this happens, you have two alternatives: to sell the puts at a profit (which will largely offset the decline in your stock) or to sell your shares at the strike price of the puts. Normally, you're better off selling the puts and keeping the shares, because you retain your dividends and, in time, the shares should rebound. The main disadvantage to puts is the cost of the premiums, which are often prohibitively expensive. For this reason, before buying puts, it's prudent to do your maths.

If you held a stock that was trading at $29 and you thought it could fall to $25, you might buy puts with a $27.50 strike price. This would make sense if you could buy the puts for 50 or 75 cents, but not if you had to pay $2 for them. At a cost of $2, the risk versus the reward would be unprofitable. Excluding commissions, here's the calculation:

Strike Price of Puts		Cost of Premium		Net Proceeds	Protection over $25
$27.50	minus	.50	=	$27.00	$2.00
$27.50	minus	.75	=	$26.75	$1.75
$27.50	minus	$2.00	=	$25.50	.50

This strategy applies to the protection of a single security, and can only be done if there are options available on that company. If you want to protect your entire portfolio, you can use the same strategy to sell calls or buy puts on the TSE 300 composite index. You won't get dollar for dollar coverage, even with puts, because your portfolio and the TSE 300 contain different securities. You can also achieve a similar hedge in the futures market, which is based on the TSE composite index, but there's no advantage for the average investor.

Buying Bonds Denominated in Foreign Currencies

If you're an income investor concerned with the level of the Canadian dollar, Canadian bonds denominated in foreign currencies offer an excellent hedge. The federal and provincial governments, as well as the banks and some leading Canadian companies issue bonds denominated in U.S. dollars, Deutschmarks, francs, yen, and sterling. With these bonds you can choose whichever you think is the strongest currency, or buy a selection of currencies, and enjoy peace of mind as well as a steady income. It also makes sense to stagger the bond maturities, so that you'll be able to redeploy your capital as the world situation changes. A good global mutual fund is an alternative, but most global funds aren't tied directly to a specific foreign currency. Currency options are yet another alternative, but they require some expertise and can be very risky.

The T-Bill/Option Hedge

So far we've just looked at ways to protect yourself against loss, but it's also possible to hedge your bets and invest for capital gain. The Treasury Bill/option hedge is one of the most popular ways to do this. However, for it to be feasible, you need at least $100,000 in cash. This money is used to buy its face value in Treasury Bills, which should be as long-term as possible—one-year, if you can get them. Because T-Bills are bought at a discount and mature at par, some money will be left over from the transaction. The surplus funds are then used to buy long-term put or call, stock or index options (LEAPs). When the T-Bills mature, you recover your original investment, and you sell your options. The option proceeds—if there are any— represent the profit in the hedge. If the options end up being worthless, you've still got your original capital because the T-Bill's maturing at par will cover your loss. This hedge is not a recipe to make big money, but it gives you a chance to achieve modest capital gains with little risk. If you choose to play the American market— which has a larger selection of options and tighter spreads—all the transactions will have to be in U.S. dollars.

FURTHER OPTIONS STRATEGIES
Timing

Harking back to the section on technical analysis, you should try to buy puts or to write calls just below a resistance level. Conversely, you should try to buy calls or write puts just above a support level. The logic behind these recommendations is obvious (providing you've read the "Forecasting Prices" chapter).

Options can also be useful for tax purposes. Suppose you have a fat capital gain on a stock, but you can't afford to sell it in the current year. At the same time, you're worried that the stock may sell off between now and next year. To protect your profit, you would buy puts that expire next year. By doing so, if the stock goes down in the interim, you will have locked in most of your capital gain.

The reverse of this situation occurs when one of your stocks is down and you want to take a tax loss. Because it's basically a good stock, you intend to buy it back; but you're worried the price may go up before you're allowed to repurchase it. (If you sell a security for a tax loss, the loss will usually be disallowed if you repurchase it within thirty days of the sale.) To get around this problem, you would buy calls on the stock. This will lock in your repurchase price and, if the stock should go through the roof, you can sell the calls for a profit.

Straddles

An option strategy known as a "straddle" can also be used to trigger a capital loss, or to shift a capital gain into the next year. A straddle involves the simultaneous purchase or sale of a put and a call on the same security, at the same strike price, with the same expiry date. It might be compared to a pair of legs straddling a centre line. In this case the losing "leg" of the straddle is liquidated in the present year—say, in late December—and the profitable "leg" is liquidated at the beginning of January. Except for the price fluctuation in the few days between the two transactions, it's a zero sum game. The effect, however, is to create a loss in the current year, and a gain the following year. *This form of tax deferral may be disallowed by Revenue Canada, and should only be considered after consulting your tax advisor.*

HEDGING STRATEGIES FOR BONDS
Convertible Bonds

Another type of hedging strategy involves the purchase of convertible bonds on margin, and the short sale of the underlying shares. This is legal, and has been done by investors and the financial community for years. The trick is to find convertible bonds trading at or below par, with little premium attached to their underlying stock—which, ideally, should be volatile. The reason for shorting the stock is that the bonds, being the senior security, will fall less than the common shares. After the shares decline sufficiently, you would cover your short sale by buying them back on the open market. The profit on the short sale more than makes up for the loss on the bonds (which, as I have said, decline less than the shares).

Should the stock you've shorted go up, instead of down, your bonds will increase by a similar amount. And if you're forced to make delivery of the shorted stock (which is borrowed from your broker), you can cover your position by converting your bonds into shares. The worst-case scenario is when the shorted stock remains stable. Should this happen, you still have to pay the carrying costs—margin charges and any dividends on the shorted shares—and this can easily put you into a loss position.

Because this hedging strategy can be confusing, it may help if I give you a theoretical example. Let's assume that you paid 98

for a bond that's convertible into 100 common shares. You short
the shares at $10 and cover your short at $7. Here are the figures:

```
Proceeds received from short sale (100 x $10)  = $1000
Cost to cover short sale (100 x $7)            = $ 700
Profit on short sale                                    $300
Cost of convertible bond @ 98                  = $ 980
Bond declines in value to 85                   = $ 850
Loss on bond                                            $130
```

Net profit on the transaction per bond ($300–$130) = $170

Regular Bonds

Now let's turn to regular, no-frills bonds. Investors sometimes find
themselves holding long-term bonds that have fallen in price.
They don't want to sell them, because it will mean a loss of capital. Unless interest rates drop, the only way to get their money
back is to wait until the bonds mature. And a long and tedious
wait it will be. Fortunately, there's a way out of this dilemma, if
you're willing to accept a *smaller* amount of annual income. What
you do is trade your long-term bonds for short-term bonds with a
lower coupon. At this writing, if you held Ontario Hydro 8.63 percent bonds due in February 2002, which are currently trading at
96⅝, you could trade them for Ontario Hydro 7¼ percent bonds
due in March 1996 at a price of 95⅜. This switch would reduce
your annual income by $13.80 per $1000 bond, but you'd get your
money back six years sooner—and you'd pocket 1¼ points
($12.50) per bond on the transaction.

This strategy will always work, providing there's a *positive* yield
curve. (A positive yield curve—when short rates are lower than
long rates—occurs 90 percent of the time). It can also be employed
in reverse, when you want to increase your annual income. It's
quite easy to switch from a low-coupon, short-term maturity to a
higher-coupon, long-term bond. A glance at today's financial page
reveals that you could swap Canada 4¾ percent bonds due in
March 1996 for Canada 7½ percent bonds due December 2003,
and take take out more than $30 per $1000 bond on the way
through. The transaction would increase your annual income per

bond by $27.50 per year, as well as your overall yield. However, in view of the upward trend in interest rates over the past forty years, I wouldn't recommend lengthening maturities, except in special circumstances. But I do recommend shortening terms.

EMPLOYEE STOCK PURCHASE PLANS

Over the years I've often been asked whether one should participate in employee stock purchase plans. I used to say that if it was a good company, you should buy as many shares as possible. But now I'm not so sure. If you invest in the place where you work, you are putting your job and your investments in the same basket. If the company's fortunes decline, both your job and your investment can go up the flue. Reversals of fortune happen to blue chip as well as junior companies. A friend who worked for IBM for nine years was recently let go. He not only lost his job, but about one third of the money he'd invested in IBM stock. I also have a friend in Halifax who worked for Coca-Cola for sixteen years and regularly bought shares in the Canadian company. In the autumn of 1993 Coca-Cola announced it was closing down the local bottling plant. My friend's Coca-Cola stock at that time was worth about one sixth of the amount he'd paid for it. Finally, I know a senior trust officer of the Royal Trust who was with the company for thirty-three years. When he retired in 1994, the company shares he'd scrimped and saved to buy were worth almost nothing. So, a company stock purchase plan, even for a blue chip company, is not necessarily a good thing. It all depends on the company.

BROKER ENDORSEMENTS

When I was a broker, clients often asked me whether I owned stock in the company I was recommending to them. They seemed to feel that if I owned shares it was a form of endorsement, or at the very least, tangible evidence of deep faith. I noticed recently a footnote in a well-known Canadian market letter, stating that the contributor not only owned all the stocks he was touting, but had made X dollars in the market for his own account. This footnote far exceeded the legal disclosure requirement, and was more of a boast than a statement.

Now let's stop for a minute and think about it. If a person owns a security, their judgement is to some extent biased. Human nature being what it is, if you own a stock, you want it to go up, and you want others to buy it. (Buying, after all, is what causes the price to rise.) A broker who owns a stock may think he knows all about it, but in truth, he's lost his objectivity. For this reason, I would be wary of recommendations from people who are already financially committed to a security. They may just be whistling past the graveyard.

IN CLOSING

Many investors also believe that to make your money work, you should be in the market all the time. Often, the smartest move is to take your money out of the market and sit on the sidelines. While you're taking a breather, your money can still be at work—in a money market fund, T-Bills, or a short-term deposit account. In this connection, the large brokerage firms usually pay competitive rates on cash balances.

When investors want to raise money—for whatever purpose—they frequently sell their winners. I can't tell you how many times I had clients study their holdings, and then make this error. What you should do is to *sell your losers, and keep your winners*. You might liken this approach to owning a woodlot. If you needed firewood, would you cut down the healthy trees, or would you cull out the dead ones? If you chose to cut down the healthy trees, eventually you'd end up with a woodlot full of dead trees. By the same token, if you persist in selling your winning investments and keeping your losers, eventually you'll end up with a portfolio of garbage.

The best market advice I ever received was given to me by an American client named Lazarus, who owned a seat on the New York Stock Exchange for many years. He was an extraordinarily shrewd trader and had made a fortune in the market. The last time I visited him in New York, which was shortly before his death, he took me to lunch at the Banker's Club. At the end of our lunch, I asked him what was the most valuable lesson he'd learned in his years on Wall Street. He thought the question over for a bit and then replied: "Take your losses quickly, and let your profits run."

GLOSSARY

ACCOUNT EXECUTIVE—pretentious title for a registered representative or broker.

ACCRUED INTEREST—interest on a bond that has accumulated from the last payment date. When you buy a bond you pay accrued interest; when you sell a bond you receive accrued interest. A bond without accrued interest is said to be trading "flat."

ACID-TEST RATIO—used to measure liquidity of a company. To get this figure, deduct inventory from current assets, and divide remainder by current liabilities.

ADR—an ADR or American Depository Receipt is a certificate of ownership of a foreign security, held in an offshore branch of an American bank. Most South African gold mining shares traded in North America are ADRs.

AFTER MARKET—Trading of a new issue after the public offering. Supply and demand determine price levels, which often differ from the initial offering price.

AGENT—broker who doesn't own the security but simply buys or sells it for the client and receives a fee (commission) for services rendered. Most stock exchange trades are done by the broker acting as agent.

ALLIGATOR SPREAD—an option spread that costs the client more in commissions than his potential profit. Should be avoided.

AMEX—also known as the ASE, which stands for the American Stock Exchange, is the second largest in the United States. Located in New York, the **Amex** trades a lot of the "swingers" as well as junior stocks, bonds, and options.

ANNUITY—an investment contract issued by an insurance company for a lump sum that pays you a fixed amount at regular intervals for the length of your life, or until you reach a certain age.

ARBITRAGE—a strategy used by professionals whereby a security is bought or sold on one market to profit from a price difference in another market. People who engage in this practice are called arbitrateurs, or "arbs."

ASSIGN—when an option is exercised, you are assigned the security, which means you must deliver the shares or buy them, depending upon whether you have written calls or puts.

AVERAGE DOWN—a strategy to reduce the average cost of a security by buying more shares as the price declines. Unrewarding if the stock ends up in the tank.

BALANCE SHEET—a financial statement that shows a company's assets, liabilities, and net worth.

BANK OF CANADA—established in 1934. Regulates the credit and currency of the nation, and exerts control over external value of the Canadian dollar. Sole issuer of currency and custodian of the country's gold reserves.

BANK RATE—the rate at which the Bank of Canada will lend money to the chartered banks, which is 25 basis points above the 91 day Treasury Bill rate. Treasury Bills are auctioned by the Bank of Canada every Tuesday.

BASIS POINT—usually applied to yields, represents one one-hundredth of 1 percent. If a yield rises from 4.37 percent to 4.47 percent the increase is 10 basis points.

BEAR—one who believes the market or a single security will decline.

BEAR RAID—concerted attack on a stock with the object of driving the price down by means of short sales. The bears often romp on the Vancouver Stock Exchange.

BETA—an indication of a stock's volatility in relation to an index such as the TSE 300 or the S&P 500. Useful word to drop at a cocktail party because it implies a knowledge of both the stock market and Greek.

BLOCK—a stock transaction of 10,000 or more shares with a value in excess of $200,000.

BLUE CHIP—a large company that is a leader in its industry, with a consistent record of earnings and dividends.

BLUE SKY—to get legal clearance for the sale of a new issue in all the provinces or states.

BOARD LOT—standard trading unit for shares. Number of shares comprising a board lot is determined by the stock exchange, and varies with the price of the shares.

BOILER ROOM—place where stock hustlers work the telephones to push speculative securities.

BOND—a debt security backed by a pledge of assets. See also **debenture**.

BOOK VALUE—total tangible assets minus all liabilities and the par value of preferred shares. To get the book value per share, divide the number of common shares into this figure.

BOTTOM FISHING—purchase of securities at perceived bargain prices. Also called Bottom Feeding.

BROAD TAPE—nickname for Dow Jones news service.

BROKER—an individual or a firm in the securities business. See also **agent** and **account executive.**

BULL—one who believes the market or a security will go up (also, what some brokers tell their clients).

CAGE—section of brokerage office where securities are physically handled. Called a cage because the area used to be enclosed by wire walls to prevent theft.

CALL OPTION—a security that gives you the right to buy the shares of a company at a fixed price for a fixed period of time.

CALLABLE—security that can be redeemed before the maturity date at the option of the issuer.

CASH FLOW—the sum of net income plus deferred taxes plus non-cash charges (such as amortization, depreciation, and depletion).

CHARTIST—one who uses a technical approach to security analysis and relies upon charts to forecast prices.

CHICAGO BOARD OF TRADE—oldest and largest commodity exchange on the continent. Parent of CBOE (Chicago Board Options Exchange), North America's largest options market.

CHICAGO MERCANTILE EXCHANGE—second largest commodity exchange in North America. Parent of International Monetary Market.

CHURNING—excessive trading of a client's account to generate commissions. Unless there is evidence that the broker prompted the trades *and* the client has lost money, churning is difficult to prove.

CIRCUIT BREAKER—commission and exchange regulations that prevent certain types of trading after the market has moved a given amount in either direction. Purpose is to dampen market swings.

CLIENT—a customer of a broker is referred to as a client because the broker (at least theoretically) provides professional advice.

COMEX—commodity exchange located in New York. Main market in North America for precious metals and financial instruments.

COMMON SHARES—see **common stock.**

COMMON STOCK—represents the equity or ownership of a company. Common shareholders normally have voting rights and, by this means, control the management of the company.

CONCEPT STOCK—a company with exciting prospects but little or no earnings. Concept stocks are high risk; when you buy one you are buying the sizzle, not the steak.

CONVERTIBLE—usually refers to bonds or preferred shares that may be converted into common shares.

COUPON—the interest rate expressed as a percentage of the face value of the security, e.g., a 6 percent coupon on a bond. Also refers to small cashable certificates attached to a bond representing interest installments.

COVERED WRITING—the sale of call options on a security that you own.

CURRENT RATIO—arrived at by dividing current liabilities into current assets. If a company had $1 million in current liabilities and $3 million in current assets, this would be a 3 to 1 current ratio.

DEBENTURE—a form of long-term debt, similar in most respects to a bond, but secured by the general credit of the issuer rather than by specific assets.

DEBT/EQUITY RATIO—usually calculated by adding total long term debt and preferred shares, and dividing the total by the value of the common shares. Indicates earnings leverage in corporate structure.

DEBT INSTRUMENT—any type of debt security, e.g., bonds, debentures, T-Bills, GICs, mortgages, etc.

DELAYED OPENING—occurs when matching an avalanche of buy or sell orders holds up the commencement of trading.

DEPLETION—accounting allowance for the amount of ore or oil withdrawn from a mine or well.

DEPRECIATION—accounting allowance that represents the reduction in value of an asset (such as a building or a piece of machinery) through wear and tear, or obsolescence. The value of the asset is written down on the company's books by this amount each year.

DERIVATIVE—security derived from another investment security e.g., options, rights, futures, stripped bonds, split shares, stock receipts, etc.

DISCRETIONARY ACCOUNT—an account for which the client gives the broker *written* authority to make investment decisions on his/her behalf. Should only be done after careful consideration of the possible consequences.

DIVIDEND—cash distribution, usually quarterly, to common and preferred shareholders made at the discretion of the board of directors.

DIVIDEND TAX CREDIT—only applicable to shares of Canadian companies. Canadian residents "gross up" and inflate the dividend by 25 percent, and then deduct 13⅓ percent of that amount from their federal tax payable.

DOUBLE PLAY—an investment opportunity with two profit potentials, e.g., a Japanese stock that may appreciate in value and may also be worth more in Canadian dollars because of an increase in the value of the yen.

DOW JONES INDUSTRIAL AVERAGE—a measurement of market movement, based on the changing values of thirty senior stocks listed on the New York Stock Exchange.

EARNINGS PER SHARE—often expressed as EPS, calculated by dividing the company's net earnings (after dividends on the preferred shares) by the number of outstanding common shares. An important statistic in analyzing the value of a stock.

EURODOLLARS—U.S. dollars held in Europe. When used to pay for oil they become Petrodollars. If used to pay for American goods they return to the United States as regular Yankee dollars. But so long as they remain offshore, they are Eurodollars.

EX-DIVIDEND—the cutoff date on the exchanges for the dividend on a stock. If you buy a stock that is ex-dividend, the former owner receives the pending dividend (but you get all future dividends).

FANNIE MAE—nickname for the Federal National Mortgage Association. Debt securities issued by the association have long been known as "Fannie Maes."

FRONT RUNNING—when a floor trader buys for his own account before entering a large institutional order. Securities commissions are not amused by the practice.

GO-GO FUNDS—volatile mutual funds that sometimes provide superior performance (and, at other times, deplorable returns).

GOVERNMENT NATIONAL MORTGAGE ASSOCIATION—a U.S. federal corporation whose securities have been nicknamed

"Ginnie Maes." Some even less imaginative people have now taken to calling CMHC securities "Cannie Maes."

GREEN SHOE—a provision that allows an underwriter to expand the size of an issue and draw down more securities. Useful if an unexpected demand develops, or if the underwriter has over-sold (shorted) the issue.

GROSS PRODUCTION—a resource company's production before royalty payments.

HOT ISSUE—a security offering that is oversubscribed and goes to a premium. Invariably scarce, and only sold to good clients.

IDA—stands for the Investment Dealers Association of Canada, which was founded in 1916. It is the self-regulating body of the Canadian securities industry.

INSIDER—one who owns more than 10 percent of a company's stock, or who is a senior officer of a company. Also applies to any person privy to confidential corporate information.

INSTITUTIONAL INVESTOR—industry term for large investors such as pension funds, insurance companies, trust companies, mutual funds, and banks.

INTEGRATED OIL—refers to the vertical integration of an oil company, that does everything from exploration through to selling of the refined products at its own gas stations.

INVESTMENT GRADE SECURITIES—high quality stocks or bonds.

KICKBACK—under-the-table remuneration of a broker or promoter for the sale or promotion of securities. Strictly illegal.

KICKER—a special feature added to a bland security to make it more attractive to investors. Might be anything from a retraction privilege to free share purchase warrants. Also known as "bells and whistles."

LATE TAPE—indicates trading is so hectic on the exchange, or in a specific security, that transactions and quotations are delayed.

LEAP—farfetched acronym for long-term equity anticipation options. These options have terms of one or two years, rather than nine months.

LEVERAGE—using a small amount of money to get the play off a larger amount. Securities bought on margin are a good example of leverage.

LIBOR—stands for London Interbank Offered Rate. Only relevant to institutions and very large investors.

LIFTING A LEG—when applied to securities, refers to liquidation of one side of a hedge. (Has different connotation when applied to dogs.)

LIQUIDITY—the ability of a security to be quickly turned into cash. Also referred to as marketability. Highly desirable.

MARGIN—can mean either the client's equity in a securities account, or a securities transaction with the aid of money lent by the broker.

MARGIN ACCOUNT—a trading account in which the broker partially finances your transactions. Special documentation and approval are required to open a margin account.

MARGIN CALL—what the broker issues when your equity falls below the minimum required in a margin account. You respond to a margin call by putting up more money (or securities), or by selling some of your position. If you don't respond, the broker can sell you out.

NAKED WRITER—a person who sells call options on a stock he doesn't own, or sells put options when he's not short the stock (or long offsetting puts).

NET WORTH—the amount a company's assets exceed its liabilities. Also called "shareholders' equity. "

NEW YORK STOCK EXCHANGE—founded in 1792, it is the largest and best-known exchange on the continent. Most of the issues listed on the NYSE are senior companies.

NIFTY FIFTY—the name for the fifty favourite stocks of the institutions. A somewhat obsolete term that came into vogue in the '70s, and is rarely heard today.

OPEC—acronym for Organization of Petroleum Exporting Countries.

OPTION—in security parlance, refers to a call or a put. Call options give you the right to *buy* the underlying stock for a fixed period of time. Put options allow you to *sell* the underlying stock under the same conditions. Selling calls or puts (which is known as "writing"), places an *obligation* on the vendor to deliver or to buy the underlying stock if the option is exercised.

OVER-THE-COUNTER—a securities market where dealers trade among themselves by telephone or telex, rather than on a stock exchange.

PAPER PROFIT—the profit in a security that has not been liquidated. The opposite is a "paper loss."

PAR VALUE—the face value of a bond or a preferred share. Meaningless when applied to common shares.

PEAC—acronym for a payment-enhanced capital security, which is the portion of a split common share that gets the dividend income.

POINT—referring to stocks, it means a move of one dollar, for example, BCE moves a point when it goes from 52½ to 53½. With regard to bonds, it means one hundred basis points, or 1 percent of the par value.

POISON PILL—amendment to a company's capital structure designed to thwart a takeover. In the event of a takeover offer, the "pill" often releases a flood of new shares that makes the company prohibitively expensive to swallow.

PREFERRED SHARE—equity in a company that ranks ahead of the common shares. Preferred shares normally have a par value, and usually don't participate in the earnings of a company except to the extent of the dividend. Often called "preference shares."

PRICE/EARNINGS RATIO—to find this ratio divide the earnings per share into the price of the stock. If a stock earns $2 and is trading at $20, then the P/E is 10 to 1.

PRIME RATE—the interest rate that the chartered banks charge their best customers. Influenced by the bank rate (the rate at which the Bank of Canada will lend money to the chartered banks), which is 25 basis points above the average treasury bill rate. Treasury bills are auctioned by the Bank of Canada every Tuesday.

PRO FORMA—a Latin phrase meaning "according to custom," used to describe financial projections in a prospectus after giving effect to the issue.

PROGRAM TRADING—large securities transactions triggered by computer programs.

PROSPECTUS—a document that provides detailed information on a securities issue. Contents of a prospectus must conform to strict legal requirements. Tedious but essential reading for prospective purchasers.

PROVEN RESERVES—amount of oil, gas, or ore that has been established by drilling, and that can be extracted with present technology.

PUT OPTION—security that gives you the right to sell a given number of shares at a fixed price for a specified period of time.

RED HERRING—industry nickname for a preliminary prospectus.

REGISTERED REPRESENTATIVE—correct name for a licensed securities salesperson.

RETRACTABLE PREFERRED—a preferred share which gives the holder the option to have it redeemed by the issuer on a certain date at a predetermined price.

RIGHT OF RESCISSION—legal right to cancel purchase of a new issue if it has been misrepresented in the prospectus.

RIGHTS OFFERING—privilege extended to existing shareholders to purchase additional shares, on a pro rated basis, at a discount from the current price. If a shareholder doesn't want to subscribe, the rights usually have some value, and can be sold on the market.

RISK/REWARD RATIO—the potential loss versus the potential gain in a transaction. If you estimated you could lose $5 but could make $15, the ratio would be 1 to 3. In most cases, you want a minimum ratio of at least 1 to 2.

ROLLOVER—usually applies to the automatic reinvestment of funds (e.g. when a Treasury Bill matures, the money is "rolled over" into another Treasury Bill).

RRSP—acronym for Registered Retirement Savings Plan.

SECONDARY OFFERING—the sale of a block of securities to the public by the existing holder. The proceeds go to the vendor, not into the treasury of the company. Can be a "bailout" by the vendor, and should be viewed with caution.

SECURITIES AND EXCHANGE COMMISSION—established in 1934. Federal agency that enforces securities regulations in the United States. Usually referred to as "the SEC."

SELLING GROUP—investment dealers who participate in an underwriting as sales agents, but are not members of the underwriting syndicate.

SHARE—an equity unit in a company. See also **common stock**.

SHORT—sale of securities a client borrows from the broker.

SINKING FUND—does not refer to a poorly performing mutual fund, but to money set aside by a company for the purchase of its outstanding bonds or preferred shares.

SOFT RETRACTION—a security that isn't retractable for cash, but may be converted into common shares (and *then* sold for cash).

SOUR GAS—natural gas contaminated with sulphur. The sulphur must be removed before the gas can be used for industrial or domestic purposes.

SPEC—acronym for a special capital gain security, which is the growth portion of a split common share.

SPLIT SHARE—a common share that is divided into two parts: one part receives all the dividends; the other, the price appreciation of the underlying shares. See **PEAC** and **SPEC**.

SPOT PRICE—when applied to commodities or financial futures, it's the current or present price.

SPREAD—the simultaneous purchase and sale of options of the same class, to benefit from any change in price of the underlying shares. Both risk and reward are limited in a spread. Term also applies to a similar commodity trading strategy.

STANDARD & POOR'S—well-known American financial service.

STOCK DIVIDEND—distribution of treasury shares rather than a cash dividend.

STOCK SPLIT—the subdivision of existing shares into smaller units, e.g., a 3 for 1 split triples the number of shares you own. A share split doesn't increase your ownership percentage in the company, but merely increases the number of shares. However, share splits improve marketability, and can enhance the total market value of your holding.

STRADDLE—the simultaneous purchase or sale of a call and a put on a stock with the same strike price and the same expiry date.

STREET—strictly speaking, Wall Street, New York. Now used in a general sense to encompass the entire financial community.

STRIKE PRICE—the price at which an option may be exercised.

STRIP—to detach the coupons from a bond and to market each unit separately, usually at a discount. Also the nickname for a zero coupon security. See also **zero coupon bond**.

SWEETENER—industry slang for a feature that makes a mundane security more attractive to buyers. See **kicker**.

SYNDICATE—a group of investment dealers who underwrite a securities issue. The syndicate buys the entire issue, and is also responsible for marketing it.

TAILGATING—when a trader or registered representative executes an order for a knowledgeable client, and then buys the same security for their own account. A rather innocuous and often futile practice.

TAKE GAS—unpleasant consequence of owning a security that falls sharply in price.

THRIFT INSTITUTION—colloquial expression for a bank, trust company, credit union, or caisse populaire.

TOMBSTONE—industry nickname for the advertisement of a new

securities issue. Names on a financial tombstone are ranked in precedence, according to their participation, from the top down.

TRADING PIT—an octagon-shaped platform, with descending steps on the inside, where futures are trades.

TRANSFER AGENT—an institution, normally a trust company, that is responsible for the issuance and cancellation of bond and stock certificates. Each company has its own particular transfer agent.

TREASURY BILL—a short-term obligation of the government of Canada. Most T-Bills are issued for a term of 91 days, but they can have terms up to 2 years. They do *not* bear interest. Their yield comes from the difference between the discount at which they were purchased and their face value at maturity.

TURKEY—a security whose price movement causes profound distress to the holder.

UNDERWRITE—the process whereby one or more investment dealers purchase a securities issue. Until the issue is sold to the public, the underwriters are normally at risk for the entire amount.

UNIT—a security that consists of more than one component, for example, an issue that includes a stock purchase warrant with each common share.

VARIABLE RATE—a security without a fixed rate of return, that pays interest or dividends based on prevailing rates. These securities use many different formulas.

VOLATILITY—the more violently a stock fluctuates in price, the greater the risk. Conversely, the more stable it is, the greater the safety. See **beta**.

WARRANT—has two meanings: either a long-term right or a *certificate for* rights.

WATERED STOCK—the issuance of additional shares without any money going into the treasury. Dilutes the equity of the existing shareholders, hence the term.

WHITE KNIGHT—a person or corporation that averts an unfriendly takeover by making a better bid for the target company.

WORKING CAPITAL—the amount remaining after current liabilities are deducted from current assets.

WRITE—when applied to options, means the sale of a put or a call.

YIELD—the return, expressed as a percentage, on a security.

ZERO COUPON BOND—a bond that has been stripped of its coupons. Both the stripped bond and the separate coupons are sold to investors. Because neither the bond nor the coupons pay interest, the return on them stems from the difference between their cost and their face value at maturity.

INDEX